THE VIEW FROM SOMEWHERE

THE VIEW FROM SOMEWHERE

Undoing the
Myth of
Journalistic
Objectivity

LEWIS RAVEN WALLACE

The University of Chicago Press
Chicago and London

The University of Chicago Press, Chicago 60637
The University of Chicago Press, Ltd., London
© 2019 by Lewis Wallace
Published 2019
Printed in the United States of America

28 27 26 25 24 23 22 21 20 19   1 2 3 4 5

ISBN-13: 978-0-226-58917-6 (cloth)
ISBN-13: 978-0-226-66743-0 (e-book)
DOI: https://doi.org/10.7208/chicago/9780226667430.001.0001

Library of Congress Cataloging-in-Publication Data

Names: Wallace, Lewis Raven, author.
Title: The view from somewhere: undoing the myth of journalistic
    objectivity / Lewis Raven Wallace.
Description: Chicago: The University of Chicago Press, 2019. | Includes index.
Identifiers: LCCN 2019014782 | ISBN 9780226589176 (cloth: alk. paper) |
    ISBN 9780226667430 (e-book)
Subjects: LCSH: Journalism—Objectivity—United States. | Journalistic
    ethics—United States. | Social movements—Press coverage—United
    States. | Social justice—Press coverage—United States.
Classification: LCC PN4784.O24 W35 2019 | DDC 302.23—dc23
LC record available at https://lccn.loc.gov/2019014782

♾ This paper meets the requirements of ANSI/NISO Z39.48-1992
(Permanence of Paper).

CONTENTS

INTRODUCTION

Ten days after Donald Trump's inauguration in January 2017, I adjusted my tie inside the unisex bathroom at an Au Bon Pain in Midtown Manhattan, messed with my salt-and-pepper hair (I was thirty-three, but my job doing daily news was aging me quickly), and tucked a cigarette behind my ear. I was walking the path of so many journalists before me, on my way to get fired. Fifteen minutes later, I calmly hung my coat over a cheap metal chair at a bistro on Lexington Avenue where I was meeting the chief executive of American Public Media's *Marketplace*, the national radio show where I'd worked as an on-air journalist for the past eight months. I sat down next to the show's VP, Deborah Clark, while a woman from HR perched nervously across the table. I had told myself I wouldn't cry or even flinch.

I knew Clark was firing me because of a blog post I'd written the previous week, questioning the role of "objectivity" in journalism. After posting it to my personal Medium blog, I'd gotten a call from the higher-ups in Los Angeles, asking me not to come in the next day. Initially I took the blog post down. But then, overwhelmed with a sense of urgency, I changed my mind, reposted it, sent a long explanatory email to *Marketplace* management, and waited. An email on Friday afternoon let me know I'd be meeting the boss Monday morning.

That weekend felt unreal, in my life and in the country: the new president, Donald J. Trump, had just introduced the so-called Muslim ban, and people rushed to airports around the country to protest. I was out interviewing people as the crowds gathered at LaGuardia, and later watched people dance in the streets when a federal court paused the ban with an injunction.

The previous weekend had been wild, too. I had taken the bus to DC, seen the middling crowds for the inauguration of the forty-fifth president of the United States and the huge crowds for the Women's March, stopping up the streets. But Trump insisted, on his first full day as president, that his had been the biggest crowd ever at an inauguration. Sean Spicer, his press secretary, pushed the point. The Sunday morning after the giant march on Washington, Trump advisor Kellyanne Conway was asked on national television about the aerial photos showing far more people at Obama's 2009 inauguration than Trump's in 2017. She said the administration was just offering "alternative facts." I came back to work early Monday to reruns of that clip: "alternative facts" had entered the lexicon.

My mind was churning with fear about how journalists would face this new reality. On my blog a few days later, I suggested that maybe the best response to "alternative facts" was not to keep doing exactly what we had been doing last week, and the week before, and five years ago.

The post was titled "Objectivity Is Dead, and I'm Okay with It." I wrote about my experience as a transgender journalist, never neutral on the subject of my own humanity and rights, even as they were being debated in "both sides" journalism. I suggested that rather than pretending there is no "why" to what we do as journalists, we should claim our values, standing firmly against those who propose to chip away at free speech, civil rights, and government transparency. How else could we help hold back a rising tide of white supremacy and transphobia, the normalization of tyranny? I knew there was a long history of "objectivity" changing to accommodate the shifting status quo, and I wanted a journalism that rigorously pursued verifiable facts while claiming a moral stance, fighting back against racism and authoritarianism. And I thought that might be a way to rebuild trust with our audiences.

When I posted the blog, I knew it might be controversial. What I didn't know was how dramatically it would change the trajectory of my life, as my own story became part of a tense national conversation over truth and journalism. I didn't know it would lead me, eventually, to this book: a dive into the history of "objectivity" in US journalism and the stories of people who have challenged and changed how we think about truth in the news.

· · ·

At the bistro that Monday morning, Deborah Clark, the boss, seemed nervous. She had clearly prepared her speech, maybe during the flight from headquarters in LA. She let me know that my blog post and subsequent communication had made it clear that, as she put it, I "didn't want to do the kind of journalism we do at *Marketplace*." She said she believes in a clear line between journalism and activism, and that I had crossed that line. By way of demonstration, she told a story: When she was in college studying journalism, she'd been an activist around the issue of apartheid. Clark is white and British and would have been in college at the University of California, Berkeley, sometime in the 1980s, the height of the anti-apartheid struggle in South Africa. She told me she had a professor who said she'd need to make a choice: stop doing anti-apartheid activism, or abandon her desire for a career in journalism. She'd chosen journalism, she said to me with a straight face, as if leaving the anti-apartheid struggle was something a white person ought to be proud of in retrospect.

As far as I know, there hadn't been any audience complaints about the blog post or about my bias as a reporter. Still, Clark fired me on the spot, effective immediately, with an offer of two weeks' severance in exchange for agreeing not to speak publicly about what had happened. My health coverage ended two days later. I had been the first and only transgender person to work on air at the show, and one of the only trans people working at any national broadcast outlet.

I wandered off into the streets of Manhattan in shock, and the next day I put the measly severance offer in the recycling bin and went public with my story in another blog post. My goal was to expose what

I saw as a troubling double standard in which cisgender white men are treated as inherently "objective" even when they're openly biased, while the rest of us are expected to remain "neutral" even when our lives or safety are under threat. I saw this playing out in real time: *Marketplace* had a white male host who was notorious for opinionated tweets.

For a brief and exhausting moment, I became the news. Hundreds of thousands of people read my Medium posts; I was featured in dozens of news outlets—including the *Washington Post*, *On the Media*, and *Democracy Now!*—and I was also asked to speak at conferences and universities. It was clear there was a hunger for an honest conversation about the limits of objectivity and impartiality, and whether they are the right frame for journalism today. There was also a desire to hear from a working journalist willing to criticize the status quo, as well as a lot of interest in the experience of transgender journalists, because we continue to be so rare even at a time when trans issues are in the news almost daily. I sort of hated being the "transgender journalist," but it felt like a job that needed done.

The View from Somewhere is my response to the demand for a more nuanced conversation about the purpose of telling news stories in the twenty-first century, who should tell them, and how they should be told. My firing is far from the first time "objectivity" in journalism has been the subject of controversy. And many of the questions I've been asking about journalism and truth are hard to answer. Has objectivity in journalism ever really existed? Is detachment purely aspirational, and if so, is it the right aspiration? Is biased journalism a slippery slope into falsehood and distortion? What is the best response to "alternative facts"? How do we get people to care about stories that are true? Can truth survive the "post-fact" era? What is trust? What is truth?

· · ·

My urge to resist the status quo didn't materialize overnight. Before I was a journalist, I was an activist, and I more or less popped out that way—I circulated my first petition when I was eight (protesting the authoritarian stance of an elementary school lunchroom supervisor) and got suspended for insubordination multiple times during high school. I didn't like any form of unfairness, and as I grew up, I saw unfairness everywhere: in the way queer and trans youth were kicked to the curb by parents and teachers, in the way Black and brown kids were policed in school hallways, in the war, in the next war. At fifteen, I cofounded the first youth-run LGBTQ youth organization in Michigan, out of a local teen center in Ann Arbor. At nineteen, I was in the streets of San Francisco, protesting the beginnings of the US war in Iraq, and I spent much of my twenties working on issues of police violence and providing anti-racist education for and with other white people. I was woken up many mornings by news of another police killing, another eviction, another demonstration on the curb, many of which I joined.

But I never quite became the person with the bullhorn. My mind wandered. I wanted to tell stories, to constantly learn. So I wrote articles about trans women in prison, recorded audio documentaries about youth and policing in Chicago, made 'zines about transformative justice. I spent time in New Orleans after Katrina and wrote about public housing, published photos of the sunflowers growing up in old house foundations in the Lower Ninth Ward. I got a degree in religious studies and learned about gender-variant medieval saints, nineteenth-century property law, William Blake and Dante and Frantz Fanon. Everything new excited me.

I always had this dream of talking on the radio. When that opportunity came my way—through a "diversity" fellowship at Chicago Public Media in 2012—I was over the moon. I remember the excitement of working the election that November, an evening I spent crunching local election numbers, printing them out, and silently running them in to the host live in the studio. The following summer, determined to get a full-time gig in radio, I applied for jobs all over the place and ended up moving from Chicago to a small town in Ohio. At WYSO, an NPR station in Yellow Springs, I moved from reporter to managing editor, filed national stories to NPR and *Marketplace*, and generally loved the fast-paced news environment. After a few years in the cornfields, I left for a job in New York City, living out a lifelong dream.

Over the years, I filed hundreds of stories heard by millions of people. I reported on the 2013 government shutdown, the disastrous rollout of the Affordable Care Act, the slow and unequal recovery from the Great Recession, John Boehner's retirement from Congress, the rise of the Black Lives Matter movement, and, finally, the tumultuous and frenzied presidential election of 2016.

During those years, I was the only out transgender person in every newsroom, every press conference, and nearly every interview. I rarely spoke about my identity. But privately, I found the idea of a truly "objective" news media laughable, a perspective that was fairly normal in my own queer and trans community. After all, transgender people had been covered for decades with almost nothing but bias and bigotry by supposedly "objective" journalists. Constantly aware of my outsider status, I still pretended to believe that objectivity was possible in order to keep doing what I loved. My poker face sucks, but I did my best.

The traditional line in journalism is that a life on the sidelines is the price we pay for a different kind of influence, the influence of being trusted as purveyors of the facts. While I was in Ohio working for a local newsroom, my doubts about this assertion grew. I began doing research, seeking to understand where the idea of journalistic "objectivity" had come from, and how it had been challenged and changed over time. This book traces that research from before I got fired, to after my firing and the publicity surrounding it.

Much of the research is about the past, but my own reflections are very much in the present, from my limited perspective as an educated white US citizen. During this process of learning and writing, I established a freelance career, realized that the "New York media bubble" is real, and moved from Brooklyn to Durham, North Carolina. My viewpoint is strongly shaped by having lived most of my life in the Midwest and finding most of my family roots, and my current home, in the American South.

. . .

One problem that plagues this book throughout is the many uses of the word "objectivity." In general, I will use it to refer to the modern journalistic ideal as it is performed and enacted in mainstream newsrooms. In his book *Just the Facts*, media historian David Mindich breaks newsroom "objectivity" down into five basic components: detachment, nonpartisanship, the use of the inverted pyramid model for news, facticity, and balance. But sometimes "objectivity" refers to the practices of journalists, and sometimes "objectivity" refers to the perceptions of audiences—in other words, journalists can attempt to be objective, while audiences can see them as unobjective and biased. And some use "objectivity" simply to mean the absence of inaccuracy and distortion, not as a synonym for impartiality. In each chapter, I attempt to pull the elements apart: Is impartiality ever possible? Is detachment the same as nonpartisanship? What is the difference between attempting "balance" and attempting to *appear* "balanced"? When "objectivity" responds to public perceptions, which public is it?

My argument against "objectivity" doesn't abandon facts, truth, or the hope that we will pursue them without undue influence from political parties or corporations. Broadly, I argue in favor of facticity and nonpartisanship, elements of "objectivity." A related idea of editorial independence also continues to resonate for me: while no one is ever entirely independent of influence, the effort for publications to remain independent from big money and political parties is important to journalistic integrity. But in public debates over news and "objectivity," this concept of institutional editorial independence is often confused with the detachment or impartiality of the individual journalist. It is this idea of a detached, impartial journalist that I take the strongest issue with, and argue vehemently against, pushing instead for transparency and self-awareness.

Lots of journalistic organizations, including the Society of Professional Journalists, have long since dropped the word "objectivity" from their ethical codes, opting instead to advocate for transparency and fairness in reporting. In the case of American Public Media's *Marketplace*, where I worked, "objectivity" wasn't actually in the ethics policy—"impartiality" was the word of choice. This makes sense, given how thoroughly "objectivity" has already been debunked. But, as I learned in my own case, the use of replacement terms such as "impartiality" or "fairness" still allows for a great deal of interpretation, which can often result in invisible double standards: Fair to whom? Impartial in whose view? This book asks whether journalism *needs* objectivity and impartiality anymore, whether and why we need to stay out of the fray.

. . .

One of the most helpful frames I came across in my research is the work of media scholar Daniel C. Hallin. In his 1986 book on Vietnam, *The "Uncensored War,"* he explains the limits of "objective" journalism in the US through a simple graphic of two concentric circles. The center is the sphere of consensus, the first ring is the sphere of legitimate controversy, and outside of both rings is the sphere of deviance.

As he explains it, the inner sphere of consensus is what American journalists deem to be so thoroughly agreed-upon that you can advocate for it in your work and still be seen as "objective": ideas like *patriotism is good* or *capitalism is better than communism.* The second circle, the sphere of legitimate controversy, is where most "objective" news reporting and most attempts at balance play out: it encompasses things like Democrats versus Republicans, and debates over constitutional rights and freedoms. In mainstream journalism, the sphere of legitimate controversy is the playing field, with prevailing norms defining the boundaries.

The outer sphere of deviance is where ideas live that aren't viewed by most journalists as legitimate and worth engaging. As Hallin writes, during wartime the idea of siding with the enemy typically lives in that sphere—the peaceniks who saw the Vietcong as revolutionaries and stood on their side weren't usually brought onto the evening news shows. The sphere of deviance has also always contained people, ideas, and structures that are close to me. When I was born, in 1984, the idea of gay rights was mostly outside the sphere of legitimate controversy. The concepts of transgender identity and gender nonconformity were pretty much entirely in the sphere of deviance. And of course, when my mother was born, in South Carolina in 1948, racial integration was just making its way from deviance into the sphere of legitimate controversy. A quarter century later, in the 1970s, she taught high school during the first year of integrated schooling in South Carolina.

The point being that the sphere of legitimate controversy changes, and it can change in any direction. In moving questions from the sphere of deviance into the sphere of legitimate controversy, journalists and other members of the public often collaborate in complex ways. And the topics and debates that fit into the spheres of consensus and controversy reflect particular ideologies and worldviews. As radio producer Ramona Martinez said to me in an interview, "Objectivity is the ideology of the status quo."

Looking at how acceptable debate shifts over time, based on often-unspoken ideological frames, puts useful context around the idea of being impartial. Impartiality at the time of our country's founding meant support for the institution of slavery. Impartiality today may mean a tacit agreement to watch people die of thirst and starvation at our national border to the south, or to send innocent people to a death sentence. Impartiality under apartheid meant accepting unequal racial segregation in every aspect of life. Claims of "objective" approaches to such questions can quickly devolve into a moral relativism that is dangerous and antithetical to a free society. And I am unabashed in my desire to live in a way that strives toward freedom, for myself and others.

· · ·

The stories in *The View from Somewhere* reflect my subjective search for particular kinds of people: rabble-rousers who resisted, challenged, or shook up standards for news production in the past. As a result, there's an element of confirmation bias to this book. I sought diverse people who'd resisted "objectivity," and I found them. Far more journalists, of many backgrounds, have either put up with or actively upheld the status quo within journalism, and that is fine with me. This book is not out to prove that their journalism was bad, but to tell stories of people who took risks to make change. I tell these stories with the shameless goal of legitimizing these debates, bringing them into focus at a time when so many of us are searching for a new way of looking at truth, fact, and identity. I also aim to highlight the ways in which "objectivity" has been used to push out and silence the voices of those who are already marginalized and oppressed. My hope is that these marginalized people and communities can reclaim journalism as our own.

The View from Somewhere starts in Ohio, where I first started researching "objectivity," race, and power in journalism. My exploration of those themes had obvious origins: the death of Michael Brown and the rise of the Black Lives Matter movement, which happened right after a police killing in a Walmart less than ten miles from where I was living. I was troubled by the way I, as a journalist and editor, did and didn't cover these incidents, and I watched as #BlackLives Matter challenged and changed the judgment of news outlets, as well as my own judgment. Black journalists like Steven Thrasher and Wesley Lowery were among many to help shift the coverage at the time.

My doubts about the ethics of how journalists cover Black lives and deaths were confirmed when I began to study history—in the earliest days of "objectivity," Ida B. Wells and other Black journalists were branded as radicals for documenting lynchings in the US. I learned about many other journalists who resisted "objectivity." Wells's editor and friend T. Thomas Fortune wrote about the difference between being nonpartisan and being neutral in the 1890s. Labor organizers and writers Marvel Cooke and Heywood Broun were part of the earliest newspaper strikes in the 1930s, just as the "objective" ideal for journalism solidified. *New York Times* reporter and disability activist Kerry Gruson spoke out against the Vietnam War while working as a journalist and had an experience covering Vietnam that changed her perspective for the rest of her life. Sandy Nelson, a lesbian socialist reporter, sacrificed her mainstream journalism career in the late 1980s to make a point about freedom of speech.

There are plenty of more contemporary examples, too: Desmond Cole of the *Toronto Star*, who insisted on the importance of protest as a Black journalist; *New York Times* reporter Linda Greenhouse, whose 2017 memoir on her life as a journalist contains a thoughtful critique of the performance of "objectivity"; journalists who reject "objectivity" in their coverage of white supremacy, including Pulitzer Prize–winner

Rachel Kaadzi Ghansah, Peabody-nominated podcaster John Biewen, *Guardian* correspondent Gary Younge; and Meredith Talusan, a former BuzzFeed reporter who has been working to create new models for storytelling as a Filipina trans person. These journalists have dramatic stories of resisting traditional journalistic "objectivity" and exciting ideas about what it could mean to be a journalist today.

Of course, I can't talk about challenges to "objectivity" without talking about its powerful opponents in right-wing media. During the so-called age of consensus—the post-WWII era in the United States when relatively liberal, anti-Communist, and pro-capitalist ideology was dominant within the white power structure—right-wing activists largely agreed with left-wing activists that objectivity was a mythology favoring the status quo. But in the 1960s, this widespread perception of a unified sphere of mainstream consensus began to fall apart. Right-wing activists then figured out a brilliant strategy to capitalize on that fragmentation: smear any media they didn't like as "biased," while claiming that any media they *did* like was fair and impartial. Notably, in the 1970s, right-wing media watchdogs and activists helped undermine public broadcasting in its earliest days by vilifying it for having a "liberal bias," a tactic that worked to pull public media to the right and to encourage censorship of people of color and LGBTQ people.

That sidelining of already marginalized voices, not just in public media but in all mainstream media, has real consequences. I take as an example what happened in the 1980s, when the AIDS crisis emerged and then exploded in the absence of big-ticket news coverage. The stories of gay media activists from that time period show how what is within the sphere of legitimate controversy can have life-or-death consequences, and how quickly the sphere of acceptable debate can change. Gay journalists and documentarians John Scagliotti, Andrew Kopkind, and Marlon Riggs animated my research into how journalists can be a part of changing the frame.

By the end of the 1990s, *Fox News* had emerged with the tagline "We Report, You Decide." It was the ultimate distortion of the mythology of objectivity: Fox was unabashed in its partisanship, but fully claimed the title of "objective." Through the story of scorned former right-wing journalist David Brock, I look at how right-wing media's "objective" charade has dangerous consequences, as the public becomes more and more cynical about truth, fact, and reality. But I argue that we can't fight that cynicism with a return to a mythical "objective" past.

Throughout *The View from Somewhere*, I attempt to pull on the threads of race, class, and gender that constantly reveal themselves in debates about whether "objectivity" is the right frame for twenty-first-century journalism. I look critically at some of my own reporting during the 2016 presidential election, and I consider the history of the coverage of transgender people, which has always been subjective and ideological. I argue that that's okay: everyone has a frame through which we think, interpret, and speak. Once we are conscious of these frames, we can choose our stories and the values they reflect.

A part of the backdrop for this book is the popular twenty-first-century belief that the news media is in crisis. This idea that the press has been pushed to a breaking point by rampant clickbait, unabashed media bias, and the decline of local print media has been the topic of many tomes over the last couple of decades. The proliferation of options for online news, combined with the growing power of social media platforms, has decimated the business model for news media, forcing many organizations to shrink, go under, or radically rethink their structures. Certainly, the funding model is broken, a problem I don't try to solve here. But some of my conclusions are hopeful.

I don't believe that there is only one truth, but I still believe that truth is worth pursuing, and its pursuit still requires the rigorous practice of reporting. The careful observation of events, gathering of commentary, verification through a variety of means, and the production and analysis of data are all aspects of "objective" journalism I would not do away with. I don't propose that everything journalists do should be a polemic or an opinion piece, however subjective all reporting may be. By vocation, journalists are looking for new facts, truths that require seeing outside of ourselves. We see and interpret these truths through our ever-subjective lens, but it is our job to go looking, to try to be honest about the search.

Abandoning "objectivity" leaves us in need of new ways to think about journalism and trust, work that many people are already doing; transparency, equity, an analysis of power and oppression, and community accountability are all elements of the movement to revive and revise journalism for the twenty-first century. Journalists in the US today need to define our values, identify and acknowledge the ideological frames from which we work, and develop tools for being accountable to the communities we cover. Verification, deep sourcing, and data-based research must increasingly be paired with radical transparency and media activism; curiosity must increasingly be paired with a sharp, and shifting, analysis of power and oppression and how they operate both in our daily lives and in our newsrooms. Rebuilding trust with audiences must begin at the grassroots.

While I don't propose a single solution to save us from the sinking ship of "objectivity," I am persuaded that "just the facts" is no longer enough to justify the existence of journalism. We need to ask ourselves: What will our facts be in service of in the future? Fascism or democracy? Capitalism or collectivity? Anti-racism or white supremacy? These aren't idle questions, but consequential ones that we can't erase by pretending they aren't there or by clinging to dated notions of consensus, notions that evolved when there were hardly any women or people of color in newsrooms.

And it matters more than ever who is making the news. Until recently, the majority of Americans were excluded from even being journalists because they were women, people of color, or LGBTQ. As I discovered through my research, gay journalists were the ones who made more room for stories about gay people and AIDS; Black anti-lynching activists were the leaders in telling stories about the terrors of Jim Crow laws; #BlackLivesMatter activists were the ones who created an opening for better reporting on police killings; and transgender writers have been leading the debate over trans issues for two decades, in spite of our exclusion from much of the supposedly "objective" discussions about our lives. A wonderful part of the end of "objectivity" is that oppressed people's voices can no longer be excluded on the false pretense that we are biased in favor of our own humanity, that we are too close to the story.

· · ·

As you may have gathered from my repeated use of the terms "fact" and "truth," I don't believe we're in a post-fact era. We have lots of facts, lots of information—more raw data about the world is available than ever before. This abundance of facts is perhaps exactly why there is so much pressure for the role of the journalist to change, and so much insecurity about who can or should be a journalist. We are no longer professional intermediaries, controlling the access to information the way print journalists did in the 1950s—Facebook and Twitter and YouTube have taken over that role, with little regard for the standards previously held dear by journalists.

Some are horrified by the idea that people can just skip stories they don't want to hear, go only to websites that reflect their own worldview. As a member of an outsider community too long misrepresented in mainstream news, I'm not horrified by this new paradigm of choice: I'm delighted by its potential and interested in its consequences. I think what we're trying to figure out today is how journalists can become people who don't just impart facts, but who interact, engage, and ultimately bring meaning and shape to information. Our stories still matter, because they tell people what world they live in, and help people imagine what other worlds might be possible. But it is more important than ever how and why these stories are produced.

The View from Somewhere is ultimately an argument against what I view as a damaging false dichotomy. I believe journalists can seek the truth without engaging in a battle against the subjective or the activist. And battles against subjectivity and activism have too often amounted to being battles against the marginalized and oppressed. That is because the center is ever shifting and "objectivity" is a false ideal that upholds the status quo. Once we accept that, I believe journalists can apply a new rigor and sense of mission to our work. I don't ask that other people's sense of mission be the same as mine. But I do hope we can take responsibility for the choices we face in shaping reality.

1

HOW BLACK LIVES MATTER
MADE THE NEWS

It was barely August, and I was doing early morning shifts as a radio host. That meant getting up right around sunrise and biking a few blocks through thick summer shadows to WYSO, the small radio station on the campus of Antioch College. Our newsroom was bare bones. A clunky PC glowed from one of the two desks, wire copy popping up on the screen in a steady stream. It was still called wire copy, as if it comes to us through an old telegraph wire, but it was actually the Associated Press sending dispatches over the internet. Every morning I'd sit in the dark, drink coffee, and run my eyes over tornados and fires and kidnappings and infanticides and voter turnout and political play-by-plays, the occasional "human interest" story. Once in a while there'd be some bit of humor or joy, usually on a slow news day.

On this particular morning shift, the story that jumped out at me was a police story, or rather a story about a man and the police, a quick AP dispatch about an event in Beavercreek, Ohio, a suburb ten miles from where I was sitting in the air-conditioned dark, with my face lit by the virtual wire. It opened something like this:

> A man in a southwest Ohio Wal-Mart store waved a rifle at customers, including children, and was fatally shot by police when he wouldn't drop the weapon, according to police and a recorded 911 call from a witness.

Authorities say a customer also died after suffering a medical problem
during the evacuation of the store Tuesday. Police identified her as
Angela Williams, 37, of Fairborn.

Police identified the man shot Tuesday night at a Wal-Mart in the Dayton suburb of Beavercreek as 22-year-old John Crawford of Cincinnati.
He died at a hospital.

He waved a rifle. He wouldn't drop the weapon. Did I revise the
wording, knowing even then to be skeptical of police narratives? I
might have added another "police say" to qualify, aware that a man
who is dead cannot tell his side of the story. I had, after all, been an
activist around this stuff for years; before I was a journalist, I co-
created and ran a website full of young people of color's stories about
harassment and violence at the hands of police in Chicago. Growing
up, my dad, an attorney, had told me, "Cops always lie." So I knew
enough to know that a police statement does not a true story make.
What I didn't know was that this was the beginning of the end of my
faith in the whole system of news-making into which I'd been trained.
That August, everything was about to change—the way the news covered policing, the way I thought about the news, and the relationship
between activism and the news. It was a tipping point, but I couldn't
see that yet.

Of course I couldn't. It was 5:30 a.m.; I was alone in the so-called
newsroom, rushed because I was prepping for a 6 a.m. hard start,
when I'd have to be ready with a four-minute newscast, the weather
for today and this week, and traffic updates, saying all this into a mic
while operating the soundboard and not making mistakes of any kind,
or at least not making the kind of mistakes people catch: a mispronun-
ciation, a wrong name, a verbal stumble, running over my time. With
an audience of several thousand even that early, people notice when
you mess up.

So that morning, in a mix of other sad stories, I read the copy
about that death in Beavercreek and didn't think too much of it—
another shitty news day. Beavercreek is an almost-entirely white sub-

urb of Dayton, Ohio. I didn't think much about who the man might be who'd been killed, but I pictured some wacked-out white dude, waving that gun at some kids. Incidents with white dudes and guns seemed to happen every day somewhere, so, sure as I was that journalists shouldn't trust police, I figured they'd stopped some shit from going down that could have been national news, could have dominated my day: "Shooter kills four children in Ohio Walmart," Lewis Wallace reports from Dayton. Instead it was just a "police-involved shooting," a blip. One life, which can begin to seem like nothing when you're reading out death every day. This is horrible, but I'm saying it because it's true and it can become part of how you think when you're doing daily news.

There are lots of true stories in the world. Daily news is where they are first pared down, selected out in a process called "news judgment": the split-second decisions about what is a story, and just how big and new that story is, how much airtime or word count it deserves. The decisions about which truths get told can have a ripple effect— sometimes a protest that gets news coverage becomes a larger protest; an act of violence or terrorism gains imitators and followers; a radical ideology propagates in the mainstream in part because it's been talked about on the news. I was astounded and humbled most days by the fact that I had this kind of power to choose what would become news. There I was, a weird transgender punk, alone in a dark room with my cup of coffee, making decisions that would, in small or large ways, shape what people believed their world was made up of, what was important and possible. I was also acutely aware of the stories that didn't get told, the dispatches that came through the wire and went nowhere. At the time, it was rare that a story about a police shooting got told in much depth. These deaths were covered like poverty or cancer: a thing that happens, too routine to highlight every time in a headline.

If you were one of the people reading newswires in the morning, it was obvious what stories and events were being left out. But for the people listening, it was like they never happened.

The day brightened. People came in and filled up the cheerful old gray-carpeted science building that the radio station was now housed in, after years in a moldy basement under the student center. WYSO was the NPR station for the cities of Dayton and Springfield, but still remained in its founding spot on a college campus, and a strange college campus at that. Antioch is known for its anarchist leanings and frequent closures due to budget problems. Even with the closures, the station had been thriving there consistently since the 1950s, and it had become a mainstay. We had a membership who trusted us, a relatively diverse staff, a robust community outreach program. We were proud that we aired voices from all over the region talking about the problems that affected our listening area, like the still-lingering recession and water pollution and abandoned homes, gas prices and troubled charter schools and closed-up strip malls. We covered immigration, welfare, health care, and the sprawling US Air Force base, the jobs that came and went with each federal budget. Dayton is in many ways the epicenter of Middle America, a perfect microcosm of every Rust Belt problem and every hopeful story about overcoming it. I loved this job.

So I moved on from the miserable wire copy that morning. The on-air shift ran from 6 to 9 a.m. and then I'd prerecord and mix some stuff for the next day, stick some stories up online that I'd aired that morning, eat something real quick, drink more coffee, and start reporting, which could mean anything: working phones, running out the door to meet the latest subject for a story, who might be city official downtown, or a farmer talking about property taxes, or a group of kids hanging out in a park in a run-down part of town, sharing their dreams of getting out. That day I went to an interview in downtown Dayton and drove back home alone through the quiet suburbs, radio humming WYSO's afternoon music into my ears. Just after 1, 2, and 3 p.m., I'd listen carefully to the five-minute NPR newscast. It was a quiet summer. No big stories going on.

On Friday, August 8, there was an update to this wire story.

A man who was fatally shot by police in a Wal-Mart store in a Dayton suburb after officers say he waved a weapon at customers was carrying an air rifle, Ohio's attorney general said Thursday. Attorney General

Mike DeWine released a brief statement after the state's crime bureau said it had taken over the investigation of the shooting at the request of Beavercreek police. Police had said John Crawford, 22, waved a rifle at customers Tuesday night and was fatally shot when he wouldn't drop the weapon. DeWine said the man had a "variable pump air rifle" made by Crosman Corp.

It had emerged that the weapon John Crawford was holding in the store was an air rifle, a BB gun—a kind that's sold at Walmart. There was more to the story, and this line further down stood out to me: "Family members and friends of Crawford had said earlier that he didn't have a real gun and suggested that the purported rifle was a toy."

We read this new copy on air, kept going with our busy day. In the days that followed, the headlines began to morph. It became clear that Crawford had picked up an unloaded BB gun/air rifle that was on display in the Walmart, and he was still on the phone with his children's mother when he was shot; the officer who had shot Crawford had been involved in the only other fatal police shooting in the department's history, five years before. An open box was found on a Walmart display. The Beavercreek Police Department declined comment, and the case was passed on to the state's attorney general.

On Saturday, August 9, a local lawyer, Michael Wright, announced he would be holding a press conference with John Crawford III's parents, saying they were skeptical of police accounts of his death. "The family wants answers," Wright said to the local TV station. "We just want to get answers. We are seeking video, witness statements and investigatory items." The radio station was quiet that day, volunteer DJs going in and out the glass doors. I was at home, cooking and gardening, glancing at my phone. No one from the station attended Monday's press conference: not enough staff to cover it.

Saturday, August 9, 2014. It flicked across my phone sometime that night, maybe the next morning. Something had happened in a place called Ferguson. That day, a baby-faced eighteen-year-old named Michael Brown had been shot and killed by police outside St. Louis, Missouri, and his neighbors and family members had watched and tweeted as his body lay crumpled and bloodied on the sidewalk for hours. That night, the police in Ferguson held a press conference, but by then, the protests had already started. Ferguson, Missouri, was opening up to the rage and sadness of Michael Brown's death, and it was happening quickly; there were rumors of rioting, property destruction. The sense that something larger was about to jump off had spread across social media. This day, this moment, would begin weeks of daily national coverage that came to be referred to just as "Ferguson" ("Did you cover Ferguson?"; "I went to Ferguson"), but Ferguson was shorthand for "Black people are dying at the hands of police, and there is now a giant and growing protest movement to stop it."

As I took it all in on Monday morning, I felt a flush of shame. Just days before Brown's death became the biggest story in the country, I had overlooked our own local version of that story. I had seen it flash by on the screen, read some lines about it on air, and assumed it was a blip. I had gone along with it as John Crawford, unarmed and now dead, was first defined in the public eye as a "suspect." I'd done something I knew better than to do: repeated an official narrative without looking any further. Suddenly the whole country was watching this same dynamic play out in another midwestern city. Activists in the street were asking: Why do the police keep killing young Black people, particularly those who are unarmed? How many, how often, how disproportionately? They were demanding that the news media cover these deaths. Twitter was on fire; Facebook was on fire; Ferguson was on fire.

What would happen in the weeks and months to follow would change not only my own approach to reporting, but the way my entire industry approached stories about police violence and race. Black Lives Matter, the movement and the organizations and people involved in it, would do what their predecessors in the civil rights movement had done decades before: pose a protracted challenge to news judgment, to which stories get told and why. This change didn't happen because white reporters like me sat in newsrooms somewhere and realized what we'd done wrong, that we'd criminalized the victims or idealized the perpetrators, and it didn't happen because there was a white awakening in the United States about what Black Americans were living through, or because there were more Black reporters in newsrooms than ever before (unfortunately, there weren't). It happened because a hashtag and a movement took hold, and part of that movement's strategy was to shift the frame, to put all Black people's deaths at the hands of the police into the sphere of legitimate controversy. Journalistic ideas about news judgment and balance would be pushed to a breaking point. "Police-involved shooting," the terminology preferred by law enforcement, would become a pointedly non-neutral phrase. Black Lives Matter functioned, in a way, as a news organization, shifting the frame by using Twitter and Facebook and Instagram and Snapchat to tell the stories being left out of the news.

· · ·

Suddenly everyone was talking about Ferguson. The national media focused on property destruction and conflicts between police and protesters; local media looked for "local angles" like protesters traveling to Missouri or holding similar protests in their own towns. And my busy, harried self knew that we had just had a police shooting in our coverage area, that the man had died, that he'd been holding an air rifle that police initially said was a firearm. But what I didn't realize until August 9, 2014, the day of Michael Brown's death, was that John Crawford III was Black and his shooter was white. The man who'd called the police on Crawford, Ronald Ritchie, was also white.

About two weeks after Brown's death, a group of Antioch students called a protest as part of the national #HandsUpWalkOut event. The students and a handful of community members were going to speak the names of Black people killed by police and hold blown-up printouts of their portraits. Michael Brown. Oscar Grant. Eric Garner. John Crawford III. These students, along with a group called the Ohio Student Association, were determined to get Crawford's name and face into the news. Another local group organized a protest for Crawford at the federal courthouse, responding in part to requests by his parents in Cincinnati—they were crushed, and convinced that racism had killed their son. They were also determined to find out what had happened: Why had a man holding a product sold in the Walmart been shot and killed? Who were the officers involved, and were they facing any consequences? Was there surveillance video showing these events? Why couldn't the public see those tapes? In that terrible moment, another person had also died—a woman who was inside the Walmart had a heart attack on her way to the door after hearing the police gunshots.

Pretty soon, the Ohio Student Association was demanding that Ohio Attorney General Mike DeWine release the surveillance video from Walmart. And suddenly John Crawford went from a few lines off the wire to the most important story we were covering: activists had come from other states to demonstrate in front of the Greene County Courthouse. Crawford's aggrieved parents were in BuzzFeed. DeWine held a press conference to announce a grand jury investigation into the case. While no new details about the shooting itself were coming out, our station covered its ripple effects: the voices of the young activists, the attorney general's restrained attempts to project empathy for the family, the occasional blustering white person dismissing the protesters as angry about nothing. At the end of September, the attorney general's office released a limited section of surveillance video from that evening. Because activists had been demanding its release, the video itself was news. The footage was immediately plastered across the internet: Black man shot by police in cold blood in a Walmart, and so on. During this time period, I had become the managing editor at WYSO, and I was tasked with sitting down with our web editor and afternoon host to decide both how to report this development and whether to post the video to our site.

That meant watching the video, multiple times, hunched over someone's laptop in the common space outside our broadcast studio. There was no sound, and our station kept blaring music through the speakers while we watched the grainy video of Crawford, with tiny twists in his hair, baggy jeans, and a T-shirt, walking distractedly through the aisle, talking on his phone. You don't see the moment when he scoops up the unloaded BB gun, but suddenly he has it. He's not apparently pointing it at anyone; he's on the phone, talking in an animated way, the BB gun hanging at his side. He's visibly distracted and does not, to me, look threatening. The moment when he gets shot is surprising even when you know it's coming: his body suddenly goes stiff with fear, he looks down the aisle toward someone, and, seemingly immediately, he drops to the floor and dips out of sight of the camera, crawling as if in the trenches of a war zone. He stands briefly and reappears, then collapses again as two police officers rush toward him, guns drawn.

That's the end of the video, which would later be coupled with audio from the phone call he was on. One of the officers handcuffed Crawford as he bled to death. His ex, still on the phone with him, was hanging out at his mom's house with the kids, and she handed the phone to his mom after she heard the shots. His mother, Tressa Sherrod, stayed on the line listening as her twenty-two-year-old son bled out in the pet food aisle.

By the next morning, there was a police statement claiming he had waved a gun and ignored orders to drop it. It is still unknown whether police were lying when they said he had a real gun, or truly didn't know at the time of their press release that it was an unloaded BB gun. It is also still unknown whether Ronald Ritchie, the 911 caller, consciously lied or exaggerated about Crawford waving it at people; we did learn later that Ritchie had lied about his former military status when the story first became public. In any case, an "active shooter" was nowhere in this video. It was blurry, yes, and the timing was hard to make out. But Ohio is an open-carry state, and what I saw was a picture of a tragedy—a murder. I was increasingly horrified that I had ever been part of telling the police version of the story: the shock and fear and vulnerability I'd seen in Crawford's young body kept me up at night. We decided not to post it but put a link to the video in our story about the news of its release.

The video brought still more attention to the case. Because of the activists who had stirred the pot, John Crawford's death had become a story, a story with obvious parallels to Michael Brown's death and the deaths of many other Black people at the hands of police, and with obvious connections to institutionalized police practices, to rules and policies or the lack thereof. My colleague Jerry Kenney did a national story for NPR about the case. We did local stories about police body cameras, about efforts to better track police violence in the state, about religious responses to Crawford's death. For one piece, I talked to a Black preacher in Dayton who was also the only Black father on his block. He lived in Beavercreek, the suburb where Crawford had been killed, and he said he was afraid for his sons, told them not to play in the yard. The killing of a twelve-year-old holding a toy gun was not unprecedented in our state: by the time I interviewed him, it had just happened to Tamir Rice in Cleveland. In December 2014, I did a piece for NPR about several multiracial families in Dayton who were heading to DC for a march on Washington about police violence. A photograph of John Crawford III holding his newborn son circulated around the internet and was turned into paintings and posters.

. . .

This shift, from John Crawford as a blip to John Crawford as a story, was part of a national strategy advanced by activists associated with the hashtag #BlackLivesMatter to make every police-involved death into a news story. Mervyn Marcano was one of the people who'd been plotting the movement's media strategy nearly from the beginning, as a communications director with several nonprofits including Color of Change, and later with his own communications firm, Blackbird, which worked largely behind the scenes through many of these key developments.

Marcano, who, like me, was in his early thirties when Michael Brown died, is clever and cynical beyond his years, with a wide smile and a soft mustache. He's also an old friend of mine, from when we were both underage queer youth who had more or less run away from home to a collective house in Detroit (but that's definitely another story). While I was managing the chaos of covering a national story from a tiny local newsroom in Ohio, he was living in Oakland and watching the developments in Ferguson on Twitter and on TV. The first two weeks, he said, it was all about the "breaking news disaster press corps." On TV and in most newspapers, the images were of a chaotic scene: trash cans burning, protesters facing off with riot cops after dark, police press conferences calling for calm. But he saw a completely different narrative on social media. There, the Ferguson story was about grief, Black death, a wounded community that had finally boiled over. Black Twitter was at a fever pitch, #BlackLivesMatter was trending, and #HandsUpDontShoot had become a refrain. On TV, it was about "violent protests" and unruly streets: a "too bad, so sad" event prompting an overreaction. Even the NPR coverage, which I followed carefully, frequently focused on the property destruction and referred to protests as "riots."

"The less violence there was, the less interesting this story was to them," Marcano said of the national media. In the first two weeks of coverage, "people were being talked about as criminals, going to war with the police. There wasn't real storytelling about Ferguson." In a moment that became notorious among journalists and activists, the *New York Times* referred to Michael Brown as "no angel" in a story discussing his upcoming memorial.

About two weeks after Brown's death, Marcano flew from Oakland to Ferguson at the request of local organizers in Missouri and stayed for six months. By that time, he said, most of the major media had left—and that was when his work with Blackbird became really important.

· · ·

After the fact, we know a lot about Ferguson. We know that in a majority-Black town with a police force of fifty-three, fifty of the cops were white. We know that Black residents there had long endured a toxic mix of racialized targeting and a municipal court system that funded itself through tickets for traffic stops and minor violations that amount to a police tax on Ferguson's poorest residents. Thanks to a federal investigation spurred by the protests, we know that police had routinely covered up abuses, particularly of Black people. And we know that the community there had reached a boiling point for a set of reasons that went way beyond the details of what happened to Michael Brown. Images of his death, the brazenness of the police who left his body laying out for hours, were a last straw. But in August

2014, virtually none of that had yet been reported in national or local media.

And so Ferguson appeared in the news as a sudden explosion, not as a pot boiling over. Before then, the St. Louis area's Black neighborhoods were largely reported on TV news as sites of crime and violence; in more liberal outlets, they were "tough" places full of poverty and disinvestment. That a lot of Black people in Missouri went to jail and prison was reported; why this was the case was largely unexplored. That "police-community relations" were bad was certainly known; again, the reasons why were rarely illuminated in a news story.

Ferguson and St. Louis were no different than most other parts of the country, where strong police unions and police organizations such as the Fraternal Order of Police had long pursued a strategy of fighting every accusation of police abuse, tooth and nail, protecting both their individual members and their profession writ large. Police organizations participated assertively in shaping narratives about "police-involved shootings," while fragmented and impoverished communities like Ferguson had fewer structures in place to counter the official narrative. What this meant for decades was that when a Black person got killed by police, the police had extensive media organization behind them, and the Black person did not. A few cases got national coverage anyway, like Rodney King, Amadou Diallo, and Oscar Grant, who was one of the first examples of police killing a Black man while cell phones recorded from all sides.

News reporting often reflected this disparity in resources, and, as such, it wasn't so much false reporting as lazy or even just under-resourced reporting. Reporters were doing what I had done when I read that wire copy about John Crawford: reflecting the information available without any attempt to overcome preexisting power dynamics. What to report and focus on was decided by default, and getting the police version was easy, while getting the rest was hard.

Mervyn Marcano and his team were PR people, in the business of communications and spin. Still, they aimed not to propagate tall tales about cops or depict them as individually bad people, but to expose institutional power structures. They wanted to right historical wrongs by filling in the gaping holes in the picture, by helping to answer the burning questions: Why had these tragedies happened? Why did they keep happening? Why were police so often protected when they killed innocent or unarmed people, especially Black people? Marcano and his team started with shifting the narrative around protest. Local police at the time would hold a nightly press conference, feeding the major outlets their version of what had happened in the last twenty-four hours. As Marcano describes it, these conferences followed a familiar formula: They'd pull out a brick that was thrown, or some other evidence of a property damage, and point to the protesters en masse as the cause. They'd list off arrests and get asked few questions by reporters filling in details for their nightly filing.

Reporters, meanwhile, weren't necessarily doing the lofty and idealistic job they'd learned about in journalism school. They were scrambling under the daily pressures of the job, getting to "the story" in the fastest and easiest way they could, under pressure from bosses and a twenty-four-hour news cycle. As a result, these stories followed a formula, too: the official facts, a comment from police, maybe an attempt to speak to a random "eyewitness" or "man on the street" to give the story authenticity and color. In this fast-moving environment, packed with national and international media, there was pressure to scoop the next development, with little incentive to slow down and investigate the context more deeply. Local news was already defunded to a devastating extent; police beat reporters were rare, and where they did exist, it took a strong mind to do anything more than keep up with the newsreel put out by police themselves. National outlets with more resources came and went based on how sensational the story was.

Marcano was sympathetic to the situation of journalists and saw his role as helping them.

"We had to educate journalists in terms of using police press releases and why that's not a good idea. This moment requires more than blotter reporting," he said. He worked the crowd at those press events, connecting the more interested journalists with local residents, individual protesters, people whose lives had been affected directly by the ongoing police abuses. He took them to people's houses, so journalists could meet with community members and get another side of the story, instead of sitting in their hotels waiting for the next police press conference. And he and Blackbird began to help journalists frame the problem differently, to connect them with sources who would explain why Michael Brown's death wasn't viewed as an isolated incident by people in Ferguson.

"That's the kind of stuff you had to train journalists to tease out," he said. These journalists weren't substandard, but they also weren't superhuman—not knowing what questions to ask, particularly when you are covering an unfamiliar situation or community, is normal. What Blackbird was trying to do was make it unacceptable not to look beneath the surface of the story. Blackbird worked closely with activists to put out daily notices with their own official version of what had happened and developed source lists and training documents for journalists. They did one-on-one meetings, helped with outreach around an upcoming action that October, and connected with activists across the country working under the #BlackLivesMatter banner.

Eventually, Marcano says, the coverage did change. Over time, the story became about the structures that led to the protests: the racism, the institutional abuse, the forced segregation and disinvestment that had built the St. Louis area into a world of extreme and visible inequality. Surrounding Brown's death were decades of torn-down housing projects, neighborhoods split by highways, white flight and the collapse of industry, a massive loss of Black wealth in the housing crash, and endemic police violence against Black communities dating back to the earliest days of the city's existence. There was a legacy of white supremacy and anti-Blackness in the county and the state, sometimes blatant, sometimes embedded in policy. Bit by bit, that larger story began to be told out of Missouri.

I wish it were true that journalists were already doing all this—the sourcing, the teasing out, the analysis, the history. I wish our assumption was that no police story can be told with just a statement from the police. I wish we had an analysis of the ways in which historical white supremacy undergirds even the simplest little news story. And yet I, too, had been guilty of blotter reporting, just weeks before all this, as I read wire copy about John Crawford in the predawn light. It's not incidental that I am white: mostly white newsrooms typically weren't sufficiently attentive to police killings, or to any racial justice issue, and they had often waited for outside pressure to cover communities of color in any thorough and deep way. The presence of Black reporters had certainly helped, but for decades now, there's been a dearth of Black journalists in both broadcast and print newsrooms, and in recent years that problem has gotten worse, not better, in many newsrooms.

Marcano says that oftentimes Blackbird was teaching journalists "how to cover Black people," how to clue into conversations already well underway in many Black communities. Wesley Lowery of the *Washington Post*, one of the journalists who did the earliest in-depth coverage of Ferguson and one of the few Black journalists covering police for a national outlet, arrived on the scene just after Brown died and was arrested two days later by Ferguson police inside a McDonald's. Marcano said he worked closely with Lowery, and the *Post* became the outlet, along with the *Guardian*, that did the most thorough and sustained coverage of the Black Lives Matter movement and its causes and goals. But these two outlets' coverage happened against the odds, and their decision to dedicate so many resources to it came in part because of ongoing mass protests in the city. Lowery's editors rarely sent him to the places where protests fizzled.

. . .

The fallout in Ferguson stretched across the country. Suddenly #Black LivesMatter was in the news almost daily. But in Chicago, where I'd spent seven years before I went to Ohio for the WYSO job, police killings were and remain so routine, it took a whole team of people from multiple organizations to begin to shift how media covered these events.

Aislinn Pulley, a lifelong Chicagoan whose parents were socialist activists, was one of the people at the forefront of those changes. Before Ferguson, she'd been taking a break from in-the-streets activism after getting burned out. But when the events in Ferguson came to Chicago via Twitter and Instagram, a group of Chicago organizers called We Charge Genocide had already been trying to draw attention to the death of one of their friends, Dominique "Damo" Franklin, who'd been killed by a police Taser at age twenty-three earlier that year. I knew of Damo from my work with an organization called Project NIA that aimed to end youth incarceration, and I had worked with many young people who knew him. Damo had been painted as a bad victim, because he had a weapon on him at the time of his death. But we all knew the back story—his hard life, his fear of police, and the simple fact that police should not be able to execute someone, accident or not. But they can, and they did. His death had traumatized this community, and it hadn't made national news.

Pulley had shown up for a community meeting about Damo, and as August 2014 unfolded, she found herself suddenly in the role of organizing a busload of activists from Chicago to go join the protests in Ferguson. After that first protest, the group coalesced into Black Lives Matter Chicago—part of a network of Black Lives Matter groups around the country.

They faced many of the same media hurdles as Ferguson organizers. Each time police shot and killed someone, Pulley said, "the news would just report what the police union press release would say, and that would be it, there would be no counter." Black Lives Matter made it their goal, alongside allied groups like the People's Response Team and We Charge Genocide, to present a counter-narrative in as many cases as possible.

Pulley says it took a while to get organized, but by early 2017, the group had its drill down. A young man named Chad Robertson was shot by Amtrak police near downtown on February 8 of that year. Police had said that he had drugs on him, a technique often used to indict a person after the fact. But another story quickly emerged: Robertson was from Minneapolis and was on a layover in Chicago, traveling home from a funeral in Memphis. He'd taken Megabus, a cheap Greyhound alternative that doesn't have its own stations or shelters, and he and other passengers had been waiting out the freezing cold inside an Amtrak station. After a tense interaction where Amtrak police asked the passengers to go back outside, officers had shot Robertson in the back as he ran away. Robertson was taken to Cook County Hospital, and Pulley and her friends' phones started blowing up as his family learned he'd been hospitalized.

Black Lives Matter put up money for an Airbnb for what turned out to be over a dozen members of Robertson's family from Minnesota and worked closely with them to set up a press conference while he sat in the hospital in critical condition. While police advanced a story that Robertson was a criminal, killed for threatening behavior, Black Lives Matter and his family told a different story: that he was a young traveler on a layover, shot in the back. "We told the truth," said Pulley, "and the media picked up on that, and that became the narrative that was published."

Five days after their first press conference, which was packed with reporters from every major outlet, Chad Robertson died in Cook County Hospital, with his mother at his side. Two days later, Pulley says, the state's attorney pressed murder charges against the officer, a very unusual move in Chicago at the time.

Because of the organizing work Black Lives Matter was doing, alternative narratives about victims of police violence had become impossible to ignore, Pulley said. But she also warned that this shifting of the frame in Chicago took sustained work; without an organized effort to get this kind of coverage, "it could very well revert back, and it more than likely will."

Which raises the question of the responsibility of journalists themselves, ourselves. If Chad Robertson's family's story was true, why wasn't the local press doing the work of telling that truth, or at least of trying?

· · ·

Steven Thrasher was one of few national journalists who'd already been questioning Black criminalization and pushing for different kinds of coverage; before Ferguson, in 2014 he'd spent months in the St. Louis area working on a story about a Black man incarcerated for purportedly spreading HIV, another type of criminalization story. After Ferguson, he also rushed to the scene, to do on-the-ground coverage for the *Guardian*, where he was on contract as a columnist.

But unlike news reporters who claimed "objectivity," Thrasher approached Ferguson with a sense of mission. He's Black and queer, and he said his goal as a writer was to write stories that are relatable for people like him. "I wanted to make people of color, especially black men, feel seen, feel that their experiences were validated. I wanted people to know that this is not aberrational. . . . [T]he thing that happened to Mike Brown is terrible, but it's completely common in our communities."

Thrasher was in Ferguson on and off for many weeks, and he noticed a profound shift during this time period, one that Mervyn Marcano also made note of: prior to Brown's death, Thrasher said, "when these shootings would happen, there was this presumption of guilt . . . that the person who was shot by police must have deserved it." And in fact, the narrative of police innocence had been so overwhelming that most police killings did not become major news stories, even in cases with victims who were young, psychologically disabled, or unarmed. These stories were not within the sphere of legitimate controversy, and they were rarely judged newsworthy beyond a few lines of copy, as illustrated by my own behavior just after John Crawford's death.

After Ferguson, at least for a period of time before the 2016 election, that news judgment changed. Almost any police killing could become fodder for a major local story, and big protests would often go national. Both Marcano and Thrasher say this was thanks to an intentional reframing of the question of innocence—Marcano says activists in his camp decided not to feed into narratives of good protesters or bad protesters, good victims or bad victims. When the *New York Times* published that article describing Brown as "no angel," the movement rejected that frame—focusing not on the message that Brown *had* been an angel, but on the idea that no kid's guilt or innocence should be tried in the court of public opinion after the police have been allowed to execute him.

"In order for us to get coverage about deaths of folks at the hands of the state, whether that's on the street or in jails or in prisons, we no longer have to go through the rigamarole of 'they were a good family man, they got straight A's.' They didn't have to have any of that," Marcano said. "These stories are more real and more in line with how we live our lives than these fantasy narratives of respectability that didn't do anything to disrupt the structural problems."

Activists had successfully shifted the frame: suddenly John Crawford was a story; Rekia Boyd was a story; Sandra Bland was a story. Black death at the hands of police was being revealed as an epidemic; the *Guardian* and the *Washington Post* both began to count and track these deaths, allowing reporters to measure the racial disparities as well as increases or changes in deaths at the hands of police. It was revealed that in 2015, one in thirteen gun deaths in the US was a police shooting (not including suicides and accidents). It was revealed that Black people were killed by police at 2.5 times the rate of white people.

"You would not have seen these kinds of pieces being written ten or even five years ago," Thrasher said. All police killings of Black people, even ones where the investigation was closed, had entered the sphere of legitimate controversy.

· · ·

How does something *become a story*? In other words, how does an issue move from the sphere of deviance, the unspeakable, or the unimportant, into the zone of controversy and legitimate debate? News judgment is one of the most unquestioned, charged, and non-neutral aspects of the daily decisions that go into creating purportedly "objective" news. News judgment is supposed to be based on a mix of factors that are usually presented to journalists and students of journalism as factual but are actually somewhat mystical. News judgment asks: What does our audience deem important? Which stories matter and are worth being told? And news judgment answers those questions quickly, decisively, sometimes in the act of a single host or journalist alone in front of the AP wire putting together a newscast, or a single editor turning down a story pitch, sometimes in the act of an editorial board or set of newsroom leaders in a morning meeting, drinking coffee and talking about what is newsworthy, which more often than not means what they think is interesting or what they think their bosses or audiences will believe that they should cover.

When I was first taught news judgment, in the newsroom at WBEZ in Chicago, where I was trained in radio, I was taught to look for a few things: novelty, surprise, relevance, and impact, and each of these elements was presented as something one could fairly easily discern. And yet I saw again and again how that process of discernment is overshadowed by so much that goes unsaid. An editor who lives in a floodplain, for example, may be more likely than another editor to assign a story about rising river waters during a rainy season. An editor who's never heard about transgender children facing discrimination may find the topic newsworthy and fascinating in a way that someone familiar with the problem might have trouble seeing. (These examples are real.) And an editor who is white may not see a Black man's death at the hands of police as anything more than a one-off, a story that might be interesting if it happened near your house but isn't newsworthy until its impact is proven. White editors have made that last call over and over again. Black Lives Matter stopped them, stopped us, in our tracks.

News judgment is the first filter all news passes through, and it usually isn't based on anything measurable: we don't look to statistics on our current or desired audience or even our most popular stories of the past to decide what to cover. Some of this is good, protecting journalists against the influence of a purely commercial way of thinking about news. But news judgment is still always about power—who controls the narrative, whose narratives matter, and how the appearance of "mattering" is created in a society rife with entrenched inequality. Black Lives Matter, in that sense, was and is a news organization that tells stories to a mass audience, striving for a more factual, thorough representation of Black life and death. And it's a movement that has changed how these stories themselves come to matter and come to be seen as true or important. It has posed a protracted challenge to the purportedly objective framework of news judgment in journalism institutions across the country. And it has changed the lives of journalists like me, who struggled to articulate and put into practice the idea that all Black lives mattered until this group called for every story about state violence against Black people to be told in context.

Still, these stories are told unevenly. In Ferguson, Justice Department investigators showed up and put out a report about how police in the St. Louis suburb use minor traffic violations and misdemeanor charges to line the city's coffers. But that reality, or a reality a lot like it, had already been playing out in cities around the country, and in some cases had already been uncovered by lawsuits and reports. Ferguson's report was national news because Ferguson was already national news; the assumption then was that "people," whoever they are, would want to know about it.

On the other hand, in Beavercreek and Dayton, protests around the death of John Crawford continued steadily through 2014 and 2015. WYSO covered many of them. We covered the release of the video of Crawford's last moments, the grainy image of him collapsing in pain. We covered the grand jury's decision not to indict the officers involved in the shooting. I remember hearing that news from my coworker Jerry's mouth through my car radio, crying bitter tears, and rushing back to the station to figure out who would go to the evening press conference. After the case was passed to the federal Department of Justice, we called the DOJ over and over for an update, hearing nothing for years, until July 2017, when the Feds quietly dropped the investigation.

In 2015 we made an hour-long documentary to release on the anniversary of John Crawford's death, August 5. And we covered the death of Crawford's girlfriend, Tasha Thomas, who was killed in a car crash on New Year's Day of 2015. Her friend who was driving had apparently been going ninety on a local street in Dayton, in a forty-mile-per-hour zone. They both died on impact, tragedy compounding tragedy. Because it was New Year's Day, we didn't have the story until the next morning, and we didn't have anyone to send out to her memorial or track down her grieving family. Sometimes news judgment is also just about limited capacity.

And sometimes it's about unspoken assumptions about what is interesting. I pitched stories about Beavercreek and John Crawford to

NPR for national airing more than once. Isn't it interesting, I posited, that in Beavercreek, Ohio, there have been no homicides in the last five years, but there have been two fatal shootings at the hands of the same police officer? Isn't it fascinating that this mostly white suburb has proven a difficult place to launch and sustain a protest movement against police violence? Shouldn't we talk about how long-term policies and practices of racial segregation in the Dayton area are connected with Crawford's death, in that he was a Black man killed for nothing but stopping off to shop in an all-white suburb? I pitched all that as a feature story to NPR, a portrait of how white segregation can lead to Black death, how protest can be silenced by segregation, and that pitch was turned down.

In April 2015, I followed the local Black Lives Matter group into a Beavercreek City Council meeting. After a brief protest surrounded by police cruisers in the parking lot, the multiracial group filled the tiny council chambers, taking nearly all the seats and sitting quietly under the fluorescent lights holding yellow "Black Lives Matter" signs. The meeting took place without a peep about John Crawford III, although outside, seemingly the entire Beavercreek police force had gathered. The items on the agenda had nothing to do with police, and all of the recognized speakers were white. Before the end of the council meeting, though, one of the protesters stood up with a bullhorn and began to speak, demanding that the city council address police misconduct and apologize to John Crawford's family. Within moments, everyone was kicked out, escorted single file by pushy cops. I recorded all the action and called up NPR's newscast desk when I got back to the office; did they want a colorful forty-five seconds about protesters getting kicked out of a city council meeting in suburban Ohio, trying to draw attention to this one young man's death? *The trouble is,* the person at the newscast desk told me, *there are riots still going on in Baltimore. That's the lead story tonight. We'll have to pass on this one.*

. . .

News judgment matters. It affects what kind of world we think we live in, and who we think populates that world. I think of all the ways

NPR's newscast would be different if a small moment of defiance like that one in the Beavercreek City Council chambers sometimes led at the top of the hour. What if the 11 p.m. newscast that day, rolling out softly into people's cars on darkened highways across the country, had told a story about twenty people in Ohio pushed to the sidelines again and again, and then gone from there to the angry streets of Baltimore? What if listeners had heard a white Beavercreek resident asking why "they can't just move on" (a quote I had recorded that night at the city council meeting), and then after that heard the police batons cracking down on people heartbroken about Freddie Gray? What if, in the years before John Crawford III and Michael Brown died, stories of people like them had been told over and over, so relentlessly that it felt like the epidemic that it was, covered so relentlessly that it mattered beyond the devastated families, the witnesses burdened forever with images of blood and flashing lights?

We can change what news judgment means, I thought. The process of how something becomes a story, depicted to the public as a product of some kind of mystically fair and yet tragically limited weighing of the scales, is one of the most subjective and unexamined collective processes I have ever observed in action. It is about power, and in my case, as the managing editor in a newsroom, I had acquired some of the exact kind of power it requires. So I tried to make change in my own small ways, pushing for us to cover almost any protest, large or small, and making sure that when someone was killed by police, we asked questions and followed up in every case. Never again, I thought, will my eyes breeze over some wire copy about this and not pause and wonder.

Black Lives Matter shifted the frame, but as Aislinn Pulley pointed out, the frame can always shift back again. Journalists, it occurred to me, need to know what we stand for; we need to search beyond our assumptions about newsworthiness to look at why a story matters, why one life matters more than another, why twenty people protesting with their voices is less newsworthy than twenty people breaking windows or lighting trash cans on fire. We need a moral compass to make these decisions with integrity. This need to define our values felt urgent to me, especially as I became someone who had a say over news assign-ments. Why, I wondered, was the utter subjectivity of news judgment so obscured in our professional training? I needed to go back and learn where this whole idea of objectivity in journalism had come from in the first place.

2

THE DEVIANTS

Race, Lynching, and the Origins of "Objectivity"

It turns out that trying to track down the origins of objectivity in news is sort of like trying to track down the origins of some of the water in a river. This is probably true of any cultural or intellectual phenomenon: the sources of an idea as it is adopted and adapted by large groups of people are many and none at the same time. But I was on a quest nonetheless. I began diligently checking out stacks of books from the library and surrounding myself at my kitchen table in Ohio, spent a winter flipping through tales of 1830s penny papers and personal vendettas among famous newspapermen and a spring digging into histories of alternative media outlets, trying to figure out this code of professional conduct that's so widely accepted today.

Living in small-town Ohio was lonely, and I had a lot of time to think—when I wasn't wandering through the damp, lush woods, I wandered through these books looking for answers. But I was also fighting loneliness, looking for people in whom I could see myself, and my own resistance to orthodoxy. I wanted to find people who'd critically asked the questions I was beginning to ask: Who is journalism for? Do we do it for the community and, if so, which community? Or is it for the market, the bosses, the business? Is the goal to maximize audiences, donations, profits? If we claim to serve the public, then which public do we serve?

At first, I found what I'd expected: lots of "great men" stories about

Edward R. Murrow and Upton Sinclair and Walter Lippmann. There was also a constant sense, especially in more recent texts, that a heyday of "real" journalism is behind us and ethics have gone to the wolves and somehow the internet is to blame, and it's such a disaster that just anyone who wants to be a journalist these days can claim the title and so on. But I did learn that the guiding ideal of "objectivity" in news, at least in those terms, was less than a hundred years old, with its precursors—ideas like independence, nonpartisanship, balance, neutrality, and detachment—only emerging in the mid- to late 1800s. Even then, there were people who disliked these developments and spoke out against them, and these disagreements had a clear connection to what I was struggling with in my own reporting: race and racism were at the center of the debate over what makes a story "objective," legitimate, or true.

I came across the book *Just the Facts: How "Objectivity" Came to Define America Journalism* by journalism scholar David Mindich. His carefully researched history became my guide. I pored over it at night before heading to work as a reporter, and I began to feel connected to a history I could understand. Mindich breaks down the early development of "objectivity" into five aspects that can all be traced to the nineteenth century: detachment, nonpartisanship, "inverted pyramid" writing, facticity, and balance. Mindich, like me, was interested in analyzing the usefulness of objectivity by looking at where it comes from. "It is no less than remarkable," he writes, "that years after consciousness was complicated by Freud, observation was problematized by Einstein, perspective was challenged by Picasso, writing was deconstructed by Derrida, and 'objectivity' was abandoned by practically everyone outside newsrooms, 'objectivity' is still the style of journalism that our newspaper articles and broadcast reporters are written in, or against."

Before the 1830s, most newspapers were either funded by political parties and geared toward white men with voting rights, or they were business journals, geared toward white men who owned businesses, ships, or real estate. But this was a time period when people were arriving in the United States, particularly New York, by the literal boatload. A new kind of industrialism was booming, and a new kind of working class was being born, at least in the North. In the 1830s, a few editors had the idea to try to reach more of this growing audience by creating a new kind of urban publication, a daily newspaper of popular interest that would be sold on the street for a penny. The paper would not be funded by a political party, but instead by advertising sales. Those ads would be valuable to advertisers because of the papers' high circulation among a growing middle class. So, alongside and in concert with the process of urbanization and industrialization, the penny paper was born—and so was nonpartisan news reporting in the US.

Mindich deals first with detachment and nonpartisanship, explaining that detachment in the 1830s wasn't what we think of now—there was a lot of hooting and hollering and immoderate language. But Mindich shows that the beginnings of detachment involved a subtle but important shift away from the hands-on approach to partisan politics and toward a new role for newspapers as observers, rather than participants. He also details the emergence of a new style of writing, that impersonal, "inverted pyramid" news writing that starts with the key facts and appears separately from editorial pages. This is still the approach of newswires today: the key information appears at the top of the story—previously, a dispatch about a battle was just as liable to be told in chronological order, beginning with the fighting and ending with who won, what today we would call "burying the lead." As the 1800s went on, a professionalized role emerged for reporters, who wrote from a stance of naïve empiricism, based on the assumption that facts are observable, and that they are either true or false—what Mindich calls facticity. Finally, he shows that by the turn of the century, journalism in the US also focused on balance, real or performed, sometimes to the detriment of actually uncovering the truth. All this was in service to journalism's new business model and changing modes of distribution.

Mindich argues that the 1890s was the period when the ideal that would become "objectivity" began to take shape. Alongside this developing notion of objectivity came an increased focus on professionalization and specialized education in the field. And Mindich emphasizes again and again that from the beginning, this increasingly neutral, objective model for news had critics, opponents, and detractors—the people I was looking for. The abolitionist newspaper editor Horace Greeley was one of those critics.

. . .

Horace Greeley was the founding editor of the *New York Tribune*, one of the first penny papers and one of the most successful media enterprises of the nineteenth century. Greeley was nothing if not a curmudgeon, with a perpetual ax to grind. Round and boisterous, he fits a fabulous stereotype of the early newspaperman: a balding white fellow with an ugly hair-ring and lots of opinions, who bellows at a crew of Oliver Twist–looking paperboys that he dispatches every day in cute hats to sell his papers on the streets of New York. He was also quirky: near the end of his life, he helped start a utopian commune in Colorado and ran for president. He founded a number of publications through the 1830s, creating the *New York Tribune* in 1841.

In the span of just that decade, purportedly impartial journalism had become something of a movement. His major competitors, including the *Sun* and the *Herald*, claimed both neutrality and political independence, and they inaugurated the separation of the news and editorial functions of their papers. But Greeley saw most neutrality claims as pure showmanship. Many of Greeley's leading competitors did have political affiliations and even political aspirations. (Greeley also accused his competitors of sending their newsboys to flog his newsboys, which, if true, strikes me as a distinctly nineteenth-century problem.)

Greeley despised neutrality, even saw it as insufficiently manly. In his 1868 memoir, Greeley wrote: "My leading idea was the establishment of a journal removed alike from servile partisanship on the one hand and from gagged, mincing neutrality on the other. I believed there was a happy medium between these extremes—a position from which a journalist might openly and heartily advocate the principles and commend the measures of that party to which his convictions allied him, yet frankly dissent from its course on a particular question, and even denounce its candidates." Instead of neutrality, he pushed for independence. His paper was openly allied with Whig Party viewpoints but didn't take funding from political parties and reserved the right to criticize the party as he saw fit. He believed that readers would benefit from knowing where the paper's editor stood.

In learning about Greeley, I began to see an important distinction that's often confused in discussions of nonpartisanship in journalism today. "Neutrality" and political independence, two aspects of the larger framework for journalistic objectivity, have not always gone hand in hand. Political independence started as largely a formal distinction: the penny papers weren't funded by political parties, so their editors and reporters were free to write what they liked and not toe the party line. It functions about the same way today, and most journalistic organizations with integrity pride themselves on the firewall between editorial departments and the people who bring in the money for publications. But as "objectivity" developed, independence and nonpartisanship also became a matter of tone—of presenting oneself as detached and neutral. Greeley pushed the idea that newspaper coverage should be independent-minded but still opinionated.

For Greeley, being an independent but opinionated newspaper editor was a moralistic stance. He was neither a centrist nor a relativist on moral questions. His biggest and most consistent cause was the abolition of slavery, though he also advocated socialism and women's rights, and opposed divorce, lotteries, and the theater. He hated the "immoral and degrading police reports" and refused to publish something that contained so much explicit violence and vice. In the 1850s and 1860s, his *Daily Tribune* inveighed passionately against the Confederates and published many works by Karl Marx. An editorial on the front page of his paper around the start of the Civil War began this way: "The war has put some over-nice gentleman in a pretty pickle. These are hard times for Mr. Facing-Both-Ways." Mr. Facing-Both-Ways—the moderate who refused to pick sides even in the face of civil war—was an enemy of Greeley and all that his paper stood for.

As Mindich shows in *Just the Facts*, the transition to a more rigid division of news and opinion as a reflection of a paper's nonpartisanship and detachment was gradual. It happened in fits and starts and was influenced by a great many changes, including the introduction of the telegram and wire services, as well as the growth of interstate train networks, which brought cities closer together. But I was surprised to learn that throughout the nineteenth century, all these ideas still operated separately—like Greeley, you could be politically independent without being neutral. You could also pursue and report empirical facts without being detached from the story. These were particularly important distinctions for Black journalists, who lived in a very different world than white journalists, both before and after the Civil War.

. . .

Far away from Horace Greeley's exciting New York City mix, a little boy was born in 1856 in Marianna, Florida, whose life provides an excellent example of how complex and contested the territory of "objectivity" has been from the start. When I met this man in books, I felt like I somehow already knew him: T. Thomas Fortune, wavy-haired and intense, was a journalist, poet, and self-identified "agitator" who often became so worked up, he had to take long bike rides to cool his nerves. James Weldon Johnson (who wrote "Lift Every Voice and Sing") remembers visiting friends as a child and rooming in the same house as a grown-up Fortune: "My two playmates and I were sometimes in a room where he sat at a desk writing, covering sheet after sheet that he dropped on the floor, and all the while running his fingers through his long hair. . . . We stood in awe of him." For me, Fortune represents an opponent of neutrality who was also a fierce advocate of nonpartisanship—and perhaps a model for journalism today.

Fortune developed his ideas about the role of the media through a remarkable life that took him from slavery to a life as one of the most prominent Black editors in New York. When he was born in 1856, Timothy Thomas Fortune's mother, Sarah Jane, was a house worker, and his father, Emanuel, ran a tannery—both for a white man's plantation. One of Timothy's earliest memories, from near the end of the Civil War, is of his mother intervening to defend him from a beating by the plantation's owner, Mr. Moore. In his autobiography Fortune recalls his wiry, tiny mother, "long hair flying and eyes flashing," attacking Mr. Moore with her dishrag, and "giving him a rasping tongue-lashing the while for daring to strike her child!" After this incident, Sarah Jane ran off and had to go into hiding for several weeks—and then the war ended, and they were free.

Marianna was a rural, wild place, where Fortune's family stayed on after Emancipation to farm, fish, and hunt for food. He went to a Freedman's Bureau school, and his father, Emanuel, became involved in local politics. But attacks on Black people and their white support-ers in Jackson County, as well as the emergence of the Ku Klux Klan, eventually drove his parents out of Marianna. Timothy himself saw the aftermath of a mass shooting by a white man at a Black picnic. "The ground was littered with dead and maimed children and grown-ups," he later wrote, and no one was ever charged for it. Under direct threat of violence against Emanuel from hostile white locals, the For-tunes gave up their land and moved to Jacksonville. Teenaged Timothy stayed behind in Tallahassee, where he worked as a page in the state senate. Out of an interest in both politics and writing, he also started to stalk the local newspaper office, the *Sentinel*, part of his developing obsession with newspapers. He eventually made his way to school at Howard University, but dropped out because he couldn't afford the tuition.

Fortune was a troublemaker, who placed a premium on telling the truth. "Timothy possessed a very large bump of honesty and it grew larger with his years," he wrote of himself. Truth-telling was a risky proposition for a young former slave: he was constantly getting into what today might be called "situations." For example, he described scandalizing a whole town when he first went north to Delaware by booking a room in a hotel that was supposed to be reserved for white people. Because Fortune was light-skinned, it took the hotel manage-ment two days to figure out that he wasn't white; he was promptly given the boot. It seems he narrowly escaped trouble—racist attacks, criminal accusations, a life of lollygagging with beautiful women—a whole bunch of times before he finally moved to New York City, as aspiring writers often do.

At age twenty-five, in 1881, Fortune and some friends launched a paper called the *Globe*. That paper later became the *New York Free-man* and then the *New York Age*, which remained in weekly publication until 1960 and was among the most influential Black papers of the 1800s. Like Greeley's *New York Tribune*, Fortune's paper led with excited editorials, and he used his columns in the *Globe* and the *Age* to rail against injustice. The convict leasing system, the plague of lynching, the rampant disenfranchisement of Black people in the South, and the treatment of laborers by corporations all became targets of his clever wrath. Fortune was a fierce critic of segregationists, who at the time were primarily southern Democrats. But he had also seen—and detested—the ways that northern Republican carpetbaggers who came to the South during Reconstruction betrayed the causes of free Black people in favor of their own self-interest. He preferred the term "Afro-American" way before its time.

Among Black people, Fortune was an important voice and intellectual leader, and his paper was read around the country. Even with a segregated audience and a lot of political opponents, there was no question as to whether he was a "real" journalist—which is where I found such a stunning contrast with twenty-first-century views on journalism. The first journalism school was yet to be founded, and the ideas of nonpartisanship and detachment in journalism were still in the process of forming, still not part of any unified school of thought. New York City papers, competing for a rapidly increasing audience, aimed to inform and entertain, interspersing opinion columns with the news.

Black papers and abolitionist journals weren't the only publications to promote a clear viewpoint. Joseph Pulitzer, who published the popular paper the *World*, put out a front-page article in 1883 advocating a relatively radical tax reform plan. But perhaps even more than Greeley or Pulitzer, who both flirted with politics and public office, Fortune was always nonpartisan. Political parties can't be trusted, he wrote in the *Globe* in 1883. "The Democratic party is a fraud—a narrow-minded, corrupt, bloody fraud; the Republican party had grown to be little better." He also wrote in 1883 that "to properly defend a people's interest, a newspaper at this juncture should be non-partisan," and he constantly inveighed against the Republican Party for letting down Black interests.

For Fortune, nonpartisanship was not so much a path to selling papers as a path to making just demands on behalf of his race. If neither party served them, he wrote again and again, Black voters (and Black writers) should refuse allegiances. Fortune cared about political equality and civil rights for Black people, full stop—so for him, nonpartisanship was a natural stance, and a political one.

T. Thomas Fortune continued writing until his death in 1928, and he was never neutral on his own humanity or on the rights of Black people. By the early 1890s, his paper was so well-known, and Fortune so beloved as an editorial writer, that the *Cincinnati Afro-American* wrote that if Fortune were white, he'd have been the editor of the *New York Times*. Perhaps—although its growing conservatism probably wouldn't have appealed to him (and, worth noting, the *New York Times* wouldn't hire its first Black executive editor until more than a hundred years later, in 2014). The *New York Times*, which was still young and competing to become the city's paper of record, did turn out to be the enemy of one of Fortune's closest allies, Ida B. Wells.

• • •

It was 1892, the year Coca-Cola incorporated and the first elevated train opened in Chicago, and paperboys still stood on corners peddling city news for a penny. The country was just coming out of a recession. Ida B. Wells rolled up by train to Jersey City, a growing industrial center with new buildings going up on its riverbanks, to meet with the famous editor T. Thomas Fortune. I imagine Wells, with her dark eyes and petticoats and composure beyond her years (she was twenty-nine at the time), being mildly amused by Fortune, a passionate and pushy man just six years older. They both had been born into slavery in the South, and likely had plenty to talk about, but even more that they probably didn't feel the need to say aloud.

Fortune had a troubling message for Wells. "Now you are here I am afraid you will have to stay," he told her. Wells owned a newspaper back home, the *Memphis Free Speech*, where she'd been running a series of insistent editorials against lynch mobs and lynch law in Tennessee. It turned out Fortune had seen a story cross the AP wire that day, while Wells was traveling, reporting that her office manager had been driven out of town and her printing office destroyed by a white mob. It wasn't safe for her to go back to Memphis.

Wells hadn't planned to start an anti-lynching campaign. She was going about her business making a local newspaper when, in March of that year, a white mob lynched three of her acquaintances. The three men were co-owners of the People's Grocery Company, a relatively new business in town, and they had scuffled with white men associated with the competing store. Things got tense in Memphis, and after a group of Black men shot at a white mob in self-defense, Thomas Moss, Calvin McDowell, and Henry Stewart were arrested. A few days later, impatient for vengeance, a large group of white men dragged the three men from the jail and killed them. Wells had never been so close to a lynching, and she later wrote about how this incident changed her forever. Before her friends were killed, she'd swallowed the story that Black men were typically lynched for raping white women, a collective crime of passion and pride.

"Like many another person who had read of lynching in the South, I had accepted the idea meant to be conveyed—that although lynching was irregular and contrary to law and order, unreasoning anger over the terrible crime of rape led to the lynching," she wrote in her autobiography. Suddenly, things looked different to her: these white men had escalated the conflict with their Black competitors, and then murdered them in cold blood after they defended themselves. "This is what opened my eyes to what lynching really was. An excuse to get rid of Negroes who were acquiring wealth and property and thus keep the race terrorized and 'keep the nigger down.'"

She started editorializing in the *Memphis Free Speech* about it, calling for Black people to boycott local white businesses. That enraged the white people who held power in Memphis. "I then began an investigation of every lynching I read about," she wrote. Wells was intrepid in her investigation of lynchings, their stated reasons, and the actual facts behind them. She read about a lynching in Mississippi, described by the Associated Press: "The big brute was lynched because he had raped the seven-year-old daughter of the sheriff." But when she went to Tunica County, Mississippi, she learned that the girl was in fact seventeen and had known the lynched man well, and that the circumstances of the accused rape were murky at best. In case after case, she found that the white woman who was purportedly raped hadn't come forward about the rape accusation until the liaison between her and the Black man in question was made public; in still other cases, she learned that there was no rape accusation or accusation of any crime at all. Wells began to see that the common narrative about lynching was a lie—one even she had believed.

Wells and Fortune must have gotten along fine, because in Jersey City that day, he offered her a job at the *Age*, and, warned off of returning to Memphis, she stayed in New York to write a series of reports that would later be turned into the powerful anti-lynching pamphlet *Southern Horrors*. She uncovered the fact that lynching was becoming an epidemic, finding, for example, that 241 people were lynched in 1892 alone.

While Wells crisscrossed the country gathering statistics on lynching, the northern white papers were scarcely covering the problem at all. When they did, there was never an investigation into the allegations against the lynched person, or into the lack of consequences for mob violence. The *New York Times* reported on lynching from the perspective that, while lynchers ought to be stopped, the penalties for the type of crimes that Black men committed should be more swift and severe. "The crime for which negroes have frequently been lynched [rape], and occasionally been put to death with frightful torture, is a crime to which negroes are particularly prone," an editorial asserted in 1894. This editorial stance was reflected in the paper's news coverage. "Black guilt was assumed in nearly every story" about lynching during the 1890s, writes Mindich. The *Times* managed a semblance of "balance" on lynching without bothering to gather the facts, while Wells, with a clear goal of ending lynching, worked tirelessly to expose facts that might otherwise have never been told.

These facts were published in Fortune's *New York Age*, in Wells's self-published pamphlets, and in speeches she gave around the world. Meanwhile, the *New York Times* ran its own small crusade not against lynch mobs, but against Ida B. Wells. Wells traveled to Britain in 1894 on a speaking tour, and after some in Britain were moved to start an anti-lynching committee, the *Times* responded with an editorial calling Wells "a slanderous and nasty-minded mulattress, who does not scruple to represent the victims of black brutes in the South as willing victims." She was painted as a deviant, and I suppose she was. She deviated from a norm that criminalized Black life while decriminalizing white murder, and she encouraged others to organize and agitate. But she was also the journalist who constructed the most thorough picture of lynching in her time, telling a factual story that was nowhere to be found in the pages of white papers.

. . .

Again and again, T. Thomas Fortune was nonpartisan without being neutral; like Horace Greeley, Fortune advocated independence but not passivity. And there was a particular risk for an African American newspaper editor in taking an aggressively nonpartisan stance at the time. Remember, nonpartisanship was still relatively new for newspapers, and party sponsorship remained a relatively common way for papers to pay the bills. This was especially true for Black papers, which frequently depended on Republican support. For white papers, being "independent" might have been part of the recipe for being successful, but that independence typically remained well within the sphere of legitimate controversy, entertaining debates between Republicans and Democrats over policy matters, including policies related to race. But rejecting the white supremacist views of both Republicans *and* Democrats was well outside the sphere, which meant that T. Thomas Fortune and Ida B. Wells, while using similar reporting tactics as many of their fellow white editors and reporters, played a very different social and political role. For them, telling the truth from a nonpartisan stance also meant pushing back on the status quo. Even as Wells used empirical standards of reporting to tell her story, she didn't give in to the "gagged, mincing" neutrality Greeley so hated, choosing instead to stand by her conviction that lynching was wrong and must be stopped.

Wells and Fortune called out and exposed lies and injustice, and helped shift the frame for what could be included in mainstream discourse about race. But in a way, journalism in their time was a less conservative, less rigid vocation than it became during the next century. Their heyday in the 1890s was still decades before the terminology of "objectivity" would be consistently applied to journalism, and newspapers, Black and white ones, largely remained a raucous mix of opinion, invective, narrative, and fact. Opinionated editors like Greeley still dominated the front pages of many dailies, the personal voice continually mixing with the reportorial one.

Learning about Ida B. Wells and T. Thomas Fortune, holed up in my Ohio home or watching spring arrive from the screened porch, my loneliness got a little smaller. The conflict that stirred in me as I worried about my own coverage of Black Lives Matter and police violence seemed to be an old conflict. In 1894, using the truth to push back against the criminalization of Black people meant being cast as slanderous, an activist. I began to see that then, as now, feigning a detached neutrality was easy for the people who wanted to sell papers, and impossible for the people whose lives were at stake, whose every word was judged as a representation of their race. But nonpartisanship and editorial independence were not the same as detachment or neutrality, and for these journalists, *not* being neutral was a path to the truth. The biographies of T. Thomas Fortune the journalist poet and Ida B. Wells the journalist activist rejuvenated me.

As I learned their stories, I also felt aware of my own deviance, my own position outside of the job I was doing every day. I had never known another transgender journalist, first of all, and in many ways, my perspective as transgender puts me in the sphere of deviance, looking from the outside in at contemporary debates over trans issues. It was becoming clear to me that journalists were constantly engaged in demonstrations of detachment and "balance," without considering that sometimes to be independent isn't the same as being neutral. To stand independent of white supremacy, for example, might mean actually standing up to it. I began to wonder whether I could live with myself, with my values, and continue in this vocation that I had experienced as a calling, as the work I was meant to do in the world.

3

THE AGITATORS

Journalists as Labor Leaders

Many journalists buy into the framework of "objectivity" and participate in it. It is still taught in journalism schools and textbooks. Some truly believe they can *be* objective; others understand objectivity as aspirational, but agree to the attempt, as I had during all my years as a daily journalist. A lot of people figure it's a tough field full of jobless searchers, and if appearing unbiased is what we must do, we will. I had done it until I couldn't anymore, and then I had been kicked to the New York City curb. Quite literally, I stood out on the street corner in the city that never sleeps, tapping out messages on my cell phone and calling my family and friends. "I just got fired," I said, picking up my pace down Lexington Avenue. "Oh my god," said my friends and former editors on the other end of the line. "Why?"

"Over something I wrote," I said.

And yet even after my research in Ohio, it still wasn't clear to me how all this became so rigid, so codified. I knew I couldn't be the first person to be fired for lacking (or opposing) objectivity—but I wanted to know who else had been. How did the frame we now call "objectivity" harden into an inviolable ideal? When and how was it encoded into the profession, turned into something that could be a basis for disqualification? As I searched through the stories of the early 1900s, I found a number of characters who risked their careers for their convictions— and found that even in the earliest days of "objectivity," not everyone agreed that it was an ideal to strive toward. As soon as an "objective" framework fell into place, it was also used against journalists who tried to organize, right here in New York City, blocks from where I stood.

. . .

In the years between the late 1800s and World War I, journalism was something between a trade and a profession, a low-class occupation unsure of its place. During this period, the first American journalism schools were started at the University of Missouri and Columbia University, and newsrooms created their first ethical policies and standards of conduct, both signs of a move toward professionalization. By the 1920s, journalism was poised to have a moment: there was an increasing public focus on and fascination with verifiable facts, along with new concern about the rise of propaganda and interest in the scientific method.

One of the first manuals attempting to codify objective standards was published in 1924. In *The Ethics of Journalism*, an academic named Nelson Antrim Crawford explained the growing public interest in the verifiable: "It is only in recent years that the significance of facts has been recognized by anybody. It is now recognized only by a minority." Before the twentieth century, many continued to turn to God, superstition, and authority figures for truth. All of that was being replaced by scientific methods, and truth wasn't gospel truth anymore—it was now something you could check out and verify. The argument followed that journalists should stop sloppy practices such as filling in small details using their imaginations or reporting stories depending on single sources.

Crawford, anxious about "ignorance, inertia, and fear" among journalists, urged a strict new set of guidelines for the profession. "However objective a man (or woman) may strive to be, he is likely to be misled at a critical moment by his own philosophy of life or his own private interests unless he is guided by some definite standard." The guidelines included a division between the publishing and editorial sides, so that the editors could not be influenced by advertisers or money; a refusal to take gifts or bribes; rigorous sourcing and fact-checking; a focus on experts; and the use of purportedly "objective" scientific methods of establishing facts through empirical observation and the use of data.

But why all this attention to the "objective" and the verifiable right at this point in time? Well, for one, over the previous ten years, mass-distributed facts had developed a powerful competitor: mass-distributed propaganda. The US government had made extensive use of propaganda during WWI; journalists who worked for the federal government on the war effort, including Walter Lippmann (who would later cofound the *New Republic*), were horrified to learn how easy it was to sway public opinion. By the 1920s, the propagandist was a known quantity, a shiny person peddling packaged "facts"—a specialist in manipulating people with claims of authority. Lippmann was so disturbed by this, he wrote an entire book, *Public Opinion*, on how easy it is to change people's minds. "Under certain conditions men respond as powerfully to fictions as they do to realities," Lippmann fretted.

He had keyed into a massive problem of the modern age: that "the real environment is altogether too big, too complex, and too fleeting for direct acquaintance." No one can know *all* the available facts, so we need people to translate and tell the story, to distill and explain the knowable world. Lippmann strove for a solution to the problem, and he thought he had one: expertise. "I argue that representative government, either in what is ordinarily called politics, or in industry, cannot be worked successfully . . . unless there is an independent, expert organization for making the unseen facts intelligible to those who have to make the decisions." Public opinion, he argued, ought to be distilled by this expert class of political scientists, and then reflected by the press. Experts, he believed, could learn the tools and techniques of objectivity and faithfully reflect the facts of the world in a way that laypeople, the public, and even journalists could not. Public opinion should be treated as a science in order to avoid the pitfalls of subjectivity and the influence of public relations.

The scientific method would be brought to bear in journalism, too. "The conviction has been reached," Crawford wrote, two years after Lippmann's book, "that the method which has been applied to scientific research may likewise be applied to studies in economics, sociology, and politics, the subjects with which everyday conversation and newspaper stories alike chiefly deal." Like Lippmann, Crawford was skeptical that the masses could understand the world—but not skeptical that the world was knowable. It's just that knowing it was a job best left to the professionals.

. . .

"Show me a man who thinks he's objective, and I'll show you a man who's deceiving himself." Those were the words of Henry Luce, a conservative thinker and eventual media mogul, when he cofounded *Time* magazine in 1923. The statement is stunning in its clarity (objectivity is a myth, says the founder of several of the nation's most influential news media products!) and in its timing: after all, the framework of objectivity had only barely emerged. Michael Schudson's detailed history of objectivity, *Discovering the News: A Social History of American Newspapers*, argues that this ideal of journalistic "objectivity"—a combination of unbiased inquiry, nonpartisan voice, factuality, and scientific method—emerged out of the factual urges of the postwar era and the anxiety about public relations articulated by Walter Lippmann. And yet, as Luce's quotation demonstrates, this belief in objectivity as an ideal to strive toward was coupled from almost the very beginning with an intense skepticism—not just about the truth, but about the human ability to recognize and tell that truth. As Schudson writes, the struggle for objectivity was also inherently an acknowledgment of subjectivity.

But the fear of subjectivity, surprise at the idea that there could be multiple ways of looking at the truth, only makes sense if you previously believed there was only one way of looking. Disillusionment in government or in the authority of presidents or gods requires that you believed in the illusion, at some point. Schudson's history acknowledges that anxiety about objectivity was often a response on the part of privileged white men, realizing for the first time that theirs were not the only voices, their truths not the only truths. As they "discovered" subjectivity, they sought out objectivity in part to reassert their authority, or at least to provide a framework for why their version of the world was correct.

. Norms and power structures were shifting: northern US cities where most major newspapers were based were suddenly teeming with immigrants, Black migrant workers from the South, women who had the right to vote, workers who went out on strikes. Skepticism wasn't only a response to propaganda—it was a response to diversity. Schudson writes that the term "objectivity" seemed to be in common use among journalists by the mid-1930s. "Objectivity" in journalism now had codes to protect it. And as those gates went up, some people would be left outside.

. . .

Heywood Broun was a firecracker columnist cursed with the inability to back down. He was also a bit of a spectacle: an East Coaster with Scottish blood, he was a tall, boisterous, doe-eyed man who dropped out of Harvard, only to later become one of the most successful newspaper columnists of the 1930s. Broun was known as a leftist and a slob; as his biographer, Richard O'Connor, writes, "It was later said that his sartorial style—a new suit immediately developed elephantine wrinkles the moment Heywood put it on—resembled that of an unmade bed." (Comments on his sloppy mode of dress are common in remembrances of Broun.)

By the time Broun wandered out of Harvard in 1910, he knew he liked gin and sports and women, and he knew he *loved* writing. Journalism at the time wasn't the obvious choice: his biographer writes that it "was a low-paid vocation, and its practitioners, to an alarming degree, succumbed to alcoholism, insanity, or careers in public relations." But Broun wandered into a newspaper office and, thanks in part to his family connections, started working as a writer and an editor. After putting in some years covering culture and sports for a few papers, he got a column of his own at the *New York Tribune* and later the *World*, which was run by Joseph Pulitzer's son. By the late 1920s, Broun was famous and beloved, one of New York's highest-paid writers.

He had a growing conviction and intensity, and in 1927 he took an interest in the trial of Nicola Sacco and Bartolomeo Vanzetti, a pair of working-class Italian immigrant anarchists who faced a murder conviction in Massachusetts that they said was a setup. They both received death sentences in a Massachusetts court, a decision that was highly politicized, with impassioned protests organized in multiple urban centers. Anti-radical and anti-immigrant fears drove public support for their execution. Dissenters, including Broun, saw the trial as a political prosecution and a witch hunt designed to strike fear in the hearts of immigrants and labor organizers. In early August 1927, Broun went to Boston to follow the case more closely. After a governor-appointed commission headed by Harvard's president returned a decision saying that the death sentence should stand, Broun wrote a defense of Sacco and Vanzetti that indicted not just the individual decision makers, but the system that would allow them to die.

"They are too bright, we shield our eyes and kill them," he wrote on August 5, 1927. "We are the dead, and in us there is no feeling nor imagination nor the terrible torment of lust for justice. And in the city where we sleep smug gardeners walk to keep the grass above our little houses sleek and cut whatever blade thrusts up a head above its fellows." In the same column, he called his alma mater Harvard a Hangman's House.

However popular his column might have been, Broun mouthing off about Harvard displeased the editors of the *World* and got the attention of the *New York Times*, which called his words evidence of "the wild and irresponsible spirit which is abroad"—a bit of that fearsome subjectivity at play, perhaps. Still, Broun continued to write about Sacco and Vanzetti. When the *World* refused to publish any further columns from him on the topic, Broun resigned in protest. "By now I am willing to admit that I am too violent, too ill-disciplined, too indiscreet to fit pleasantly into the *World*'s philosophy of daily journalism," he wrote in his final *World* column.

Now he was a columnist with a mission. Broun eventually secured a new column in the *New York Telegram*, and in 1930 he decided to run for Congress as a Socialist. The *Telegram* expressed its displeasure with him both privately and then publicly. Broun came back with a response the next day, critiquing "the weakness of an individual or organization construing independence as meaning a permanent place on the sidelines." He agreed not to promote his own candidacy in the *Telegram*, kept his column, and went on to run a kind of goofy campaign, giving speeches from the roof of his limousine at random stops in the city, getting arrested alongside striking workers in the Silk Stocking District, and ultimately losing badly to a Democrat.

In 1937, just a couple years before his death, Broun penned a column about himself entitled "The Imperfect Reporter." "There are almost no situations in which I am neutral by the widest stretch of the imagination," he wrote. "It has been said that the perfect reporter ought to be patterned more or less along the physical and chemical lines of a plate glass window. . . . I am not altogether certain whether these entrance requirements are wise and shrewd in every detail. But my skepticism may be based upon a doubt as to my own ability to pass the entrance examinations. I fear I am not glass, either clear or opaque."

Heywood Broun pushed the limits of what a columnist could be even then, and columnists these days are usually discouraged or even banned from political involvement. Still, there is nothing surprising in that a leftist columnist in the 1920s and '30s should be controversial from time to time, and perhaps even clash with his employers. But what happened next was what got me hooked on this funny Heywood fellow: he became a union organizer.

. . .

Heywood Broun brushed shoulders in New York with all kinds of people, from Eleanor Roosevelt to Mayor Fiorello La Guardia, up and down the white power structure. He had fewer ties to Black leaders and writers; New York City media continued to be almost entirely segregated by race. But Broun did cross paths, early in her career, with a woman who would go on to be the first Black woman to work at a major white paper in the city. The two didn't know each other well, but they shared a common drive to agitate.

Marvel Cooke had come to New York from Mankato, Minnesota, where she'd been the first Black girl to go to her high school, and one of the only Black women at the University of Minnesota. Her father was a Socialist; trained as a lawyer, he worked as a railroad porter instead due to racism in the legal industry. Her mother was a schoolteacher on a Native American reservation. Marvel was raised solidly middle class, in a mostly white community. She walked a fine line as a Black woman in a world that had room for sloppiness in Heywood Broun but didn't allow the same leeway for her: she was always carefully dressed and coiffed, warm but controlled in her words and actions. Cooke came to New York City in the 1920s and moved into the heart of Harlem Renaissance culture, living for many years in the same apartment building as W. E. B. DuBois, who had once courted her mother. She started out working at DuBois's newspaper, *The Crisis*, the official paper of the NAACP at the time, and after a while moved on to a non-partisan Harlem daily, the *Amsterdam News*.

Cooke quickly developed a reputation for being a fast and clever writer. She was typically the only woman doing anything other than secretarial work in the newsroom. Once she had the chance, Cooke turned out to be an intrepid reporter, and she got sent out on the *Amsterdam News* daily beats to cover crime, politics, the arts. But like Broun, she had an itch to agitate.

In an interview in 1989 with an oral historian, Cooke recalled feeling that her calling was to be a writer who tried to change things. The mainstream *Amsterdam News* frustrated her. "I grew up feeling that one must do something for our people, you know, join a crusade. I grew up in a crusading family, and here I found that here's a black paper just following the dictates of society, not making any impression at all, not addressing the problems that faced people in this area. I wasn't happy about it. It was just a paycheck for me." And that paycheck was mediocre—just eighteen dollars a week for work that often stretched into evenings and weekends.

The lousy paycheck was the thing that ultimately brought the figure of Broun slouching into her life. It was 1935, and journalists had been hit hard by the Great Depression, and the closures and consolidation that came with it. Plus, as Broun's biographer writes, "no one was quite sure whether newspapermen were working at a trade or were members of a low-grade profession, somewhere between chiropractors and horse doctors, though in a lower economic grouping." Journalists were not a group of people with power or with a clear identity. But the reporters at the *Amsterdam News* had heard about a guy who was organizing a trade union for journalists: Heywood Broun, the famous columnist. Cooke promptly organized a guild meeting in her living room in Harlem.

The *Amsterdam News* chapter of the American Newspaper Guild began by asking the paper's owner for recognition. In response, the owner fired the entire editorial staff. The reporters went out on the picket line, in what Cooke explained was technically a lockout rather than a strike. Many days of the week, Broun joined them, eager to be seen on 135th Street standing in solidarity with his fellow newspaper workers. Legally, only two people could picket at a time, and the cops would come down from a nearby police station whenever a crowd gathered in front of the building. That made it easy to get press. "Whenever we wanted to get a little publicity, we would throw out a big picket line, and almost immediately the police would appear to arrest us," Cooke recalled. "Heywood Broun tried his best to get arrested on that line. He would go around the corner and hide in the shade of a drugstore, and when he saw the police coming, he would try to sneak into the line, but he never made it. He was very disappointed."

Cooke was similarly delighted by the task of organizing a union, even sharing Broun's relish for jail. "It was not ladylike to don picket signs and march up and down. It thrilled me. I never minded getting out there on the picket line, and I enjoyed going to jail, even though I know that the women's editor shivered at the thought." She remembered when she and two other women from the paper were arrested, and some "local society ladies" brought them food in jail, terrified to see such proper women in such an improper place. But the best part was that eventually they won—the owner sold the paper and the employees got a raise from the new boss when they came back on staff. Cooke's salary nearly doubled. It was one of the first times in US history that Black workers had won their demands in a strike, and possibly the first strike of journalists of any race.

Cooke and Broun loved both the idea and the practice of being in a union. But getting journalists to unionize proved a tough task overall. Journalists were trained to be individualistic and competitive with one another. Publishers generally opposed unions because they didn't want to pay higher wages. But they gave another reason, too: they claimed union members could not be objective. "Objectivity" had scarcely come into being—and it had already become a bludgeon.

. . .

The newspaper business was as resistant as any business to the dawn of collective bargaining, and editors and publishers teamed up fast to rebut the idea of unionized journalists. The American Newspaper Guild, under the leadership of Broun, held its first convention in 1934; the editor of *Editor and Publisher*, Marlen Pew, spoke out against the idea of a trade union of journalists before this meeting even occurred, as did Roy Howard, chairman of the Scripps-Howard newspaper chain. Both argued that a union would compromise impartiality, a key part of "objectivity" for journalists.

At this point, a very important distinction comes into play: the concept of an objective *approach* was still relatively new. The concept of the objective *individual*, the reporter with no attachments whatsoever, was even newer—and this, in particular, appeared to be a direct rebuttal to the presence of organized labor in the newsroom, a display of anxiety over what the activist-journalist might mean for the editor and publisher in a rapidly changing world.

In 1935 the firings began. Morris Watson, a reporter for the AP, seems to have been the first reporter ever fired purportedly on the basis that he, as an individual, couldn't *be* "objective." After Watson started working with the Newspaper Guild, the AP said his affiliations made him biased—or at least that his work had the potential for bias. Free speech law in the United States generally protects the rights of publications to fire people for work they don't like or don't want to publish. But the AP blundered, putting too thin a veil over the fact that they'd actually fired Watson for his organizing with the Newspaper Guild. Watson sued them, and the newly created National Labor Relations Board (NLRB) took his case against the Associated Press to the Supreme Court in 1937. It became a case about labor rights rather than free speech. In *Associated Press v. National Labor Relations Board*, the majority opinion read, in part, "The [Associated Press] did not assert and does not now claim that [Morris Watson] had shown bias in the past. It does not claim that by reason of his connection with the union he will be likely, as the petitioner honestly believes, to show bias in the future. The actual reason for his discharge, as shown by the unattacked finding of the Board, was his Guild activity and his agitation for collective bargaining." The majority view was that the AP was simply using the argument of *potential* bias to thwart organizing, and Watson was reinstated. He left the AP and later became the longtime editor of the newspaper for the International Longshoreman and Warehouseman Union in San Francisco.

. . .

News outlets, grappling with questions of trust and authority in the twentieth century, sought out a new stable ground. They adopted "objectivity" first as an aspiration, but they transformed it too quickly into a bludgeon, a weapon to regulate who gets to tell stories. And as journalism professionalized, "objectivity" was defined by the bosses, the people in management (usually white men) who generally sought to maintain the status quo. It quickly became a tool for gatekeeping.

By the time I learned the story of Morris Watson, I was some months out from being fired myself. I had moved to North Carolina from New York and was carrying out my research in the deep quiet of my new home in Durham, gathering stacks of books from the university library and spending hot afternoons flipping through the pages, looking for people who'd questioned objectivity.

I was excited to learn all of this; nothing comforts the fired or laid-off like learning about other people's firings (and finding them so deeply unjust that your own experience pales in comparison). But more importantly, there seemed to be a principle at play: that even though objectivity emerged for many of the right reasons, as an ideal and an aspiration, it was quickly turned into a weapon—or maybe better put, a gate. Some would be allowed inside of the world of objective observers, others pushed out.

The shift from an effort to aspire to objectively reported news and information to a claim that news organizations must only hire and employ those who could *be* objective was subtle, but important. Watson won his case because of labor protections, but his victory didn't protect others from being fired for their affiliations, for their potential biases, for the simple *fact* of being unobjective. And as Henry Luce had said, "Show me a man who thinks he's objective, and I'll show you a man who's deceiving himself." Now the trick wasn't to aspire to fairness, truth, and nonpartisanship—it was to not be caught by your boss being a human with opinions, especially if those opinions went against the grain in some way.

. . .

"I was a slave." That was the opening line of Marvel Cooke's series for the *Daily Compass* on what she termed the "Bronx Slave Market," a block where unemployed Black women would go stand out and wait to be hired by white women for day labor in their homes. These workers had no job security, no protection from violence and abuse, and often went unpaid or underpaid with no accountability.

Cooke left the *Amsterdam News* for the *People's Voice* and in 1949 took a job at the *Daily Compass*, a leftist white-run paper, where she became the first Black woman to work as a reporter for a mainstream white paper. She wanted to use her Black womanhood to expose the Bronx Slave Market for what it was, so she went undercover. She stood out for days with the women who gathered in front of Woolworths in the Bronx and waited to be picked up. In the resulting five-part series, she started off curious and descriptive, but she quickly became emotional. "Twice I was hired by the hour at less than the wage asked by the women of the market. Both times I went home mad—mad for all the Negro women down through the ages who have been lashed by the stinging whip of economic oppression," she wrote. Her first day, she walked off the job because she felt the boss was trying to cheat her, but then she didn't get work for the rest of the day and found herself standing out with women who were desperate and stone-faced. The next day, she took a cleaning job that made every muscle in her body ache.

After a few days, she wrote, "Woolworth's on 170th St. was beginning to feel like home to me. It seemed natural to be standing there with my sister slaves, all of us with paper bags, containing our work clothes, under our arms. I recognized many of the people who passed. I no longer felt 'new.' But I was not at peace. Hundreds of years of history weighed upon me. I was the slave traded for two truck horses on a Memphis street corner in 1849. I was the slave trading my brawn for a pittance on a Bronx street corner in 1949. As I stood there waiting to be bought, I lived through a century of indignity."

It was a powerful piece of reporting, and the final story in the series suggested reforms and regulations that could help Black women find work more safely, with more protection from exploitation. The mayor of New York City, William O'Dwyer, read Cooke's series and implemented some of these reforms. Her reporting, deeply truthful and emotional, took readers inside an experience that only a Black woman could have. When the *Daily Compass* shut down in 1952, Cooke found herself out of a job and unemployable in the newspaper industry—anyone affiliated with the paper had a hard time finding work, but especially her, as a Black woman already facing other forms of discrimination.

Cooke was called before Senator Joseph McCarthy's Permanent Subcommittee on Investigations in 1953 and asked to testify against her fellow journalists. She went to Washington, donned a conservative dress for the day, and fiercely and politely took the Fifth. "I thought he was a little sleaze ball," she later said of McCarthy. But she also never worked as a journalist again. "There was really no place for me to go in New York City," she explained. "No place."

Predominantly white and male journalists in the 1920s and '30s used "objectivity" to seek authority, to prove their right to tell the truth. But Marvel Cooke's work depended on a perspective only a Black woman could access in midcentury New York City. It was a personal, accessible voice, one that would rarely be allowed on the front pages of a newspaper today. But what if the non-authoritative, subjective voice could be trusted? What if there was no one path to truth?

Cooke died in 2000, still in Harlem, in relative obscurity and with fifty years between her and her days as a muckraker. In a 1989 interview in Cooke's Harlem apartment, journalist and oral historian Kathleen Currie of the Washington Press Club Foundation asked Marvel whether her political affiliations made it hard for her to be a good "objective" reporter. Cooke rejected the premise: "I think it made me a better reporter, because I was interested in the conditions under which people had to work and live. That would come through in the things I would write." Currie pushed back, almost condescending. "There's a kind of vaunted rule of journalism that journalists are objective," Currie said in the transcript. "That's right," Cooke replied. "That's right."

"Did you ever have problems being objective on any of these stories?" Currie asked.

"No," Cooke answered. "I think some editors had problems with me reporting things as I saw them."

4

DROWNING IN FACTS

"Objectivity," Ambiguity, and Vietnam

Covering Vietnam nearly killed Kerry Gruson. Deep into my research, I traveled from Durham to Miami to meet her in her home after exchanging a few emails. Compared to North Carolina, Miami was noisy, humid, and bright—I stayed in a neighborhood full of painted bungalows and murals and freeway sounds. Gruson lived in a high-rise apartment with terra-cotta floors and two wide decks with water views, on a causeway looking out over downtown Miami. Her attendant came to the door to greet me, and as I approached Gruson in the next room, I realized I'd need to get close; her disability necessitates either leaning in to hear her or having her speak through a microphone. I put together my recording equipment and settled in next to her wheelchair, mic in hand.

There was a blue theme: Gruson's wet blue eyes, soft around the pupils, were like the water that surrounded us, glittery and deep. She pointed out the birds soaring over the causeway, swooping toward the bright water. "I miss sailing," she said—she used to have a boat called *Blew Bayou*. It took me a minute to adjust to the way she speaks—not just softly, but slowly, with some strain to get each word out. Her cadence and the way she holds her head at almost a forty-five-degree angle are a result of what Gruson calls her "accident" at the end of the Vietnam War.

She's told the story of her accident many times, and I actually came to Miami to ask about something else. I found out about Gruson from a newspaper article that appeared long before her accident. In 1969 she was in the *Wall Street Journal* talking about objectivity. The date was October 21, the headline: "Journalists: Objectivity and Activism." "Objectivity is a myth," declared Gruson, then a twenty-one-year-old reporter at the *Raleigh News and Observer*. Kerry's father, Sydney Gruson, an executive at the *New York Times*, was also quoted. "Pure objectivity might not exist, but you have to strive for it anyway," Sydney told the writer of the article, Stanford Sesser. The conflict between father and daughter over whether journalists could be activists was emblematic of the times, and the article went on to describe what it called a "widespread debate," largely divided along generational lines, over whether journalists should be involved in the issues of the day such as Vietnam, women's liberation, and civil rights. At Time, Inc., 462 employees had signed a petition asking to use the company's auditorium for an event during a day of protest against the war. Time granted the request.

"To say that newspapermen aren't allowed to think just because they're newspapermen is completely ridiculous," Gruson said, criticizing her father's decision not to allow a group of *New York Times* reporters to host a similar event in the Times auditorium.

Gruson came by her gutsiness honestly: both of her parents had been successful journalists, her mother, Flora Lewis, was the first woman to become a *New York Times* bureau chief (in Paris in 1972); her father, a foreign correspondent who later became Arthur "Punch" Sulzberger's right-hand man at the *New York Times*. Gruson was born in England, where her parents had moved to cover the end of WWII, and grew up moving around the world—her younger siblings were born in Israel and Mexico, and she was schooled in Poland and Germany. By the time she was twenty-one, she was worldly and fearless. She says jokingly of her parents, "They bred their own contradiction." She doesn't remember being interviewed for the *Wall Street Journal* article, but she does remember how she felt at age twenty-one: the Vietnam War was well underway, and she was obsessed with ending it.

. . .

Many argue that "objectivity" is just an ideal to strive toward: a combination of being detached enough not to bend the truth to our desires, and meticulous enough to track down and triple-check the facts. It's a way to get to the truth, a methodology and an aspiration. Of course, methodology and meticulousness are key to good reporting; even as a nonbeliever in "objectivity," I wouldn't propose that we throw the baby out with the bathwater. Reporters may be interpreters, but interpretation is still a skill: you can learn to check in with multiple sources, track down hard-to-find data, and double-check facts, and you can get better and more careful in these practices. It's the ideal of detachment and remove that Gruson took issue with, but her mother, Flora Lewis, believed fiercely in the aspiration of "objectivity," detachment and all. As Lewis wrote in 1984 in the *Chicago Tribune*, "Objectivity may be a humanly unattainable goal, but it is worth the constant striving." Her view was especially influenced by her experience covering fascist and totalitarian governments abroad— without a constant pursuit of objectivity, Lewis believed, you could too easily descend into working as a mouthpiece for the government. For her, the ideal of a detached, uninvolved individual reporter was a way to protect the truth.

But can anyone be truly detached from a story? I was surprised to learn that depending on whom you ask, the Vietnam War was either the victory of objectivity or the end of objectivity for US journalists. Broadly speaking, people on the left tend to see Vietnam reporting as a victory: a courageous press overwhelmed government propaganda to bring the story of an unjust war home. People on the right tend to see Vietnam reporting as the end of objectivity: reporters, predominantly antiwar, were a damaging, biased influence that contributed to shifting public opinion against the war, making it unwinnable. But there's still another way of looking at the war: today some historians believe that the predominant dynamic during Vietnam was that of press censorship, not press freedom, and that the US successfully manipulated journalistic coverage throughout the war. Daniel C. Hallin's study of Vietnam coverage in *The "Uncensored War"* focuses on how journalists collaborated with authority figures even as they experienced unprecedented access to the war front.

Arguably the beginning of the 1960s, the period during which Kerry Gruson became a journalist, was the heyday of journalistic "objectivity" in the US. Since the Second World War, there had been a sense of "consensus" among liberal institutions and establishments, a strong political center reflecting the values of white America. In line with this, most national outlets and local newspapers strove to present their reporting as nonpartisan, unbiased, and fair. But this was a tenuous and temporary arrangement at best, and in the '60s it began to break down. College kids like Gruson were getting turned on to civil rights and Black Power, and it seemed like half the country's young people were being sent off to war while the other half were protesting.

By the end of the 1960s, nobody agreed on the basic facts of the situation: Was the US winning or losing? How many people had died? Everyone had an opinion on the war, and facts were constantly called upon in support of those opinions, which meant the reporters on the ground in Vietnam played a very important role. And as historian Clarence R. Wyatt explains in his book *Paper Soldiers*, there may have been lots of war correspondents in Vietnam, but the job was in many ways even harder than it looked. Press coverage from the war front provides evidence for just how sticky the question of objective, neutral reporting is; in Vietnam, the warring parties fought over even the most basic facts.

. . .

One of the most well-known Vietnam correspondents, journalist Peter Arnett, renowned for his Pulitzer Prize–winning coverage of the war, was constantly caught up in this battle over fact. Arnett was a self-described "rough-hewn" kid from New Zealand, a shoe-leather reporter who'd been living in Asia for years already before he was brought on to cover Vietnam for the AP in 1962. In pictures he looks hobbit-like and gruff, wide-eyed, and his memoirs are a study in masculinist memory (women are generally described in terms of their looks, or the price of having sex with them).

At the time, the US was advising and steering the South Vietnamese to fight the North but had yet to send any American ground troops over to fight. Still, the situation was already a mess. When Arnett arrived, the AP's Saigon correspondent, Malcolm Browne, handed him a twenty-four-page document: "A Short Guide to News Coverage in Vietnam." As recounted in Arnett's memoir, the pamphlet gave a vivid sense of the challenges for journalists. "You will find quickly that most 'facts' in Vietnam are based at least in part on misinformation or mis-understandings." Browne's guide cautioned against depending solely on official sources, noting that "figures on casualties and reports of military engagements are especially subject to distortion. In covering a military engagement you must make every effort to count the bodies yourself before accepting any tabulation of results."

Arnett was just twenty-six, but he was already dogged, filing stories for the AP from the battlefields and jungles of Vietnam, building a network of official and unofficial sources, witnessing the violence and drama of the ramp-up of the war. His reports were assiduously factual, often based in firsthand observation. As he tells it, he was not invested in protecting either the American or South Vietnamese government, or the North Vietnamese.

But a reporter's opinion on the war wasn't the only factor that affected what stories and facts came back across the wires. As Wyatt writes, truth in Vietnam was a tangle, and partly because the US and South Vietnamese governments wanted it that way. Wire reporters tended to focus on combat, and the pressure to file stories daily meant that they were often willing to take information hand-fed to them by government sources in press conferences without the ability or time to independently verify it. The alternative to press conferences was battlefield coverage, Arnett's specialty. But that, too, had significant limitations—a key one being that this war was never fought on a neatly defined front, so winners and losers were rarely clear. Reporters view-ing a single skirmish or attack could scarcely begin to explain its mean-ing in context.

Wyatt also points out that most English-language reporters showed up with no knowledge of local cultures or of the Vietnamese language, and they rarely remained for more than eighteen months, depending on translators and fixers to get them closer to local knowledge. Location also limited reporters' information: most reporters for English-speaking outlets worked in Saigon, the South Vietnamese capital. A North Vietnamese perspective was rarely reported in the war, and reporters who did travel to Hanoi and publish the results of interviews with Vietcong leaders were often excoriated at home both by the government and by fellow journalists, ironically criticizing them for depending too much on official sources.

Thus, in spite of Browne's warnings against it, many reporters depended heavily on US military sources for a series of facts, and those facts often didn't add up to a clear picture. For government officials, and even some reporters, what was true mattered less than what was good for the US war effort. Public information officers for the US military had their own agenda: they needed public support and a justification for growing numbers of American deaths. Sowing doubt and red-baiting journalists who were critical of the US war strategy became a part of their jobs. As the war dragged on and became less and less winnable for the US and South Vietnamese, military officials went after reporters who breathed even a hint of pessimism and rewarded with access those who repeated the official line of optimism. The military meted out just enough facts that reporters had a story, but not enough that they had a full picture of what was going on. As editor William Tuohy of the *Los Angeles Times* complained: "We're drowning in facts here, but we're starved for information."

In many ways, this was the most significant limitation of "objective" reporting in Vietnam: anything US journalists reported—especially if it reflected negatively on the war effort—could have a direct influence on the war effort, which depended heavily on public support to continue. That meant every choice about which sources to trust, and which facts to rely on, was a judgment call based on the anticipated reaction of the US government, which imposed its own definition of objectivity: a "fair" story would take US claims at face value and not contradict the narrative that the war was going well.

As a result, Arnett's reporting, which exposed some of the US's missteps in Vietnam, became a target of accusations of bias. In 1965 he and Morley Safer, then a CBS TV reporter, both got on the wrong side of the government. Safer filed a report on US soldiers burning North Vietnamese villages to the ground while innocent villagers stood by and watched. Arnett broke a story on US soldiers experimenting with chemical weapons. President Lyndon Johnson himself called up the president of CBS News about Safer, reportedly waking him up early in the morning and saying, "Your boys shat on the American flag," and accusing Safer of being a Communist. Arnett was investigated by Johnson's FBI, but background checks on Safer and Arnett turned up nothing, and the Johnson administration tried in vain to tie them to the Vietcong as well as to find errors in their reporting. The AP's personnel chief, Keith Fuller, sent along a warning from New York that Arnett and his editors should take extra care to "balance" their reports.

This desired appearance of "balance" could take precedence over telling stories that were true. In one case, after Arnett and AP photographer Horst Faas witnessed and photographed a horrifying scene in which American soldiers beheaded a Vietcong fighter and danced around the severed head, AP foreign editor Wes Gallagher removed the most gory and controversial parts of the story and declined to run the photos. His concern was that the piece "had too heavy a taste." Arnett disagreed, but let it slide; certainly, it wasn't helping his relationships with official sources to constantly run stories making them look bad. In 1970 Arnett finally became truly fed up with the AP's timidity. One day he witnessed US soldiers looting a Cambodian town after an air raid, boisterously stealing from the blown-out remains. The foreign editor killed the copy about looting, sending a memo to Saigon referencing a "highly charged situation in the United States regarding Southeast Asia" and stating that the AP "must guard our copy to see that it is down the middle and subdues emotion." Arnett expressed his displeasure with the censorship to his higher-ups, then leaked the whole story to Kevin Buckley at *Newsweek*.

· · ·

Decades later, Peter Arnett would describe his own work in terms of a sort of classical objectivity: "From the beginning of the war to the end I looked at Vietnam as a news story, not a crusade for one side or the other. I believed that gathering information was a worthwhile pursuit, and truth the greatest goal I could aspire to." But not long after the Cambodia incident, Arnett writes, he felt his own detachment "cracking." "I feared that I would no longer be an unbiased observer, that my reporter's values were swamped in the bloodshed. Like others who had become disenchanted before me, I felt anger that the war seemed impervious to solution, that the reporting and terrible sacrifices seemed to do so little to end it." By the time he stopped covering Vietnam, he'd been reporting in-country for twelve years.

Despite his commitment to the ideal, Arnett would later be fired twice for supposedly lacking "objectivity": he got the boot from CNN in 1999 and from NBC in 2003. The CNN firing came after Arnett participated in a documentary critical of US forces' use of chemical weapons in Laos. The NBC firing came just after the beginning of the US war in Iraq, when Arnett went on state-sponsored Iraqi television and criticized the US coalition's plan of attack. NBC first defended his comments as an example of a reporter providing analysis, but after *Fox News* made firing Arnett into a cause, NBC did just that.

And even in objectivity's supposed golden age, the ideal was elusive. In spite of the tough work of reporters like Arnett, a remarkable amount of information about Vietnam was either never reported or never even known: casualty numbers, enemy counts, even basic questions such as who won or lost a battle were contested in the moment, with governments on both sides lobbying journalists to tell their version of the story. Even Arnett could only trust what he could see with his own eyes, and no single reporter could be present on every front. Telling one true story about Vietnam was an impossibility; getting across multiple true stories, flashes of fact or narrative, was a tough job even for a whole press corps.

The binary framing of "objectivity" (Was it or wasn't it objective? Was he or wasn't he an objective reporter?) reveals a part of the problem, because Vietnam isn't the story of victorious truth in news reporting or of propagandistic lies—it's the story of both. And just as it had in the 1930s, objectivity quickly became a blunt weapon rather than a subtle ideal. US authorities used "objectivity" to accuse reporters of bias, while reporters used "objectivity" to defend themselves against those same accusations. It's not clear that either practice brought the public closer to the truth.

It's a paradox that continues today. Reporters, especially daily news reporters, produce partial truths by necessity, but then we are expected to have asserted absolute truth. When someone doesn't like our partial truths, we're accused of being biased. Then, like Arnett, we defend ourselves by saying we are not biased, even though we know it's an impossible dream.

· · ·

While Peter Arnett was trekking through the jungle watching the horrors unfold, Kerry Gruson was a college student, writing for the *Harvard Crimson* and engaging in endless discussions about the war and its discontents with her campus friends. She spent the summer of 1967 in Alabama, reporting for a civil rights newspaper called the *Southern Courier*. The following year there was a presidential election; Johnson was out and his VP, Hubert Humphrey, lost to Richard Nixon. By the time Gruson graduated, in the spring of 1969, opposition to the war was at a fever pitch. A stubborn opponent of the war, Gruson decided she couldn't go into her intended career in diplomacy. Instead, she followed in her parents' footsteps and became a reporter, returning to the South to work at the *Raleigh News and Observer*.

In the fall of 1969, a large coalition planned a protest, a "Moratorium on Business as Usual," set for October 15. At that point, a poll showed a majority of Americans saw the war as a mistake, but that didn't necessarily mean they advocated a hasty withdrawal. A far larger percentage supported a crackdown on protests. Gruson wore a black armband to work on October 15 in solidarity with the protests, though she told the *Wall Street Journal* that "most North Carolinians thought she was mourning a dead relative."

And even though she didn't like her parents' philosophy of objectivity, being a journalist during this time period felt important.

"Journalism is not just a profession, it's a mind-set, it's how you look at the world," she told me in Miami. She had been raised to question things, to be a contrarian. "I liked to be outside, not be a part of the crowd. So it was not just a hereditary thing, but also a question of temperament. I would not have made a very good diplomat." She loved her job in Raleigh, investigating labor conditions and environmental problems and crimes and cops.

Still, already at twenty-one she was sure enough of her views on objectivity to oppose her father in a public forum. "My father of course, as a part of the *Times*, held that objectivity was sacrosanct. And I, in part because of my background, because I'd been brought up in so many different cultures, I saw the world as a very complex place, where cultures and histories interact to change your vision of reality," Gruson said. "I was much less sure of what was right, what was wrong.... I felt that subjectivity really determines your vision of the world, that you see the world through your own eyes."

She wasn't disciplined or fired for her stand on "objectivity," and later Gruson moved from North Carolina back to Boston, where she worked at the *Boston Herald*, then at a small alternative weekly called *Boston After Dark*, and then a more mainstream weekly, the *Boston Phoenix*. She continued to agitate against the war and to support the movements for civil rights and women's rights. "From being an objective journalist, I became what I call a committed journalist," Gruson said, a journalist who was committed to social change.

In Boston she was restless. The damage of the war in Vietnam stuck with her, and she wanted to go there, to report on the wind-down of the war and its aftermath, which she felt was being overlooked by the press. She wasn't sure what it would look like, but she knew she had to go to Vietnam. "I felt strongly that you can't stand by on the sidelines when you perceive wrong; you have to act."

This was the trip that changed everything. In 1974 she said good-bye to a man she loved, lined up freelance gigs with a few papers including the *Boston Globe* and the *Chicago Tribune*, and set off for Vietnam via Hawaii. In Hawaii she decided to start working, talking to returning troops. One evening she invited a Green Beret to her hotel room to interview him about his combat experience. In a sudden trauma-induced flashback, he mistook her for the enemy in a war zone, attacked her, and tried to strangle her. The soldier left her for dead in her room. When Gruson came to, she was in a hospital in New York. The attack left her paralyzed in much of her body, initially unable to speak, walk, or hold things in her hands.

Gruson still doesn't remember the attack—she had managed to stumble out of her room and onto the street in Waikiki, and her life was saved by an officer who found her and sent her to the hospital, thinking she was jacked up on drugs. Later her mother—ever a journalist—spent time in Hawaii putting the story back together, figuring out as much as she could of the what and why of it all. The veteran who attacked her was deemed unfit to stand trial due to his mental state and spent a few months in a mental institution before being released. She's never spoken to him again, but these days Gruson sees both herself and her aggressor as victims. "It wasn't an attack or a vicious attempt to do me harm. It really was an accident. I felt we were both victims of the war," she said. Seeing it that way helps her feel empathy for the man who took away the life she thought she'd have—she describes transforming anger into empathy again and again. "It gave me a deeper understanding of the meaning of the war."

Gruson didn't stop working as a journalist. As she recovered from the accident, she relearned how to speak and gained control over a few limited motions of her hands and body. She moved to Miami and worked on a local paper, until her father later helped her get a job in the *New York Times'* new Miami bureau, where she was a news assistant for more than three decades, occasionally filing a story of her own. In 1985 she wrote a first-person feature story for the *New York Times Magazine* about her accident and her recovery, her voice humble and introspective. "My friends talk to me of my 'courage,'" she wrote. "This puzzles me; I have never felt very courageous." She retired from journalism in 2005 and has since shifted her focus to athletics—she initially raced sailboats and went scuba diving but more recently has concentrated on endurance sports, marathons and triathlons, building teams comprised of both the able and the "differently able" (a term she prefers over the disabled, explaining that we all have abilities as well as disabilities). In 2015 she cofounded a nonprofit called ThumbsUp International to involve more people in that work.

. . .

Gruson remains insistent, even after her decades at the *New York Times*, that "objectivity" is the wrong goal. "It's a useless ideal, I think. Because it is void of compassion, and compassion is necessary in human relations.... If a journalist can look at the world with compassion, you can get things changed, and change is necessary."

By the end of our interview, I adapted my body somewhat to Gruson's worldview—I found myself leaning in close to listen, holding my head to the side at an angle to make direct, parallel eye contact with her. Her speech includes long pauses and it can be hard to tell when she's still partway through an idea, so she flicked her bright eyes my way to indicate when she was done with a thought. In a way, her life has been all about looking at other people's worlds and ways of life from the outside, an experience that, approached with humility, reminds you constantly of your own subjectivity. She grew up cross-culturally, and now looks at the world oceans away from where she started—an American at home, rather than abroad; a woman with disabilities; a lifelong journalist whose career was interrupted and life forever altered by the story she always knew she needed to tell, the story of US intervention in Vietnam.

Much ink has been spilled around the idea of journalists changing or influencing the story in Vietnam. Kerry Gruson makes me think, in the rawest terms, about what happens when the story changes us. "My accident shifted my perspective on the world, on my future, on everything I see and do," she said. "But I don't think it's a bad thing, just a different perspective. I see my physical disability as a positive, because it opens my eyes to a different perspective, literally."

Gruson loves to talk about black and white, light and shadow—she's fascinated with shadows, showing me pictures of the shadows on her morning runs with friends pushing her, the long, thin shadow of a friend of hers who has no arms, the jaunty shadow of the cart she rides in to run marathons. "I love the interplay of light and dark," she said. She loves shadows because they change; because they are gray areas; because they give us a different perspective. They show how the shape of a thing always depends on the light in which it's seen.

I keep turning over the questions in my mind: Was Vietnam an example of the power of objectivity to reveal an unjust war, or just another battle over versions of the truth, in which propaganda had a role on all sides? Could anyone be clear-eyed, and was it helpful, as Gruson's father insisted, to promote the idea that a clear-eyed view was possible? If objectivity idealizes a flat, unmoving picture, Kerry Gruson idealizes ambiguity, a picture of the shadow rather than the thing itself.

There were too many true stories in Vietnam for most journalists to assess their meaning, or even describe their basic context. What readers and TV viewers back home ended up seeing was not a clear view through the glass windowpanes of objectivity, but a series of flashes and images, viewed as through dark water. There was confusion and distortion, but there was also simply too much to know, and not enough light to cast on it all. It occurs to me that the truth is like an ocean—ever-changing the deeper you go, unrecognizable at each new stage of light and darkness. In the end the whole picture is unknowable, and those who claim to know it are probably telling tall tales. The story of Vietnam is a humbling reminder that nobody owns the truth, just as nobody owns the ocean. Even those who try.

"I'm a scuba diver," Gruson said, when I shared the metaphor. "I experience in very physical terms what you're talking about." Gruson scuba dives even though she is mostly paralyzed from the neck down.

Maybe this is what all journalism is: describing the world's shadows, seeking a story out of our limited view of the light. Certainly that's what journalism in Vietnam was like. Nobody knew anything for sure, in part because of the role of propaganda, in part because of the fog and fear and danger of war, and in part because of the limitations of journalists themselves. I felt like Gruson was the kind of journalist

I wanted to become—aware of her limitations and her perspective. Gruson is comfortable in the gray areas. Perhaps objectivity would be the right goal in a static, unmoving world; but to Kerry Gruson, and to me, the purpose of telling stories is, in part, to change the world.

I look around and I see a sea of subjectivity; I have a million questions. I told Gruson what I was struggling with: that this kind of constant inquiry is hard to stick with when you're trying to make it as a writer—not just because of the frame of objectivity, but because of the way news moves on the internet, the way facts and ideas are sold. Being sure of things, in this media environment, is a form of currency. President Trump cashes in on it all the time: "Fake news!!!" he tweets out with confidence. Headlines blast us with statements of sureness: "Everything you know about food is wrong," or "Five reasons to love San Diego," or "Hillary lied." I rarely see space for the quality of being unsure, for the expression of true inquisitiveness. As soon as we become too sure of ourselves, we stop asking questions. And isn't that what the reporter should do in the world—ask questions, approach things anew? And just try to be fair and do right along the way?

"The question then becomes, fairness to whom?" Gruson said, flicking her eyes at me and smiling while we watched the light move against the ocean waves through the windows. Neither of us tried to answer the question.

5

"PUBLIC RADIO VOICE"

When I was fired from *Marketplace*, I suddenly found myself publicly defending the end of an ideal I'd scarcely wrapped my head around. And I was whiplashed. How had a nuanced post on my personal blog about objectivity lost me my dream job? Many of my coworkers had expressed their displeasure with my firing in private, and it was hardly a secret that many of us questioned "objectivity" and its pitfalls. So why were my colleagues, even the ones who agreed with me, afraid of discussing these questions in public, or even in their newsrooms? The journalists in public radio were some of the most intelligent, flexible, and creative people I'd ever been around. What was the hang-up, especially in an environment that claimed to value diversity of experience and opinion?

I needed to go back and try to understand why this conversation within public media was buried in so much silence. Public broadcasting had started as an idealist, mission-driven effort, intended in part to counter the commercialism of other broadcast news. But I found that from the 1970s through the 1990s, attacks from conservatives had left public media haunted by the ghost of false "balance"—too often, Black and brown and queer people's stories and perspectives had been "balanced" with racist or homophobic views, or simply censored altogether. As a result, countless people have left public radio and TV, sick of the doublespeak on "diversity" or uncomfortable with the expectation of remaining neutral on our own humanity. In short, public media had a beautiful dream that was never fully realized.

. . .

My first day in public radio was one of my favorite days of my life. On a sunny September day, I rode my bike to WBEZ on Chicago's Navy Pier from Rogers Park, a Chicago neighborhood, about ten miles. I knew I was going to a Real Office with Adults in it, and I was nervous. I had never had a cubicle before. I rode most of the way along the lakeshore trail in cutoff shorts, admiring the glittering water, and then stopped off and changed my clothes next to the bike trail and smoked half a cigarette. In my opinion, it was bad weather for wearing a button-down shirt and respectable pants (though maybe my true punk-rock belief is that it is never *really* a good time for respectable pants), but it seemed like the right move.

I got there and I wish it had been the sigh of relief that's like, "Who cares what I wore?" but instead it was more like, "Good thing I changed out of cutoffs!" People did seem well-dressed, at least by my standards, and like they had curated their body odors before coming to work. I got to see radio hosts at work for the first time, stand in the studio through two live shows and a top-of-the-hour newscast, listen to arguments in editorial meetings. One of the largest teacher strikes in history had just started, and the two education reporters were running around frantically. The controlled chaos of it, the adrenaline rush of daily deadlines and hourly newscasts and live interviews, was all so exciting I thought I'd died and gone to heaven. By the end of the day, I wanted nothing more than to get in that seat in front of one of those fancy microphones with some respectable pants on and be a radio star.

But there was also the stress of any first day, and the usual background transgender stress. It's never been a secret that I am transgender, but because I have spent most of my life passing as female, people often simply ignore my trans identity and treat me as a woman. As a result, I'm faced with all these choices about what to say to people about my pronouns, whether to say anything, and questions about what they already know. There are issues in my health insurance documentation (Male or female? Insurance companies want to know!). There's the question of what bathroom to use, and the risk of making someone else—a potential mentor or superior—uncomfortable through that choice. And then, the quiet, lonely investigation into who I can trust with these concerns as they arise. I'd been around long enough to know that your allies aren't always who you think they're going to be, and you have to pay careful attention.

In theory, my trans identity was a part of the package. I had come to WBEZ as a Pritzker Journalism Fellow, a program envisioned by *This American Life* co-creator and then-CEO of WBEZ, Torey Malatia, as a way to bring diverse community voices into the station. Two fellows who had experience in community-based work in Chicago would spend nine months in rigorous paid training in WBEZ's newsrooms, adopting any skills we found useful. The program would connect WBEZ to new communities and give community organizers media skills to bring back out into the world. I'd been recommended for the gig by my friend and mentor Mariame Kaba, a well-known prison abolition activist. My understanding was that I was at WBEZ to bring the energy and knowledge of my community-organizing work to bear. The other fellow, Adriana Cardona-Maguigad, came from a bilingual community paper in Back of the Yards.

I filed my first story for air a couple months later, and after I heard myself on 91.5 FM the next morning, I became a complete fiend for the news, filing news stories nearly every day. I loved being out in the field recording conversations with strangers, recording my own shy voice in the studio, cutting tape rapid-fire before the afternoon newscasts, vying to get a question in at crowded press conferences. I started blowing up the phones of Chicago's aldermen, city press offices, the EPA, NOAA—anyone with information I needed to get my hands on. Being a reporter felt like a calling, something I needed to do urgently, and do well.

But a funny thing happened on my way to becoming a reporter. The interaction went something like this. My immediate supervisor at the station, Lynette Kalsnes, brought me into a meeting with the managing editor, Sally Eisele, to talk about conflicts of interest.

Everyone at WBEZ was smart: Lynnette was a quiet genius and Sally
was a loud one. Sally asked me about my activist work, and I told her
I'd been working with youth, making stories about Chicago police and
incarceration. And I'd been a trainer for years, teaching people about
transgender issues and white privilege at workshops and conferences.
Sally said that all of that activity had to stop. Okay, fine: I was only
there at WBEZ for nine months, trying on journalism for size. But
Sally's interpretation of the conflict-of-interest policy was that I was
also not supposed to do stories for the station about any of the issues
I'd previously been involved with. Lynette pushed back on this a little.
I hadn't, for example, done any lobbying on LGBT issues—I was a
trainer, not a policy advocate. But Sally still thought I should steer
clear. It became clear to me that the concern wasn't about the actual
"bias" I might bring, but about how my work would be perceived if
people connected the dots.

This was my first glimpse of a Catch-22 related to "diversity" in
public media: I had been brought in as a part of the station's efforts
to diversify and connect to community work. And yet I was discouraged from doing stories about those communities or that work. This
meant that my extensive network of contacts from underrepresented
groups couldn't come to the radio through me, because it was supposedly all a conflict of interest. I was supposed to steer away from doing
stories about the things I knew the most about—prisons and police,
queer and trans issues. My connections to marginalized communities
were valued in theory, but in practice, I was expected to hide them,
lest they compromise my perceived professionalism as a journalist. I
didn't mind the restrictions on posting to Facebook about my political
views—but the principle of distancing myself from fundamental parts
of my identity didn't make sense in the context of their stated desire
for diversity. I came from a different mind-set, in which media created
for, by, and about marginalized communities was the norm. This was
opposite day.

It seemed absurd, but I didn't think it was my place to say so. I
agreed to focus on issues outside of my past activism, although I did
file a handful of stories about queer and trans people during my time

there thanks to Lynette's advocacy. I made myself into a reporter, focused mostly on science and the environment, and by the time I left WBEZ nine months later, I'd filed one or two stories a day for almost the entire time, and about a dozen features. Over the years, I filed hundreds of stories on controversial topics from postal worker strikes to environmental contamination, tax levies to racial discrimination. No audience member ever expressed concern about my activist past or identity (easily traceable online). And no one ever accused me of political bias in my reporting. (Well, not entirely true: I once made a crack about lawyers on air, having grown up in a family full of lawyers where lawyer jokes were super-normal, but lawyers listening took offense. And I once got a call from a PR rep for the Styrofoam industry after a piece I did about the paper cup industry—they felt that I should have presented a stronger case for the hypothetical possibility of recycling Styrofoam.)

I understood and understand the purpose of conflict-of-interest policies. It's hard to do a story about your enemies, and even harder to do a story about your friends. The idea that reporters shouldn't take bribes or report on things that could directly benefit us financially is a no-brainer, and I believe in deep introspection and checking our biases as journalists. Overall, I also sincerely trusted that public radio editors were trying to do right by the truth and move with integrity.

But something about these rules always felt off to me. Maybe they worked in a vacuum, but they didn't make sense in the context of organizations like WBEZ, WYSO, or *Marketplace*, all of which purported to be trying to do something fresh and new, trying to represent and reach more diverse audiences. Some identities are more politicized than others—for example, white people are rarely asked to consider the possible conflict of interest in doing stories about white people, and children of lawyers are rarely stopped from doing stories about lawyers (I can attest). But because I'd been an advocate for the trans community, I was considered suspect—more liable to be biased than someone who'd never heard of transgender issues before. Which, of course, is ludicrous.

In spite of this initial shock, for most of my time in public radio, I believed in what we were doing. I believed that, even if we didn't fully articulate them, the values that drove our work were more or less the right ones: support for human rights and free speech, dislike for racial and economic inequity, distrust of authority, and love of truth, however complex and multifaceted. I also found the environment, overall, to be remarkably friendly and open-minded about my trans experience. I figured our efforts to present ourselves as unbiased were just about avoiding unnecessary controversy, and even though I didn't love that dance, I accepted it. So I was surprised when I realized how important it was to these institutions—and in some cases, to individuals I knew personally—to insist on our detachment and "neutrality." This version of "objectivity" was as laughable to me the day I got fired as it was the day I started.

And I found it ironic. The people I worked with were liberals, mostly. I find it comical that public radio pretends not to be liberal. For the most part, it *is* liberal, or at least the people who work there are. From my perspective, that creates a few problems. One is that everyone in public radio is in the business of trying to hide the politics of the people in public radio, to avoid accusations of liberal bias. Another is that it is guilty of the very thing it strives to defend itself from: representing a relatively homogeneous worldview, in more ways than one. Working journalists are mostly college graduates, many with master's degrees. Lots of them, like me, grew up in cities or college towns, liberal bubbles of some kind. A majority are people for whom poverty coverage is a cause and "diversity" is a cause. And seeming not to have any liberal slant is also a cause in many public radio newsrooms. That's every bit as ridiculous as it sounds.

The further irony for me was that I had never seen myself as a liberal. I'm viciously anti-partisan as a journalist, unattached to a political party in my private life, and hypercritical of partisan platforms and approaches. My views on many individual issues were so far to the left, lots of my Hillary-loving colleagues could never have guessed what they were. I held it all close to my chest—I didn't need people knowing I didn't even believe in capitalism or monogamy or prisons or the nuclear family. I actually thought I was good at political reporting in part *because* I cared so little for party politicians in general. I wasn't neutral, but I was skeptical as hell.

. . .

Why were people in public radio holding on to the idea of objectivity so tightly? The first thing I learned through research was that public radio and television in the United States are unlike anything else in the world. In most other countries, public media outlets are *majority* public-funded, and many are under direct state control. In the US, "public media" is a public-private partnership. After a flurry of lobbying in the last century to figure out how to regulate the airwaves, the final language of the Communications Act of 1934 signified a loss for those who supported truly public airwaves: it was basically a laissez-faire piece of legislation that said channels could be licensed to anyone, although federal regulators made *some* effort to require commercial stations to broadcast in the public interest. It was the rising popularity of television decades later that activated people to really push for public-access stations with consistent taxpayer support.

The Public Broadcasting Act of 1967 was the beginning of dedicated taxpayer funding for television and radio programming. One of the last acts of Lyndon B. Johnson's Great Society legislation, it created the Corporation for Public Broadcasting, and it stated that the CPB should pursue programming with "strict adherence to objectivity and balance in all programs or series of programs of a controversial nature." Johnson waxed poetic when he announced the act's passage, bragging that the new service "will be free, and it will be independent—and it will belong to all of our people." But in reality, the CPB never had a dedicated federal funding source, which meant it depended on Congress to appropriate money for it in each federal budget. The money never came at the levels suggested by the original law. As a result, public broadcasting has never been fully "public"—and even the slim public funding has always been politicized. Public media quickly became a toy for partisans to bat around at budget time.

One of the CPB's first big moves was to create the public television network, PBS. In almost no time, the language of "objectivity" was used to challenge PBS programming. In 1971 a conservative media watchdog called Accuracy in Media (AIM) went after PBS for two documentary programs it claimed lacked "objectivity." One was about youth incarceration, another about sex education. When the Federal Communications Commission (FCC) declined to intervene, AIM sued. A federal appeals court in 1975 found that the "objectivity and balance" admonition in the Public Broadcasting Act was not something the FCC could enforce the way AIM wanted; it was a goal to aspire to, not a standard subject to regulation. The drafters of the Public Broadcasting Act had never defined objectivity, and it would persist throughout public media's history as a nebulous concept, meaningless as a legal "standard" but useful as a mode of attack against programming one didn't like.

Public radio began almost as an afterthought. When National Public Radio was incorporated on March 3, 1970, nobody reported on it except for CPB's own publication. Perhaps due to how overlooked radio was as a medium, it was at NPR that some of the more idealistic aspects of public broadcasting in the US were put into practice, beginning with its original mission statement written by Bill Siemering. The founding document of NPR envisioned a pluralistic public resource focused on curiosity and social change.

"I saw radio as an agent for change," Siemering said when I called him on the phone at his house in Pennsylvania, and listened carefully to his gentle, shaky voice, his appreciative memory of NPR's idealism. Many still point to the lovely language in Siemering's "NPR Purposes" document, which opens: "National Public Radio will serve the individual: it will promote personal growth; it will regard the individual differences among men with respect and joy rather than derision and hate; it will celebrate the human experience as infinitely varied rather than vacuous and banal; it will encourage a sense of active constructive participation, rather than apathetic helplessness."

When NPR's first news show, *All Things Considered,* went on the air in 1971, the afternoon news show reflected Siemering's vision: it was a quirky blend of news, documentary, commentary, and shoe-leather reporting. The very first broadcast included many minutes of tape from an antiwar protest in DC earlier that day. It encapsulated a new vision for radio in the US—a type of radio that felt like a public square, commercial-free, diverse, and equal parts sober and strange.

But there was a problem with the idea of forming public media into a kind of broadcast public square. Public space in the United States was (and is) contested from all sides. From the start, there was conservative opposition and accusations that it wasn't "objective" enough. Soon after, the country elected President Richard Nixon, who didn't support NPR's mission and also didn't want public funding for anything critical of him. In 1972 he vetoed CPB funding entirely and set up a new funding structure that would permanently limit how much CPB could bring in directly from the federal government.

As a result, fear of defunding hovers over every public media controversy. Public radio and TV face a constant tension between providing an "alternative" to corporate news media versus producing programs that are popular and uncontroversial enough to garner sponsorship from private entities. Public media has to grapple with the question of who the "public" is, but that debate has always been tainted by partisan politics, which means NPR's (nonpartisan) founding values would only ever get so far. Within a decade, public media went from presenting itself as an alternative to striving for mainstream recognition and an "objective" voice.

· · ·

The mainstream "objective" voice at the time was also a white male East Coast voice. So, early challenges to public broadcasting also came from another angle: broadcasters of color who wanted a seat at the table after decades of exclusion from commercial radio and TV stations. In 1968 the National Advisory Commission on Civil Disorders, popularly known as the Kerner Commission, listed media among the culprits in the overall environment of racism and marginalization that led to the urban uprisings of 1967. "Most newspaper articles and most television programming ignore the fact that an appreciable part of their audience is black," the Kerner Report read. "The world that television and newspapers offer to their black audience is almost totally white, in both appearance and attitude. . . . [O]ur evidence shows that the so-called 'white press' is at best mistrusted and at worst held in contempt by many black Americans." Black Americans, as well as Latinos and other people of color, saw in public media an opportunity to get a foot in the door.

A Latina TV producer named Cecilia Garcia was among several people I contacted to learn about this early history—we connected by phone after I found her name on a list of participants in a minority task force for the Corporation for Public Broadcasting in the 1970s. She'd been a media activist and producer for decades, mostly in her hometown of Detroit.

Back then Detroit was hot, crowded—a site of protests and riots and union organizing, with a still-robust auto industry about to begin its long collapse. Garcia was born in Detroit and went to high school on the southwest side, where there's a large Mexican American community. But she read the *Detroit Free Press* and saw the way white editors and reporters talked about people in Black and brown communities as criminals and outsiders; she flipped through TV stations and didn't see her community represented at all. But, she explained, "I knew instinctively that the airwaves belong to all of us." In the early '70s, just out of college, she decided to do something about it.

She and a group of about fifteen friends started sending letters to their local public television station, WTVS, demanding a Latino program of their own. They walked into the station and asked for a meeting. At the time, organizations around the country were taking advantage of the Civil Rights Act to file lawsuits accusing broadcasters of racial discrimination in employment and programming. Partly to avoid unwanted controversy, WTVS eventually took Garcia and her friends under its wing. With the station's technical support, they started a bilingual TV program called *Para Mi Pueblo*, which aired weekly starting in 1973.

For the six years that Garcia produced *Para Mi Pueblo*, she made no bones about her work being for and by the community, often advocating for issues relevant to Detroit's southwest side. "I knew in southwest Detroit, we needed a health clinic. We presented that; we talked about that; we really dug into that issue. At the end of my time on the air, a health clinic had opened, which I saw as a big success," Garcia said. "Was that bias? Yes. It was bias in favor of health care for my community."

Around the country, producers of color were also seizing the moment to push for better distribution of shows about communities of color and facing varying levels of resistance. Garcia joined with a national group called the Latino Consortium, which distributed programming by and for Latinos; similar consortia were founded for Black, Asian American, and Native American producers. It was hard to get programs about people of color picked up for national distribution, and it was prohibitively expensive to copy tapes. Garcia describes the various consortia "bicycling" their tapes across the country, which meant sending a single video recording by mail. She'd send a film from Detroit to a consortium member or friend at WGBH in Boston; they'd air it and mail it to someone in Wisconsin or Nebraska or California; and so on. It was time-consuming, but oftentimes it was the only way to get their programs on the air.

"We came together because we felt we could not rely on PBS to distribute our programs," she said. "Breaking into distribution at the national level seemed impossible for producers of color." She explained that programmers were torn between the pressure to be representative and the desire to be popular, and too often the conflict was settled in rooms with entirely white station managers, programmers, or board members who could not imagine a Latino show as a popular show. "If it's a group of white men primarily making programming decisions, it becomes almost impossible for our voices, voices of producers of color, to be heard."

Her work revealed, again, the bias inherent in news judgment; like Ida B. Wells before her, and Black Lives Matter after, she knew that sometimes the only solution was to make the news yourself.

. . .

Public radio had a different structure than TV, because it produced its own national programs from the start (PBS was a distributor, not a producer). In NPR's newsroom during the first few years, the biggest debates were not outwardly about diversity. One divide surrounded the line between cultural production and hard news reporting: some in the newsroom thought the organization should focus *All Things Considered* on hard news and attempt to compete with other daily news organizations, while others felt a major part of the show's calling was to cover culture, music, and arts, as well as human-interest stories. The debates could become quite contentious; at one point, the now-famous correspondent Nina Totenberg was nearly fired for leaking the internal battles of the 1970s to the press.

This debate was about diversity in a way, because most of the trained news reporters came from a more traditional background, and most of them were white. One of the news directors brought in to sharpen NPR's political focus, Robert Zelnick, would later write a book arguing against affirmative action. Bill Siemering recalled only that the two Black reporters on NPR's original staff "didn't last long."

Jack Mitchell, the first NPR staff member and longtime producer of *All Things Considered*, said most of the newsroom at the beginning were people who came from the left, many from the world of educational and community radio (public radio's precursors). "With the possible exception of a few engineers, NPR's staff, to a person, disliked Nixon and hated the war he failed to end," he wrote in his 2005 book *Listener Supported: The Culture and History of Public Radio*. "While not consciously skewed, the program content undoubtedly reflected this antipathy." At the time, public radio was so small-scale that Nixon hadn't even noticed, in spite of his open hatred for public TV.

NPR's experimental days were relatively short-lived. The culture wars started early and came up often, and by the end of the '70s, the organization had burned through a couple of presidents and many of its original staff, including Siemering and Mitchell. Siemering's vision of working closely with local stations in order to better represent all parts of the country was never fully realized. "NPR started as an alternative, and switched," Mitchell told me when I called him. When a new president named Frank Mankiewicz took over in 1977, Siemering's vision of an alternative to commercial broadcasting largely gave way to an effort to take the programming mainstream. As that mainstreaming took place, diverse voices faded into the background.

. . .

By the end of the 1970s, more than a few people were fed up with the struggle to diversify services that were intended to be representative of the public from the get-go. The vision of public media as a smart, balanced alternative to commercial media seemed half-baked if the voices were still mostly white, so public media did what it does well: it commissioned a study. Cecilia Garcia was among twenty-eight people invited to sit on a Task Force on Minorities for the CPB. In 1978 the final report of the task force opened with this line: "The task force must conclude that the public broadcast system is asleep at the transmitter." The executive summary calls PBS's and NPR's minority programming numbers "appalling," noting that in 1977 less than 5 percent of the 1,500 hours of programming NPR distributed was produced by or focused on racial or ethnic minorities. More than half of public radio licensees and 16 percent of public TV stations had zero people of color on the staff. At the national level, among fifteen executives running the CPB, PBS, and NPR, there was only one person of color.

The Task Force on Minorities made dozens of specific recommendations, including new funding for training programs for reporters and producers of color, improved tools for evaluating audiences that went beyond just counting and tracking demographics, and, of course, more people of color in leadership. Many of the recommendations were never implemented. Forty years later, a discussion is still underway in public radio about why "public radio voice" is so homogeneously white and East Coast sounding. The percentage of Black people in NPR's newsroom peaked at 12 percent in 2012, and in 2017 was down to 8.8 percent. The percentage of Latinos crawled up from 5 percent in 2012 to 6 percent in 2017, when Latinos were around 18 percent of the US population. PBS stations have lots of diversity trainings and diversity policies, but still not a lot of diversity.

In some ways, Garcia thinks this lack of representation is baked into the way public broadcasting is funded; the combination of unprotected public funding and unrestricted private funding means it faces both pressure to be uncontroversial and pressure to be popular with the mainstream. It reduces risk-taking and creates a paradox for the stated goals of diversity. "There are winners and losers when we fund things the way we do here, and, inevitably, people of color have been on the losing end of that equation," Garcia said.

Her critiques echo countless stories I've now heard from people of color who do or did work in public radio; after I was fired, several people expressly told me that they had left public media due to racism or tokenism in newsrooms. Others have shared stories about being the only person of color in a newsroom in a major urban area, and how their white colleagues didn't see that as a problem. Still others have talked about the gatekeeping they've experienced from white editors and editorial boards, who—like most of us—take an interest in the stories they can identify with or connect to, undervaluing or ignoring the ideas brought to them by journalists of color. Public radio puts out its mediocre diversity numbers every year, and people respond with ideas for how to improve through recruitment. But the problem is more systemic.

Jack Mitchell, NPR's first employee, said it's clear to him that diversity is and always has been political. He recalled that the original rationale for diversifying newsrooms in the 1970s was affirmative action, not representation in and of itself. Early on, the idea of affirmative action had to do with acknowledging the existence of discrimination, and accounting for it through policies designed to counterbalance past wrongs. But gradually, diversity efforts shifted from an attempt to redress harm, to an effort to create workplaces in which everyone would benefit from multiculturalism, often while denying or ignoring systemic oppression. Mitchell noted that in public radio, diversity gradually ceased being about social justice and shifted to being about representation. And as he pointed out, you can't bring people in for the purpose of "diversifying" and expect the institution to operate exactly the same way it always has. It defeats even the stated purpose.

And this is the paradox of "objectivity" and diversity. Real diversity means fighting against institutional oppression and discrimination, which is a political act. From almost the very beginning, public broadcasting found itself entrenched in a complex, often frustrating attempt to appear apolitical—for fear of being defunded or of outright attacks by the right wing. You can't depoliticize diversity, but public media has tried.

. . .

The right wing started using "objectivity" to try to destroy public media almost immediately. James Ledbetter's 1997 history of public media, *Made Possible By . . .*, explains that it was often queer and Black voices who were the target of these attacks. There was plenty of rancor in the '70s, but in the '80s conservatives began to really push the culture wars. Ronald Reagan installed a chair of the Corporation for Public Broadcasting, Sonia Landau, who openly challenged programming the administration didn't like on the basis of a lack of "balance," while simultaneously pushing for PBS to air propaganda in support of Reagan's policies.

Landau was also part of a push for an ongoing "scientific" analysis of whether the content on PBS was balanced and objective, an effort with strong support from conservative members of Congress. These studies would count the number of conservative versus liberal voices on air (which Ledbetter called a "quixotic pursuit," particularly given the Reagan administration's push to get rid of the Fairness Doctrine requiring balance for private broadcasters). Pretty quickly, quantitative analysis of whether or not programming is "balanced" became a threat dangled over PBS leaders' heads, who responded by making more space for right-wing guests regardless of their relationship to truth or facts. These efforts at balance are especially notable given PBS's dicey record of pursuing programming that is representative of the country's diversity—one kind of balance was openly sacrificed for another.

Members of the Reagan administration also went after individual programs on PBS, including documentaries on Cuba, Guatemala, and a nine-part series focused on the politics of the African continent from an African viewpoint—virtually any anti-US or anti-Western sentiment was met with the demand that it be more "balanced." Out-side conservative groups joined the chorus. In 1983 PBS aired a series about Vietnam, and Accuracy in Media produced an hour-long rebut-tal, funded by the National Endowment for the Humanities, narrated by Charlton Heston, and aired on PBS. AIM used what would become a classic tactic: it critiqued the creators and their motives as unobjec-tive, rather than critiquing the accuracy of the series itself.

But instead of defending itself against partisan attacks, PBS often responded by simply agreeing to carry more conservative content. It already had shows that pitted liberal and conservative views against each other; why not programs that pitted conservative and even *more* conservative views against each other? General Electric, the same company that became a primary underwriter for the new radio show *Marketplace* in the late 1980s, underwrote and helped promote the hit TV show *The McLaughlin Group*, a conservative-dominated yell-fest. It premiered on PBS in 1981 and became an early platform for Pat Buchanan, who during the 1980s advocated the idea that AIDS was God's retribution against sinful homosexuals. A conservative TV production company called the Blackwell Corporation used fund-ing from conservative foundations to produce PBS documentaries throughout the 1980s, pushing neocon views on Central American politics, telecommunications, and South African apartheid. And Led-better writes that PBS itself began to support conservative counter-programming, giving hundreds of thousands of dollars in grants for the production of right-wing shows by the early '90s.

At NPR the battles were quieter but concerned many of the same issues. Inside the newsroom, Mitchell recalled battles over covering gay rights, with some dismissing such coverage as a form of advocacy even as covering conservative issues was being pushed as a form of balance. In 1986, after a *New Republic* article by Fred Barnes criticized NPR for its sympathetic coverage of Latin American uprisings, news director Robert Siegel warned the staff against being biased or doing advocacy journalism; Mitchell wrote that an independent reporter named Paul McIsaac was blackballed by Siegel for his Latin American coverage.

Fear of bad press from conservatives led PBS and NPR down a path of caution and self-censorship from which they have yet to return. While happy to air programs that were sponsored by General Electric or even the ultraconservative Heritage Foundation, Ledbetter writes that PBS refused to air a series of Academy Award–winning documentaries: a 1991 exposé about General Electric and nuclear weapons, a 1992 film about the US invasion of Panama, and a 1993 documentary about domestic violence survivors. The rationale for not airing the latter documentary, *Defending Our Lives*, was that its coproducers included an anti–domestic violence organization; the rationale for not airing the documentary about General Electric was that a consumer advocacy group pushing for a boycott of GE had been part of the production. The question was not whether the documentaries were factual, or even whether the journalism was slanted in some way; it was whether the documentaries might be fodder for conservative activists to attack. This fear of angering major sponsors or politicians set up a dangerous precedent: cautions against not checking one's facts gave way to cautions against doing anything that might be accused of "bias."

. . .

Bias is in the eye of the beholder, and right-wing activists saw bias in any programming they didn't like, especially programming that concerned Black people and gay people. There was nothing conservatives hated more than filmmaker Marlon Riggs, who produced unapologetic, raw imagery about Black gay life and sexuality. Riggs's 1989 documentary about queer Black men, *Tongues Untied*, became a cause for right-wing censors—by the time it went to broadcast on PBS in 1991, almost two-thirds of stations refused to air it, and years later Republican congressmen were still complaining that it had been aired at all, calling it a violation of decency and community standards. PBS also canceled a *POV* documentary called *Stop the Church*, about an ACT UP action in New York City in 1989 trying to draw attention to the AIDS crisis. The stated reason for the censorship was that stations simply couldn't handle the attention that would be generated by distributing the film.

Riggs responded personally to the vitriol. Writing for *Current*, a public media rag, in 1991, he criticized the idea of "community standards" that was used to attack his film: "The question such broadcasters never asked, because the answers are too revealing, is: Whose community and whose standards are they upholding?" He called for a "public" television that was actually for all of us—not just a boxing ring for white conservatives and white liberals. But public media as public square, with all of the chaos that entails, was by then a far cry from public media in practice. PBS's *The McLaughlin Group* and *NewsHour* and NPR's *Morning Edition* and *All Things Considered* all took pains to balance Democrats with Republicans but rarely balanced white voices with people of color, or male voices with women's.

"Paradoxically," Riggs wrote, "the *Tongues Untied* censorship hysteria has helped rekindle an essential public debate: who is to have access to so-called 'public' media, and on what terms? Who should represent and define 'minority' perspectives and experience? Above all, who has the authority to draw the thin line between innocuous 'diversity' and unacceptable 'deviance'?"

During the AIDS crisis, "Silence=Death" became a refrain of the queer movement. The idea of telling our stories and exposing our truths was central to queer activism, and the risk of death was real: the biggest queer story of the 1980s was the story of AIDS. There were frequent murders of gay and gender-nonconforming people. Queer communities have also long been plagued with the crisis of suicide, which feeds off silence and isolation. Making media about our sexualities was considered a way to save lives, and that meant filmmakers like Marlon Riggs and the creator of the censored ACT UP documentary, Robert Hilferty, were inclined to value voice over political party. Wouldn't it be wonderful, I thought, to talk to Riggs or Hilferty about their films, the PBS censorship, the attacks from Congress? After learning about them in James Ledbetter's book about public media, I Googled the two censored artists. Marlon Riggs had died in 1994 of complications related to AIDS. Robert Hilferty died in 2009, of suicide.

. . .

During my years of working in public radio, I never once heard a newsroom leader talk about "balance" in terms of anything other than left versus right, accuser versus accused, or critic versus criticized. This reflects a problem not just with public media, but with the news media's understanding of the concept of "balance" more generally. In 2017 I published an article that asked, "What if balance was about process, rather than outcome?" I proposed that to do truly "balanced" work, journalists should stop focusing on the appearance of balance, and focus more on the process of reporting itself. Rather than trying to just *seem* fair by pitting opposing positions or left and right against one another, I argued that our efforts at balance should be about making journalism more representative, more accessible, and more collaborative, some of the values I understood to be at the heart of public radio when it was founded.

Focusing on the balance of left and right tends to keep us within Daniel C. Hallin's sphere of legitimate controversy—whatever we assume "the public" sees as a legitimate debate is fair game. But it tends not to acknowledge that our ideas about who makes up "the public" are easily skewed in homogeneous newsrooms, and there are powerful forces already tipping the scales toward overrepresentation of white cisgender men. Queer people and people of color have often been excluded from legitimacy, not just by media but by our political parties, too. A truly "balanced" public media has the potential to be representative in ways that many public institutions currently are not. What if people in prison, undocumented immigrants, youth, transgender people, Black people, rural and elderly people had disproportionate or even proportional presences in our newsrooms? I think the dream of a quirky, idealistic public media depends on the pursuit of this kind of balance.

And yet public media's history provides ample examples of how marginalized voices were "balanced" not with people who had differing experiences, but with conservative ideology. Conservatives set the terms of the debate around media bias to focus on left versus right, and the liberals in charge of public broadcasting programs went along with it.

This choice matters, because the partisan framing obscures the fact that concrete, material power struggles in the US aren't really between Democrats and Republicans. Both parties have elite power structures and Washington lobbyists and fancy fund-raisers. Real power struggles have more often been between rich and poor, white and Black, native-born and immigrant. Conservative activists painted the issue of balance as a battle between Republicans and Democrats, when in fact they were engaged in a battle between people with institutional power and people without.

I'm concerned not so much with the consequences of that trend for political partisans and parties as the consequences for the rest of us. I don't care if Democrats or Republicans win the debate; I care that marginalized people become pawns in a debate that's not really about us. This framing continues to constrain oppressed identities under a yoke of "partisanship" as a means to censor our voices. And too often, public media's defense against these blatant attacks on the truth hasn't been more truth-telling. It has been less. Meanwhile, too many people have left journalism and public radio, or never started in the first place, fed up with its hypocrisy on "diversity." Programs such as the one that brought me into public radio continue to pop up, but actual representative newsrooms have yet to arrive—when people talk about "public radio voice," they *still* mean a white East Coast or midwestern person with a smooth tone. People who speak up about racism, transphobia, or class issues in newsrooms can still be fired for doing so.

Perhaps all this caution about giving conservatives the impression of "balance" has paid off financially, but what about morally, ethically, in terms of the service mission of public media? Has depoliticizing diversity led to increased trust? The threat to defund public media returns every budget season, still a useful whipping post. But instead of everyone trusting NPR and PBS as neutral arbiters of the public good, that trust continues to decline. In a 2017 survey conducted by Gallup and the Knight Foundation, more people surveyed cited *Fox News* as an unbiased news source than NPR.

6

STRAIGHT NEWS, GAY MEDIA, AND THE AIDS CRISIS

Truth can be propaganda. And that doesn't make it not true.
JOHN SCAGLIOTTI, 2018

John Scagliotti and Andrew Kopkind's love story is a picture of the raunchy gay '70s. John was living in Boston and his roommate, Charley Shively (a writer, history professor, and collective member with the occasional newspaper *Fag Rag*), told him about this part of the Fens, a public park near Fenway Park ballfield, where men would go to cruise. Charley was older, John just barely legal.

"I was into older guys," Scagliotti told me. He was amazed to learn that Charley would go get his cock sucked from 2 to 3 p.m. most days in the park (even in winter) and decided to try it. He didn't want to run into Charley, so he went down to the Fens around 5, when the professional men were getting off work. He was basically a kid in a candy store.

One day a tall, beautiful man followed him into the park. "I was down on my knees, adoring him," Scagliotti said, looking pleased. And then this tall drink of water grabbed him under his armpits and pulled him up to face level, saying one word: "Cops!"

The police were there to bust up the orgy, so Scagliotti and the tall fellow and about seventy-five others went skittering every which way, out of this brushy brambly part of the Fens and back toward the street. There were so many men, so much copulating going on, the cops couldn't catch anyone as they ran for every exit.

"That was funny," said the handsome mustachioed man. Scagliotti laughed too, if nervously—it *was* funny. And then the man surprised him, asking, "Wanna go get a cup of coffee?"

He got coffee with *New Republic* reporter Andrew Kopkind and they were together, Scagliotti says, pretty much from then on.

Scagliotti told me this story in his kitchen in Vermont, on the farm he calls the Kopkind Colony after his late partner. I came to see him after Kerry Gruson suggested it—they had been roommates in Boston in the early 1970s, before she left for Vietnam and her accident. She said I should look up Andy Kopkind, too: a luminary queer writer whose reporting, mostly for *The Nation*, created an incredible record of twentieth-century social justice movements. So I drove from North Carolina to Guilford, which is in this Vermont version of a holler, a gorgeous topographical dip full of grassy knolls and exposed rocks. John and Andy bought it in the '70s and transformed the old farm into a writer's retreat.

I was trying to understand the relationship between journalism and activism. During Scagliotti's lifetime, coverage of gay issues had transformed dramatically. The reporters who covered queer communities were mostly outside of mainstream newsrooms, working for alternative gay papers, and these papers led the way in covering AIDS. And queer media activism in the form of boycotts, protests, and independent media coverage eventually led to more truth-telling, more probing, and more expansive and just reporting. I wanted to understand how gay journalists had moved queer issues and AIDS from the sphere of deviance into the sphere of legitimate controversy, and how they saw their own work—were they activists, journalists, or both? Traditional "objectivity" has asserted that detachment leads to more accurate storytelling. But what about the moments when connection, rather than detachment, led journalists to stories that were true and important?

. . .

Inside a gorgeous restored barn at the Kopkind Colony, there was a bulletin board covered in pictures of John with Audre Lorde in the '80s, John with his former producers of the first gay TV show ever, John outside of Stonewall with Andy. John painted this picture for me of gay life when they started out: how outside, how deviant they were as gay men, and how they had to make their own way in journalism.

"Everyone agreed that homosexuals are disgusting and horrible," he told me through his New England accent and thick salt-and-pepper beard. "They certainly should be put in mental institutions and in hospitals and in jail, and they are child molesters. That was pretty much it, at the time when we started out."

That first date at the Fens wasn't Kopkind's first time getting busted, or near-busted, for cruising. In the early 1960s, he was working for *Time* magazine in the LA bureau when he got picked up and charged with public indecency. *Time* didn't want to fire a great reporter, so they got him to agree to clean himself up—he found a therapist who claimed to help gay people go straight, and *Time* paid the bill. Apparently the shrink would try to get Kopkind to practice being straight by picking up an airline stewardess or another similarly womanly persona. During the therapy sessions, the male psychologist would play the stewardess, and Andy would have to compliment her and try to act manly and see where it all went. "It worked just fine in the office; not so well in midair," Kopkind quips in his collection *The Thirty Years' Wars*.

Conversion therapy didn't work, and Kopkind quit *Time* after just three years and became a writer for the *New Republic*. This new gig was a breakthrough: on one of his first major assignments, he was sent to Alabama to cover the civil rights movement in Selma, where he first witnessed the movements that transformed him. He became dedicated to the goals of social justice and civil rights shared by the protesters in Selma, even as he continued to work for magazines and papers. He was among the first people to write about Students for a Democratic Society for a national audience. He immersed himself in social justice movements, committed to understanding them from within while also communicating their visions to a larger audience.

"It wasn't just about civil rights, not just about laws, but about power, and power to the people, power to the community. And they were analyzing the white power structure," he recalled in his book. "I was still the journalist, but I was part of the movement too."

Under Kopkind's mentorship, Scagliotti also shaped himself into a reporter, taking a job producing news with WBCN, a popular rock radio station in Boston. Scagliotti eventually became the news director, and Andy would record commentaries, his chronic stutter mysteriously fading away as he gave sharp one-take speeches on one topic or another. For fun, they developed an hour-long show about gay life that aired on Sunday nights. From 10 to 11 p.m., Scagliotti said, "kids could put their headphones on and go off and listen and feel empowered." *The Lavender Hour* was one of the first gay radio shows ever.

As Scagliotti described it, Andy was a shimmery genius and an incredible reporter. He often talked with a stutter, but he mostly didn't talk; he listened incessantly, and then he could sit down at a typewriter and hammer out something that didn't even need edits. In photographs, Kopkind looks naughty: a big grin, a skinny cigar, a half-unbuttoned shirt.

"He never even misspelled words," Scagliotti said. "It was amazing." I loved the way his gravelly voice turned sweet with these memories—he loved Andy Kopkind, and it was obvious.

He remembered Kopkind being on the phone all day long—with his sources and contacts, people around the country and in Europe, finding out what they were talking about, keying into the zeitgeist. Kopkind was an insightful writer on the topic of the right wing and the far left, a critic of liberal establishments as well as conservative ones, and a careful observer of culture. He was creative, incisive, and strange. He didn't present himself as a "gay" writer, but after the early '70s, he was out in his professional life. In the '70s he began to write regularly for *The Nation*.

In June 1979, a decade after the Stonewall riots brought gay activism to a mainstream audience, Kopkind wrote a hilariously seething critique of the *New York Times'* ongoing refusal to acknowledge gay people as anything other than deviants. "Last winter," he wrote in the *Village Voice*, "*The New York Times Magazine* published a cover story on the city's 'renaissance,' replete with color photographs of all the fashionable features of born-again Gotham: discos, musical comedies, Bloomingdale's, rehabbed brownstones, warehouse neighborhoods, Deco restaurants, designer boutiques, gourmet kitchens. There was hardly an item on the list that was not tinged with gay sensibility—or created by it. And yet the influence of the new sexual community on the revitalized city was never once mentioned—not even in the coy euphemisms ('neighborhoods of single adults') that the genteel press prefers. Gays who read the *Times* were astounded by the omission."

Before Stonewall, there was a virtual prohibition on covering gay issues in news media, and that prohibition remained in most mainstream media even after. But the '70s and '80s saw the rise of gay alternative media and shows like *The Lavender Hour* and small-print weeklies filled the gap where straight news refused to go. "Objective" journalism at the time didn't deal with gay people at all, because they existed in the sphere of deviance. So, the coverage was left to the deviant, "activist" papers and shows—not because it wasn't true, but because it was socially unacceptable.

"Consciousness changes, huge consciousness changes move the debate line for journalism," Scagliotti said. During his time with Andy Kopkind, the idea of being gay went from being viewed as a deviant perversion, an impossibility in the world of journalism, to an inevitability, a fact of life even in mainstream media. "That line keeps moving a lot for LGBT people, but very quickly it went from total disgust and invisibility, to some visibility, to a lot of backlash."

. . .

When I left John Scagliotti and the verdant Kopkind Colony, I drove across Ontario to Michigan for a fellowship researching the history of gay alternative media in an archive called the Joseph A. Labadie Collection at the University of Michigan. I spent a month digging through volumes of gay newspapers, pamphlets, and publications from the 1980s, looking at how gay papers differed from or were the same as mainstream news media, and how gay people pushed back on coverage they felt misrepresented them. The line of acceptable coverage of

LGBT people kept moving. But how had it moved? Who had moved it? I knew journalists had been a part of that movement, that to tell the truth about gay life had required gay journalists taking on the role of media advocates, much as trans writers have done during my lifetime.

Certainly, the sea change in coverage of gay identity didn't happen as an inevitable result of mainstream journalists seeking the facts about queer lives. Instead, the shift came out of a prolonged struggle. Throughout the 1980s, gay activists protested the *New York Times* and other newspapers, pushing for more accurate and fair coverage. They organized with their unions to get anti-discrimination protections at places like the Associated Press and the major papers. They wrote outsider articles for gay outlets and 'zines until those outsider stories became stories deemed worth covering in bigger papers. They published the first and most in-depth coverage of AIDS as it became one of the biggest news stories of the century.

These journalist-activists largely rejected "objectivity." But even as they advocated for factual, contextual reporting, they remained at the margins of journalism.

. . .

A 1949 *Newsweek* article entitled "Queer People" opened with this line: "The sex pervert, whether a homosexual, an exhibitionist, or even a dangerous sadist, is too often regarded as merely a 'queer' person who never hurts anyone but himself."

In 1956 a *Time* magazine article quoted author Edmund Bergler from his book *Homosexuality: Disease or Way of Life?* "There are no happy homosexuals."

In December 1963, the *New York Times* ran a rare cover story about homosexuality, headlined "Growth of Homosexuality in City Provokes Wide Concern." It used the words "homosexual" and "deviate" interchangeably, as did much coverage of the time. A 1964 *Miami Herald* article opened: "Miami's homosexual world is a sad and frantic place."

Through most of the twentieth century, gay people were imagined by most news media as an abject group of effeminate men suffering from an embarrassing sexual perversion. Gradually, the "homosexual" became a person, and that person became a member of a community. From the 1960s on, activists pushed hard for new cultural and political space to live openly as gay in the United States. Homosexuality was removed from the list of psychiatric disorders in 1980, and the term "gay" came further into vogue at that time. From the beginning, the news media was seen as one of the most important fronts in this battle: news coverage, and the nature of the coverage, mattered greatly to gay people, who wanted social change and civil rights.

A 1982 publication called *Talk Back! The Gay Person's Guide to Media Action*, which I found in the Labadie Collection, provides a window into the developing strategy to change media coverage. The book-length pamphlet begins by breaking down the immediate problems with media coverage, from the perspective of a group of Boston-based activists. They criticize the low placement of gay stories, stereotypes about gay and lesbian people, the tendency to present gay people as isolated phenomena, and the near-total invisibility of lesbians in news coverage. One news media habit is described as "Hitler's opinion": reporters would call in a bigot from the Moral Majority or the psychiatric profession for a "balanced" take in any article that mentioned being gay, while presenting gay voices exclusively as subjective and non-expert.

Talk Back! also critiques sensationalism and a formulation they call "the homosexual adjective": newspapers, which rarely referred to a gay community or even a homosexual community, had no problem asserting the existence of "homosexual murder, homosexual torture, homosexual rape, even, we are told, gay arson." When a gay person killed someone, it was reported as "homosexual murder"; when a gay person was killed for being gay, it was not reported at all. If journalism is the first draft of history, there was an entire history of anti-gay violence never recorded—instead, we had "gay arson." The pamphlet also addresses the lack of openly gay representation in newsrooms: "As this book is being written, the *San Francisco Chronicle* is the only daily newspaper in the U.S. that has actively sought to hire a gay reporter. Few papers have even one openly gay person in their editorial department."

By way of strategy, *Talk Back!* suggests developing relationships with local papers, but also warns that reporters may have a hard time working with them. "Those reporters who are sympathetic have probably been harassed for not being 'objective' or may be suspected of being gay themselves." Few workplaces had protections against discrimination for being gay, and reporters who came out or were outed were frequently fired or demoted. It was also widely assumed that a gay reporter could not possibly be "objective" around issues of sexuality. *Talk Back!* challenges that notion, asserting instead that *no one* can be objective on the topic. "A reporter's ability to be 'objective' is notoriously affected by numerous *subjective* factors, and around the issue of sexual orientation there are few neutral opinions."

. . .

A 1983 undergraduate thesis I found in the University of Michigan's Labadie Collection, by Barry Yeoman, named one newspaper in particular as the great pariah of gay people seeking better coverage: the *New York Times*. "It is difficult to discuss gay news coverage without singling out the *Times*. More than any other paper, it is cited by gay observers for homophobic journalism," he wrote. (When I contacted Yeoman, who is now a freelance journalist in North Carolina, he laughed with delight that his NYU undergrad thesis had ended up in an archive, available for study—apparently he'd sold several copies via a written notice in the local gay paper, and these copies have made their way to libraries around the country.)

The *New York Times* was indeed notorious for its negligent coverage of gay communities, a trend-setter that had largely ignored one of New York's biggest trends. A gay community paper called the *New York Native* published a media criticism column in every biweekly issue, which frequently critiqued the *Times*. The author, David Rothenberg, had a cover story in June 1981: "Homophobia at the *New York Times*."

"Lesbians and gay men at the *Times* are allowed little—if any—positive influence over the paper's coverage of gay people," he wrote, noting that he'd reached out to several *Times* staffers, who were all closeted, afraid of losing status at the paper if they were to be outed.

"Needless to say, there is a significant correlation between the closeted status of gay and lesbian *Times* staffers and the historic inability of that most influential newspaper to deal accurately, honestly, or fairly with our existence."

An especially unpopular facet of the *Times* coverage of gay people during this era was its refusal to use the word "gay," insisting instead on "homosexual" even where it created linguistic awkwardness. And, Rothenberg wrote, the paper looked past huge political developments in its own backyard: "Gays were stunned at the *Times* coverage of the largest gay march in history. An estimated 100,000 gay men and lesbians gathered in Washington, D.C., on October 14, 1979. The *Times* ran a short, inside-page story and gave coverage to a handful of born-again homophobes who taunted gays at the march. A week after that event, the paper ran a page-one story about fifty tenants who marched on Washington."

The October 1982 issue of the *New York Native* has another damning mention of the *Times*. An article entitled "Midtown Cops Go Berserk in Gay Bar," by Andy Humm, is a dramatic description of a group of Black queer people "being savagely beaten by a commando squad of precinct police" after a neighbor called the cops. More than twenty officers descended on Blue's Bar and terrorized the patrons seemingly unprovoked.

Remarkably, Blue's Bar was across the street from the offices of the *New York Times*. Humm reported that the manager of the bar, Lew Olive, called the *Times* as the police assault was underway, asking them to send a reporter—perhaps one of the ones hanging out at the bar next door. The paper said no one was available. "The next day, Blue's looked as if it had been bombed," Humm wrote. The mayor's office declined to investigate, and there were no arrests. The *Times* had no story on it the next day, offering only the tiniest bit of coverage a couple of weeks later when there were giant protests over the incident.

When I called him up in 2018, Humm remembered the incident like it happened yesterday—and still held it against the *New York Times*. "They didn't like having a trans bar across the street," he said. "It was a NIMBY thing for them. There were massive demonstrations in the wake of that. It's something people remember, at least people of a certain age remember, about fighting back. It was the worst raid of a bar since Stonewall, and they busted it up, they smashed it up."

By 1983 gay activists were calling for a boycott of the *New York Times* to demand better and more nuanced representation, a change of language from "homosexual" to "gay," and an end to discrimination against gay journalists. In June of that year, a group of gay activists including Humm met with none other than Sydney Gruson, Kerry Gruson's father, to register their protest and explain their demands. When nothing came out of the meeting, an out gay reporter at the *New York Post* (a paper that loves to gossip about its competitors) found out about it and quoted Humm in an article. After the *Post* article, executive editor Abe Rosenthal himself met with a few of the activists (Humm excluded) and then directed his editors to seek out more stories about gay issues. But given the crisis that was already well underway in the gay community, it may have been too little, too late.

. . .

There were no knights in shining armor or perfect examples of fair news coverage in the early days of the AIDS crisis. As the disease emerged, it was initially confusing, undiagnosed, and untestable—a mysterious interconnected web of deaths that seemed to be primarily affecting gay men. No one knew why, so reporters were faced with many difficult choices about how to characterize the disease, how much to cover it, and what to say about its victims. That said, the gay papers and papers that had gay people working for them drove the coverage of the crisis from the very beginning and played a key role in pressuring more mainstream publications to get on board.

The *Gay Community News*, published every week in Boston from 1973 until 1992 (and periodically through 1999), is archived at the University of Michigan, and it was a delight to flip through—funny, political, and eclectic. It included wandering features, tight news clips, unpredictable opinion pieces, and sometimes prolonged arguments in the letters over topics ranging from racism to political correctness to porn. *GCN* covered AIDS thoroughly before the first case even came to Boston, putting the *New York Times* to shame.

Veterans of the paper went on to be well-known activists and leaders in the community, and I reached out to many of them; the person I contacted with the clearest memory of the early days of AIDS was Larry Goldsmith. He lives in Mexico City now, and we connected by Skype. He became a history professor after his time as a journalist, and he's whiskered and wire-rimmed and slightly awkward, a nerdy friendly visage, soft-spoken. He was an isolated out gay man in college in the late '70s, and after he finished school in LA, he described getting in his car and driving clear across the country to Boston—he'd read the *Gay Community News* and gathered that Boston was a hotbed for political gay people, so he decided to just go. He got off at the wrong exit in Boston and ended up driving through the South End by accident, trying to get to Harvard Square. Looking around at the burned-out houses, Goldsmith wondered if he'd made a mistake.

Two weeks later, he got an interview for a position at *GCN* as a local reporter. The youthful and energetic staff asked him about objectivity in the interview, did he believe in it? No, he said, there's no such thing. We try to tell different sides of the story, but there's always another way of looking. Everything is ideological, he told them. He got the job.

There was a lot to write about: it was the era of vice squads and bar raids, regular reports of anti-queer violence from across the country. *GCN* covered all of it, from any source they could get it from, week after week. One article details the arrests of thirty men in a bar raid; another, a suicide after a gay man was arrested for cruising; another, a story about a young woman's parents hiring "deprogrammers" to kidnap and rape her because they believed she was a lesbian. Sometimes the people who beat and killed gay and lesbian people were convicted, but often they were acquitted. Once in a while, a city passed a pro-gay ordinance or shot down an anti-gay one, but just as often, it went the other way.

GCN was housed in a funky office shared with *Fag Rag*, where John Scagliotti's old roommate Charley Shively periodically came in to produce an issue of the quixotic paper. By contrast, *GCN* was busy all day, every day. Goldsmith said they got copies of all the major papers daily and scanned them closely for gay items, even those that had coded language.

Just a few weeks after Goldsmith started at *GCN*, in June 1981, the team gathered around the cluttered table full of dailies to look at a strange headline in the *New York Times*: "Rare Cancer Seen in 41 Homosexuals." Vulnerability to the cancer was a symptom of the disease that later came to be known as AIDS—and this was the first time any of them had heard about it.

"It was hard to take it seriously," Larry said, grinning sadly, "because it was the *New York Times*. It was not a place you looked to for accurate news about our community."

Not long after that, on June 27, 1981, *GCN* published its first article about the disease. It was four paragraphs based on the same recent CDC report the *New York Times* had reported on. "While no specific relationship has been demonstrated between these two diseases, it is almost certain that some aspects of the gay male lifestyle . . . link *Pneumocystis carinii* to the population of gay men," wrote *GCN* in a piece with no byline.

Over the following months, he became the reporter to focus on AIDS. He didn't exactly choose it: his undergrad background in science made him slightly more qualified than his coworkers, and he got subscriptions to the various medical journals and started following the development of the still unexplained disease.

Goldsmith was like most people at *Gay Community News*—he didn't last more than a few years due to the constant stress and low pay. In 1982 the *GCN* and *Fag Rag* office was burned down—arson was a common anti-gay crime at the time, though the fire remains an unsolved mystery. After the fire, Goldsmith said, and the stress that went with it, nothing was ever the same.

. . .

While gay activists led the way in covering AIDS, the mainstream press and television lagged.

"'Has the *New York Times* done it yet?' is a question writers and correspondents are often asked when they propose stories. A negative response can veto a too-new idea," James Kinsella wrote in 1989. His book *Covering the Plague: AIDS and the American Media* was published in the midst of a still-growing epidemic, and it's a cutting exposé of the homophobia and negligence that fed into media coverage (and lack of coverage) of the AIDS epidemic. Whether the *Times* had covered something could indeed sway news judgment at smaller papers as well as TV stations, and the *Times* wasn't interested in the AIDS story for years after it began.

At first, the negligence was excusable: the *Gay Community News* and even the *New York Native*, which first broke the story of the "gay pneumonia," didn't know what to do with the AIDS story when it was a handful of men with a rare pneumonia (that first *Native* headline, on May 18, 1981: "Disease Rumors Largely Unfounded"). But through the end of 1981 the epidemic grew, and quickly. People started dying, and the *GCN* and the *New York Native* started paying attention.

The mainstream papers didn't, and this neglect went on far beyond the window in which "we don't know enough" was an excuse not to report it. By the end of 1982, nearly 800 people had confirmed cases of AIDS, and the number of people infected was rising exponentially. The death rate for those infected appeared to be above 50 percent. Kinsella found that at that point in the outbreak, the Associated Press had published a total of nineteen stories, UPI (then the other major wire service), ten stories. At the end of 1982, the *New York Times* had done five stories, none of them on the front page. By way of comparison, in 1982 the *Times* did four front-page articles, and fifty articles in total, on the Tylenol scare, which killed a total of seven people. The biweekly *New York Native* had stories on AIDS in almost every issue by the end of that year.

The refusal to cover AIDS at the *Times* became almost an insistence. In March 1983, the Gay Men's Health Crisis took over the Ringling Bros. and Barnum & Bailey Circus in Madison Square Garden for a fund-raiser—the largest fund-raiser to date for AIDS victims. Much of the big NYC media covered that event, but not the *Times*.

Kinsella concluded that despite the "objective" front of the wire services and major papers, relationships, perceptions, and biases mattered. In coverage of AIDS, all of these factors showed through clearly. "For the past decade," he wrote, "the AIDS story has challenged the ground rules of American journalism. It has forced reporters to acknowledge that their treatment of the news, far from being objective, is often shaped by their personal prejudices and their assumptions about their audience. Such biases are often elusive, but in AIDS reporting, they have taken on exceptional importance."

Kinsella's most important conclusion was that, contrary to the common belief that the best coverage of an issue comes from a dispassionate observer, AIDS coverage almost necessitated someone who was close to the issue: "AIDS was discussed most promptly, vigorously, and forthrightly where journalists had direct personal experience with people suffering from the disease."

He concedes that AIDS was difficult and confusing to cover—the science was unclear for many years, there was no test to confirm infection, and even the name of the disease changed several times. But he's also clear that many outlets, particularly in the early days, simply didn't try to keep up with the research into the killer disease. AIDS at first only affected people who were seen as social outcasts, gay people and later IV drug users and Haitians. When the disease was reported in babies, and then later in celebrities, it started to receive some attention. "Every surge of AIDS coverage at almost every newspaper, magazine, or TV and radio station came when the disease seemed to move closer to individual newsmakers or to the people journalists perceive as their audience."

The gay papers, meanwhile, were watching their audience's worlds rocked by the trauma of the disease and the soaring death rate. The *New York Native* covered the epidemic doggedly, with detailed reports about the latest science and continuing critiques from David Rothenberg of the negligent mainstream media. The lagging mainstream media coverage had real effects on the politics: a sense of crisis about the disease was slow to come to Washington, and research wasn't funded quickly or robustly enough. President Ronald Reagan didn't say "AIDS" publicly until September 1985, at which point the death toll was in the thousands and included Reagan's personal friend Rock Hudson. The gay papers published nearly constantly about the dearth of funds for AIDS research, and they weren't ignored—but they couldn't have the impact that the *New York Times* would, had it decided to focus on the stories of the AIDS crisis during the early years.

"By 1986, some reporters in the mainstream media admitted to watching the gay press for tips on the epidemic," wrote Kinsella. "Scores of journalists across the country . . . said they regularly read the *Native* or other gay publications. Gay journalists had become more professional during the AIDS crisis. They had to, because reporters for publications like the *Advocate* and the *Native* were now covering the life-and-death story of the decade."

Here, decisions about newsworthiness were truly life-and-death. People close to the epidemic saw it, while others did not.

"People died and nobody paid attention because the mass media did not like covering stories about homosexuals and was especially skittish about stories that involved gay sexuality," wrote Randy Shilts, a gay reporter who covered AIDS for over a decade at the *San Francisco Chronicle*. A controversial figure in his own right, he ultimately wrote the definitive history of AIDS in the 1980s, *And the Band Played On*.

Gradually, and thanks in part to the work of reporters like Shilts and the media activists who pushed from the outside, the coverage did come: the *New York Times* did an about-face in the late '80s after Abe Rosenthal retired as editor and Max Frankel took over. The paper started covering the epidemic more seriously, asking questions of government officials and telling the stories of patients. In 1988 Rosenthal himself, who had been known as a homophobe, called AIDS "the story of the decade."

The shift at the *Times* became even more evident in 1990, when a longtime reporter and editor, Jeffrey Schmalz, was diagnosed with AIDS after he collapsed suddenly in the *Times* newsroom—at this point, he also came out as gay. Somewhat shockingly, his editors decided to assign him to write about the epidemic, developing an

AIDS beat for the first time in the paper's then ten-year history of covering AIDS. Schmalz died three years later at thirty-nine.

The year before he died, Schmalz wrote about the meaning of his own assignment for the *Times*: "Now I see the world through the prism of AIDS. I feel an obligation to those with AIDS to write about it and an obligation to the newspaper to write what just about no other reporter in America can cover in quite the same way." Covering one's own community, he felt, was "the cutting edge of journalism." A cutting edge, certainly, for the *Times*, though the gay papers had been doing it for decades.

. . .

What happens when the personal, the connected, and the empathic actually bring us closer to stories that are true?

"That concept of the personal, that moment of discovering that you are part of this as opposed to just an observer, is a very important moment," John Scagliotti said to me, almost immediately after I sat down in his kitchen. I knew what he meant: since I had come out as queer at age twelve, becoming identified with a political struggle over my own identity, I hadn't really known the feeling of being "just an observer," and had always felt myself in conflict with a world that claimed there was such a thing as being truly separate and detached.

But that concept of the personal isn't about whether or not one is gay and covering a gay story, or an AIDS victim covering an AIDS story. It's not just about identity, but about the broader question of whether and how one is implicated in the stories we tell. And of course, all of us are implicated, in one way or another. Those who realized that the AIDS crisis could touch their own lives were more likely to write about it; ignorance of the risk it posed was not so much an "objective" stance as a clueless one, influenced by the privilege of distance. Sometimes it isn't detachment, but the opposite of detachment—connection and closeness—that gets us closer to the truth.

When a gunman killed forty-nine gay people in Orlando's Pulse nightclub early on a Sunday morning in 2016, I was one of the people who was out at a bar that night too—happy to be queer in New York, a dream I'd had for much of my life. The next morning, I remember the creeping realization of what had happened and who it had happened to; it was flashing on my Twitter and Facebook feeds, taking form in guarded words of mourning from my friends. Of course I knew someone who knew someone who was at Pulse; it felt like we all did. On Monday I called in sick to grieve, and a few weeks later I was in Orlando myself, interviewing people through their grief and heavy drinking, taking a surreal walk through the burgeoning public memorial, the sadness tight in my bones.

I've since quit drinking, but at the Parliament House, the seedy gay motel and bar where I was staying in Orlando, I drank myself silly with a couple of people who had just come from another memorial. They had fresh tattoos of a rainbow-colored sound wave showing a pulse, a heartbeat. I knew that I couldn't wrap my mind around their loss, but I felt connected to it. My stories for *Marketplace* were burning with my desire to show what this community had been through.

That concept of the personal, that awareness that I was a part of the story, was driving me, as it so often does—to deeper coverage, to more sensitive stories, and to new ideas. On my second night in Florida, I recorded people at a Gay Pride March, the choked sounds of sobbing during a silent vigil for the Pulse victims and the beating of endless techno and margarita-enhanced laughter as the night went on. I ended that night dancing, wild and alone, in a rowdy crowd of queer people of all genders. It felt brave to be out there so soon after Pulse, and it was a reminder that the concept of the personal is also with us when we're just dancing and drinking.

Andy Kopkind died of cancer in 1994, and not long before his death, he reflected on the changes wrought by the gay movement in his lifetime.

"What has changed the climate in America is the long experience of gay struggle, the necessary means having been, first, coming out, and second, making a scene," he wrote for *The Nation* in 1993. I love this idea of making a scene, and it feels clear that sometimes it is journalists who must make a scene—our mission of truth-telling mixing with a mission to advocate for ourselves and our communities. And yet, when journalists do this, we are accused—usually by other journalists—of being activists *instead* of journalists, propagandists *instead* of truth-tellers. Why the dichotomy, when history shows so clearly that you can be both?

"Truth can be propaganda. And that doesn't make it not true," John Scagliotti said, just before I left the Kopkind Colony. Indeed, sometimes we tell truths with a goal, a particular orientation, even truths that are meant to persuade: people told stories about the AIDS crisis and gay life to try to access necessary resources, change public minds, and stop people from dying. And that's one way to make a scene: tell a true story that others aren't quite ready to hear, help force something from the sphere of deviance into the zone of legitimate debate and controversy. It may seem biased—it may *be* biased—but it's not the same as abandoning factual, rigorous journalism.

It struck me that maybe we need to stop talking about "bias" and even "propaganda" as if these are in themselves the problem with news media today. In the search for bias, we typically end up simply critiquing meanings we don't like. This is a punishing cycle with few benefits, I think, for the critics or the criticized. I know that if you look for bias in our news media, you will find it. But in pretending to be objective, we ignore the implications of our subjectivity, refusing to acknowledge that it matters who is making the news.

7

JOURNALISM'S PURITY RITUAL

Why was it so often women, people of color, and LGBTQ people who became the targets of campaigns against journalistic "bias"? To an extent, each case of firing or exclusion, even my own, made obvious sense: every profession has its standards, and holding to them is a part of how professional organizations define their identities. But I also began to see that targeting journalists for violation of conflict-of-interest or impartiality policies serves more than one purpose. It reinforces professional standards and boundaries, and it also discourages solidarity and organizing among media workers, reinforcing the idea that all of our jobs are unstable and we should fear our employers' power. Finally, for news organizations, these public acts of discipline can serve as a sort of ritual, a scapegoating: demonstrate that you are willing to get rid of people, and you will appear pure and free of conflicts of interest, even though that can't possibly be true. Wash your hands of the contaminated elements. I had been one of those elements; it wasn't hard to find others who had, too.

. . .

Sandy Nelson has sharp eyes, short hair, and a pointed, serious way of speaking. She lives with her wife in a small town in Colorado and works what she called a fairly skull-numbing day job as a technical editor. But when she was my age, her early thirties, she was on a career path as a journalist, working a competitive beat as an education journalist in Tacoma, Washington, filing a story a day and keeping up with local and statewide news. She was organized and fed off the energy of reporting. "I always tried to do as hard-hitting stuff as I could," she said, describing day after day of lining up interviews, getting out in the field to report, coming back and filing a story on deadline.

Nelson came out as a lesbian in 1974, right after she went to college. She studied journalism at the University of Washington and it was while she was there that she first became interested in socialism. After graduation she was determined to become a reporter, convinced of the potential to make real social change as a journalist. She also joined a Trotskyist socialist organization and participated in activism around feminist and socialist issues—rejecting the rules of objectivity she'd learned in school. She stuck with both the cause of journalism and the cause of socialism.

After a few years at a small-town paper, Nelson got a job at the *Tacoma News Tribune* in 1983, when the paper was still locally owned. She started as a feature writer and then moved to education, and she loved covering school board meetings, protests, and politics, getting out of the office and into the street to find out what people were talking about and doing. She said she scrupulously separated her two worlds of activism and journalism. Plus, when she started, her union contract had protections for journalists' off-the-job activities. As long as journalists were careful to avoid direct conflicts of interest in their news reporting or disclose any that they had, the publishers couldn't dictate what they could do in their off time. For many years, Nelson was a by-the-books reporter. She thought you could strive to be fair, balanced, and thorough, and try to get the facts right as much as possible. And she believed that reporting, gathering information, is a different practice than writing polemics or writing to make a point. She kept her worlds separate: as an activist, she was trying to make social change through protest and advocacy, while as a journalist, she was serving the institutional needs of a paper that provided local news in a centrist tone, a divide she was generally comfortable with.

I came across her story accidentally, when I stumbled onto a 1996

piece in the *New York Times*: "Gay Reporter Wants to Be Activist."
The lede induced a joyful smirk, at least for me: "To labor leaders in
this old blue-collar port, a shot-and-beer stronghold, Sandy Nelson
is an unlikely hero—a lesbian, Socialist journalist. But to the top editors at The News Tribune, where Ms. Nelson works, she is a walking
conflict of interest whose off-duty activities threaten the credibility of
journalism."

Indeed, her peaceful days at the *Tacoma News Tribune* were short-
lived. In 1986 the paper got bought out by the McClatchy Company.
Everyone, including her, had to reapply for their jobs. Nelson was
rehired, even though McClatchy was not as keen on activist journalists, and she'd been "out" as a radical socialist activist. She resumed her
daily work, but she had a feeling the calm wouldn't last. McClatchy
wanted a new contract with the editorial staff that included strict limitations on their off-the-job activities. The workers, who were members of the Newspaper Guild, opposed that and other contract stipu-
lations, and negotiations for a new union contract began and stalled,
began and stalled.

At the same time, Nelson became involved in a prolonged battle
for a human rights ordinance in the city of Tacoma, an ordinance that
protected gay workers from job discrimination. It had already passed,
but in 1989 right-wingers were pushing a ballot initiative to repeal it,
and her organization was trying to stop that. She attended protests
and ran petition drives as she always had, though she avoided public
speaking about her activism. None of this was a secret, but one day her
editor called her into the office and told her that due to her off-duty
political activities, she was being removed from her job as a reporter
and sent to the copy desk to edit. This was in 1990, seven years into
her tenure as a journalist at the paper. The copy desk wasn't a pay cut,
but it took her away from the work she loved—she said it was clearly
a punishment. "When they stripped me of my right to be a reporter,
it was really painful because I wasn't going to be out there doing my
thing anymore."

At that point, Nelson said, she had a decision to make: Go quietly,
or make noise. She chose making noise, in part as a gay rights issue

(she didn't think it was fair to be told that she couldn't fight for her own rights as a gay person, and she suspected discrimination), but more largely, as an issue of freedom of speech and workers' rights. She thought she was being targeted as the union shop steward in addition to her gay identity and the content of her activism. If an employer can curtail a worker's off-duty activities, she thought, even free speech activities, where does it stop?

"I wasn't just doing this for fun," she said. Her off-duty free speech mattered to her. "We were fighting for abortion rights, labor, gay and lesbian rights. I was fighting for my survival."

So, rather than quit after she was put on the copy desk, Nelson stayed at the paper—and filed a lawsuit. That process dragged on for seven years, and she remained on the copy desk at the paper the entire time, facing the people she was up against in person each day.

"I'm not really a quitter, per se," she told me, with a fierce deadpan.

She believed that both hypocrisy and a double standard were driving her treatment. Nelson said she had never had a complaint from a reader about bias in her actual stories, nor was the *News Tribune* able to produce any examples of complaints as part of their legal response to her. She also said she was able to point to many fellow reporters who were involved in causes, albeit less controversial ones than socialism or gay rights.

"They didn't go after people who were involved in their churches, or people who were in Boy Scouts. They can be political, can't they?"

After Nelson fought the case for years, in 1997 the Supreme Court of Washington State decided against her, finding that a state law protecting employees from job discrimination based on political expression could legally exclude journalists. The reasoning was that the free speech right of publications (the right *not* to publish the work of people they don't want to publish) takes precedence over freedom of expression for individual reporters. These reporters must choose either their professional responsibility or their personal convictions, and their bosses, protected by the First Amendment, can require them to choose.

And yet, there was a blatant double standard regarding institutional versus individual freedom of speech and expression. In the case of the *Tacoma News Tribune*, the paper's publisher at the time of Nelson's tenure was actively involved in advocating for taxpayer support for a new stadium in Seattle. In 1995 taxpayers in the county voted against providing direct support to the Seattle Mariners for the stadium, but they were overridden by state legislators, who passed several new taxes to be used to support the private enterprise.

Nelson disagrees that employers have the "right" to prevent political activity among their employees and was pleased with the part of the decision that clarified that her case should only be interpreted as a narrow exception for journalists (it protected political expression for workers in other sectors in Washington). Still, she thought the argument for a publisher exclusion was thin—they have "the freedom to publish, not to make a profit," she wrote, paraphrasing her lawyer's argument. She argued that publisher freedom of speech shouldn't extend to the ability to target people if those people could hurt their bottom line—it is, after all, a slippery slope into legalized discrimination. In her mind, publishers' fears about losing revenue over activist-journalists were winning out over those journalists' freedom to express themselves politically.

It was journalists' free speech versus the bosses' free speech, and her case set a dangerous precedent.

"I never signed away my rights as a citizen when I became a professional journalist 16 years ago," Nelson wrote in 1996. "I never surrendered my right to political self-defense in the face of attacks from the government or the right wing—so why should I make an exception if I am attacked by the management of the communications medium I work for?"

Nelson lost. The Supreme Court of the United States refused to hear her appeal, and it remains true that reporters can be fired for off-the-job acts of personal or political expression. Nelson believes the *News Tribune* and McClatchy were making an example of her. "Objectivity is a myth, and it's usually used as a way to go after people who have unpopular or radical ideas that threaten the status quo," she said. "During the McCarthy era they went after people in the same way."

When we talked on a Google Hangout in 2018, Nelson said she was glad I was continuing her fight. "People like you and I get targeted, because they think we are easy targets." The fierce twinkle in her eye matched mine. We weren't easy targets—and we both knew it. I felt warm when I talked to Sandy Nelson, even though our conversation was relatively formal. I had found another kindred spirit.

. . .

Conflict-of-interest rules limiting political expression for reporters are still a standard in the news media, but one that's become more and more tricky in the age of social media. Reporters are expected to tweet and have an online presence, but also to walk a fine line between expressing their personalities and expressing their personal opinions. Reporters of color have been chastised for calling an incident "racist," women chastised for expressing opinions about the #MeToo movement and sexual assault. After Donald Trump was elected, many journalists attended the giant Women's March in Washington, DC, or New York following his inauguration. Still others signed petitions and wore hats and T-shirts and made political donations—but plenty did not, due to restrictions from their employers. Interest in the march was so high that a variety of outlets issued specific warnings against political activity during that time period. My own editor knew I would be at the march making recordings, and just advised that I not end up getting photographed for anyone else's news article.

The argument for limiting conflicts of interest in journalism on its surface is fairly simple: the journalist's role is as a purveyor of truth, not an advocate or a polemicist. Personal involvements—whether they are financial, familial, or political—can divide the journalist's loyalties; they may be motivated to write a certain story, or present a case in a certain way, by something that falls short of a supposedly pure truth-telling motive. In a traditional conflict-of-interest framing, the journalist is caught between her role as a public servant and her role as a private citizen.

This framing tends to allow that public service is in fact the primary motive of most journalists (and not, say, profit or reward of some kind), and it tends to assume that, aside from a few discrete choices about "involvement," a person becomes a journalist as a sort of neutral player, an entanglement-free, apolitical body. These are assumptions we need to interrogate carefully, given that most news organizations are motivated by making a profit and given that nobody is neutral. We *all* have a race and a gender and a sexuality, and we all have ideas about race and gender and sexuality and politics that we are attached to, to varying degrees.

The argument against conflicting entanglements is nonetheless broadly persuasive: the offer of a payout, the fear of judgment from a close friend or family member, or the sense of doing a favor for a cause or group could all legitimately influence or even interfere with fact-finding and truth-telling, and they are the kinds of bias that audience members might understandably want to know about. Many news organizations reason that it's easiest to simply limit or avoid such entanglements. Of course, even this argument is complicated—take the example of a small-town reporter, who's likely to be writing stories about their neighbors, mother's bridge buddies, and kids' teachers. Such a person earns trust not by eliminating all entanglements, but by reporting as fairly as possible given the scenario and disclosing conflicts where possible. Avoiding payouts or personal financial benefit for a story is a clear-enough rule, but avoiding all conflicts of interest is impossible. Relationships, entanglements, and complicated ethical questions are inevitable, no matter the size of a reporter's beat, no matter how antisocial and uninvolved they strive to be.

But there is another, more insidious argument for limiting conflicts of interest in journalism—that of appearances and perception. Many ethical policies warn against conflicts of interest, "real or perceived." This argument concerns itself not with real conflicts of interests as identified by reporters, but with the slippery concept of "perception," whether audiences might believe there is a conflict of interest or bias in a given journalist. If the problem isn't actual conflicts (something only the journalist herself can possibly know and disclose) but perceived ones, who's to be the judge? How can you know if I'm struggling to separate my role as a reporter from my role as something else? The focus on appearances can also backfire, encouraging journalists with minor conflicts of interest to keep them a secret in order to avoid being scolded, fired, or taken off a story. I know full well that many journalists attended the 2017 Women's March in secret—avoiding the appearance of a conflict rather than the (potential) conflict itself.

News organizations again and again use highly subjective criteria to decide whether a conflict of interest could create a problem of perception. These criteria depend on assumptions about what is socially and politically acceptable in your environment, and they are value judgments rather than the "objective" standards they claim to be. As in Sandy Nelson's case, the results are troubling, leading almost inevitably to the scapegoating of the most vulnerable people in newsrooms— LGBTQ people (who are often not protected from workplace discrimination), people of color who have been systematically excluded from newsrooms, young people, people with disabilities, Muslims, immigrants, among others. The homogeneity of newsrooms is, in turn, protected by this thinking: white cisgender men remain the ones who can be "objective," while others are subjective and suspect.

. . .

Linda Greenhouse had been the Supreme Court correspondent for the *New York Times* for over a decade when she decided, in spring 1989, to join a national march for reproductive rights in Washington, DC, where she lived. She didn't go as press, and she knew other women from the *Times* who also attended. She was open about her plans, even inviting the editors in her bureau to the march.

But then something turned: some of her female friends at the *Washington Post* got in trouble with their supervisors for attending, and in the ensuing debate, they told the *Post* that the *Times* had let reporters march with no issue. Next thing you know the *Post* ran a story quoting Greenhouse's boss, Howell Raines. When the *Post* called him, Greenhouse writes in her 2017 memoir *Just a Journalist*, he did an about-face and suddenly indicated a belief that Greenhouse was out of bounds. "What evidently had not been a mistake when it happened was now, after the fact, a big one," she says. Greenhouse was asked to apologize and refrain from future political demonstrations.

The flap received international coverage and became a part of a heated ongoing debate, punctuated by headlines like the *L.A. Times'* 1990 stunner, "Can Women Reporters Write Objectively on Abortion Issue?" (The author, David Shaw, later won a Pulitzer Prize for his media criticism.)

The same questions aren't asked about the men in Washington who attend private dinners with politicians, the Midtown Manhattan reporters who are drinking buddies with Wall Street guys, the small-town beat reporters whose dad and brother and uncle are all cops. And in fact, the same questions aren't asked about men and abortion: clearly, a man can get someone pregnant, so shouldn't he have a stake? Maybe conflict-of-interest questions ought to be asked of everyone, but the point is, it's complicated. If women can't report on abortion because they have too much personal stake in it, who can report on anything? Awareness or disclosure of the conflicts is one thing, but punishment and censorship is another, and it's too often women, people of color, and queer and trans people who are the targets of the kind of mottled, extreme thinking that leads to "Can Women Reporters Write Objectively on Abortion Issue?"

Greenhouse, who covered nearly every contentious issue in US politics during her forty years at the *Times*, began to question "objectivity" at that time in a way she hadn't before. "When do professional norms, having evolved to buttress the credibility of a craft that only in modern times has laid claim to the status of a profession, unduly constrain not only journalism's practitioners but journalism itself? Does 'objectivity,' with its mantra of 'fairness and balance,' too often inhibit journalists from separating fact from fiction and from fulfilling the duty to help maintain an informed citizenry in a democracy?" she writes.

Nonetheless, Greenhouse mostly just got in line: the attention around the abortion march was unwanted, and she stopped taking risks in her political expression. At the end of her career, though, she found herself in hot water over political speech a second time.

In June 2006, she was invited to give an address at Radcliffe, her alma mater, as a recipient of the Radcliffe Institute Medal, the school's highest honor for graduates. In the speech, she described the George W. Bush administration as "creating law-free zones at Guantanamo Bay, Abu Ghraib, Haditha, and other places around the world." Greenhouse, speaking to an invite-only audience, went on: "And let's not forget the sustained attack on women's reproductive freedom and the hijacking of public policy by religious fundamentalism. To say that these last years have been dispiriting is an understatement."

She gave the speech, and that was that. As Greenhouse writes, "The mountains didn't tremble. In fact, nothing happened. June passed, then July, August, and most of September. Then I received a call from a man identifying himself as the NPR media reporter." David Folkenflik had seen a video of her speech because his mother went to Radcliffe. She was curt with him, not seeing the wrong in anything she had done, and he ran a story shortly afterward on NPR's website called "Critics Question Reporter's Airing of Personal Views." Folkenflik had called up a series of current and former editors and read to them from Greenhouse's speech; each gave the opinion that she should have refrained from criticizing the Bush administration, to protect the perceived integrity of her employer.

Greenhouse was indignant: "The reputation of the *Times* was at stake because two years after the Supreme Court held that the Bush administration couldn't maintain a law-free zone at Guantanamo, the paper's Supreme Court correspondent criticized the administration for having tried to maintain a law-free zone? Strong stuff."

Once again, the flap spun out into a full-on controversy, producing several days of coverage from a variety of outlets. Daniel Okrent, former public editor of the *Times*, weighed in defending Greenhouse, but Byron Calame, then the current public editor, published a column scolding her for airing her personal opinions in any context. "During the current term," he wrote, "allowing her to cover court topics on which she voiced opinions in June risks giving the paper's critics fresh opportunities to snipe at its public policy coverage."

"In other words," Greenhouse writes, "there were schoolyard bullies abroad in the land, and this was no time to stand up to them. Might such a time ever come? He didn't say."

Even though the paper's public editor weighed in, her own editors didn't—she was neither taken off the beat nor told not to say similar things in the future, at least not directly.

"But neither did any *Times* editor come to my defense," she writes, noting that one of her editors said to her, "not in the current climate," by way of explanation.

Her story raises the question: What is the climate in which editors at newspapers and radio shows should consider standing up for something they believe in? Does the temperature need to rise above a certain level, globally, before our collective survival starts feeling more important than our individual careers? Or, taking the use of the word "climate" less literally, are these ethical individuals awaiting a more liberal environment before they air their liberal views, so that they can do so without consequence? Or maybe they're awaiting a more authoritarian environment—a world of more disappeared children or "enhanced interrogation" or perhaps more white supremacist or homophobic violence—before they stand up for a reporter who would dare to question those forms of violence.

Regardless, "not in the current climate" reflects the kind of moral relativism and weakness with which I have grown impatient, earlier in my career than either Sandy Nelson or Linda Greenhouse. Waiting around for the climate to change is a privilege some of us simply can't afford.

．　．　．

After I got fired and made the choice to talk about it publicly, I heard from hundreds of people, most of them sympathetic. Many were audience members who were infuriated by my firing and wrote to tell me of their frustration; others were journalists, some of whom had worked at *Marketplace* or in public radio before and had similar critiques of those environments; a small handful were trans people, thanking me for standing up for our community in a context that has tended to ignore us, or asking for my advice on navigating the journalism world as an out trans person.

For months, people also sent me link after link about other journalists who'd been arrested, fired, scolded, or demoted in ways that evoked what had happened to me. Perhaps the most resonant for me was the story of Desmond Cole, a freelance columnist who announced his intention to resign from the *Toronto Star* in May 2017 with a post to his personal blog, entitled "I Choose Activism for Black Liberation."

Cole had started writing for the *Star* after he penned a breakthrough piece about racial profiling, "The Skin I'm In," in 2015, for another Toronto publication. That column, a searing description of his experience growing up in small-town Canada as a dark-skinned Black man, made a splash because it called out Canadian racism and racial profiling. In the piece, he explained he'd been stopped no less than fifty times by Canadian police—and never charged with any crime. He moved to Toronto to try to get away from the small-mindedness, but the harassment continued. Cole, furious about his treatment as a Black man, became a committed activist. The *Star* invited him to write a regular column for them after "The Skin I'm In" led to a book deal and a documentary.

In his blog post of May 4, 2017, Cole explained that he had by then been a columnist for the *Star* for over a year, writing a popular weekly and later biweekly column that was often about racial justice issues. Then this happened: he disrupted a Toronto Police Services Board meeting on April 20. The issue at hand was a practice called carding, whereby police stop people (disproportionately young, Black and brown) and take down their information even if they aren't being charged with a crime. Toronto activists had been demanding an end to carding, a demand they won. Now they were demanding that the police department get rid of personal information previously collected, arguing that the information was collected illegally. Cole, who had been carded himself, made a brief statement at the meeting, then informed the board he wouldn't leave until he got a response. He raised a fist in silent protest and stood still. He was eventually escorted out by police.

Cole was subsequently called in for a meeting with his editor at the *Star*, who reminded him of the paper's editorial policies, which include a prohibition on activism among its writers—even opinion writers. He wasn't fired or reprimanded—simply reminded of what the policy was. A remarkable aspect of the story is that Cole said he had "never signed any contract or agreement" during his year of writing a weekly column for the *Star*, nor had he been directed to any of the paper's formal editorial policies. That said, Cole wrote, "I knew my police protest was activism, and I could have guessed the *Star* wouldn't appreciate it."

Cole, in turn, didn't appreciate the suggestion that he would need to choose between activism and opinion writing, and resigned. "If I must choose between a newspaper column and the actions I must take to liberate myself and my community, I choose activism in the service of Black liberation," he wrote in his blog.

He didn't accuse the paper of a double standard, but after his public announcement, someone else did. The following week, another former *Star* columnist, a white woman, penned a column for *NOW Magazine* responding to Cole's treatment with a pointed accusation.

"In pushing Cole out, the Star seems to have applied a double standard on its own policies, and I speak as someone who spent 25 years as a columnist and activist at the paper," Michele Landsberg wrote. She said for her entire twenty-five years at the paper, her editors encouraged her feminist activism, even printing petitions she was promoting in the pages of the paper. "I marched on picket lines; I protested at Queen's Park. I know I brought large numbers of readers to the paper. I know the paper valued and rewarded me."

As a white woman, it appears, she was not only allowed the freedom to act in this way, but she was encouraged in her activism—a pattern she says is right and good, until it's applied inconsistently. Landsberg accused the *Star* of undermining trust with the diverse readership it most needed to reach.

The *Star* made its institutional views known with a column from public editor Kathy English entitled "Journalists Shouldn't Become the News." The opening paragraph: "It has long been Toronto Star policy that journalists do not take public stands on public issues or become the news. This policy is aligned with longstanding journalistic values and the ethics policies of most credible news organizations in Canada, the U.S. and around the world."

In other words, we have rules, and we stand by these rules because other news organizations have similar rules. And yet it seems as though the rules were applied inconsistently, and sometimes not at all. The rules were subject to a smell test.

English wrote that she and others at the *Star* became "somewhat uneasy" when they learned Cole had disrupted a meeting of the Toronto Police Services Board. And yet, isn't uneasiness the only way that change happens? Isn't disruption the only path to transformation? I have made many people uncomfortable with my personal advocacy as a transgender person; plenty of white people in the US and Canada are made uneasy, at least a bit, by any Black person who raises their voice. An unease test for what crosses the line into activism nearly always favors the powerful and the status quo.

And then came the diversity apologetics, a form that the *Star* public editor seems to have mastered. To summarize, people in power tend to say things like this: "We like diversity, and we are sorry that our policies, practices, and behaviors can't support it at this time." Here's what English actually wrote: "I am sorry Cole's strong voice will no longer be a regular part of the Star. While the Star has made considerable strides forward in publishing a greater diversity of voices, I believe it still needs more diverse voices in both its news and opinion pages."

A solution to the conundrum of feeling "sorry" to lose a diverse voice could be to revisit the paper's policies or to look closely at the inconsistency with which they'd been applied, or reconsider the decision because each case is, in fact, different. But no such revisiting would take place on English's watch: she cynically stated that policies shouldn't be made or amended "on the fly simply to accommodate any one voice or any one cause," without calling for any broad reconsideration of the policy or its application. She avoided weighing in on whether these are the right rules by simply saying that they are the rules, and rules ought not to change too quickly. It's a classic dodge, used again and again by people resistant to social change but unwilling to admit it.

· · ·

Linda Greenhouse describes a sense of relief when she finally took a buyout at the *Times* and retired in 2008—suddenly, she was able to fully participate in the political process, to speak her mind as she wanted. She talked proudly about her career-long donations to Planned Parenthood and stood up to critics who contended that somehow all her years of credible Supreme Court reporting were undone by this revelation.

But Greenhouse is, in many ways, one of the lucky ones. After 1990, Sandy Nelson didn't work full-time as a reporter again. She had imagined working at a big paper someday—the *Washington Post* or the *New York Times*. But when she was punished for her activism, she said, that ambition dissolved. "I grieved the end of that career, and then just decided that my next career was as a warrior."

Desmond Cole's work as an activist and journalist continued (he has his own radio show and still contributes to many Canadian publications), but he calls his treatment "bad news for emerging local Black journalists and journalism students, most of whom are Black women and many of whom tell me they are also being shunned, not for their actions but for their radical and emancipatory content." These young Black writers have received the message, loud and clear, that they would be asked to choose between the cause of Black liberation and the practice of being a writer, even an opinion writer.

Freelancers are among the people who are most vulnerable to these blanket policies, and these days more and more journalists are freelancers. In 2011 a freelance journalist named Caitlin Curran was fired from her gig as a part-time web producer at *The Takeaway*, a national radio news show from WNYC, after being photographed holding a sign at an Occupy Wall Street protest. That same week, music host Lisa Simeone's show, which was distributed by NPR, was removed from distribution after NPR learned that Simeone had also participated in an Occupy demonstration. "What is NPR afraid I'll do—insert a seditious comment into a synopsis of *Madame Butterfly*?" Simeone wrote in a statement. She also pointed out that she was a contract worker, not even working directly for NPR but for a station affiliate.

And of course, every rule has its exceptions, as Simeone herself pointed out: "Mara Liaason reports on politics for NPR yet appears as a commentator on FoxTV, Scott Simon hosts an NPR news show yet writes political op-eds for national newspapers, Cokie Roberts reports on politics for NPR yet accepts large speaking fees from businesses." NPR responded that these were unique situations; Simeone pointed out that it is quite difficult to tell why that is.

As we move toward a world in which nearly half of workers in the US are freelance and contract workers, the power these policies give employers is troubling. Can a person who's stretched between fifteen gigs, none of them offering livable wages or health insurance, be expected to remain an endlessly clean slate, avoiding both past and future violations of ethical policies for all potential employers? As NYU journalism professor Jay Rosen said to *On the Media* after Curran's firing, "It might be a good rule for WNYC to not try and control the lives of people that you don't give health insurance to." Todd Gitlin, a Columbia University journalism professor, called the extension of ethics codes to freelancers "appalling."

After the Simeone flap, NPR clarified that its ethics code barring participation in protest on any issue the network covers *does* apply to independent producers and station reporters. If the code were applied consistently, Caitlin Curran, Sandy Nelson, Lisa Simeone, I, and presumably Linda Greenhouse can be forever blocked from contracting with the network, even for a single story about an issue to which we have no personal connection.

"In the name of free speech and a free press, some of the nation's most powerful employers are trying to subvert the political rights of an entire class of workers—those of us at the front line of gathering and sharing public information," Sandy Nelson wrote in 1996 in *On the Issues*, a feminist magazine. Big media companies, whether McClatchy or Sinclair or NPR, command power over large workforces, which in turn wield a great amount of power over public perception and opinion. Maintaining journalists as a class of people unable to stand up for ourselves as employees or as human beings may work well for the management, but it stands to be damaging for the public.

Nelson lost her case, but maybe the remedy isn't legal but social: we need a culture that recognizes that a reporter, even one doing non-opinion reporting, can challenge distorting biases in their journalistic work while continuing to exist and participate as a member of the public in their non-journalistic work. We aren't talking, after all, about requiring outlets to *publish* everything one of their reporters says. The question is about the right to be and exist, even to blunder and make mistakes in public—it is about the idea that we are all more than one thing, that we are vulnerable, whole human beings in addition to being journalists.

. . .

Journalism scholar Jay Rosen has written about a phenomenon in political reporting that he calls the "production of innocence." Rather than face the consequences of their own inevitable perspective and slant, or carefully engage with practices of disclosure and transparency, news organizations ritually perform innocence in order to protect themselves from accusations of bias. Rosen has described how that performance plays out in the form of false equivalencies and fake balance, the sort of faux objectivity that's been much maligned by media critics. Journalists often parrot the words of presidents and self-made experts in order to seem "fair," or insert a "second opinion" on a topic like climate change or gay rights in order to demonstrate balance, sometimes even at the expense of accuracy.

"The quest for innocence in political journalism means the desire to be manifestly agenda-less and thus 'prove' in the way you describe things that journalism is not an ideological trade," Rosen wrote in his blog, *PressThink*.

Rosen suggests that performing innocence is an act of persuasion, an attempt to make a point, rather than a demonstration of ethical consistency. I think this performance also plays out when news organizations periodically fire those who are taken to be too controversial for such a neutral, nonpartisan news organization to tolerate. Juan Williams at NPR, Octavia Nasr at CNN, Keith Olbermann at MSNBC, Dan Rather at CBS, and Peter Arnett at NBC are other examples from the last two decades—and such stories reach back as far as objectivity itself. Whatever you think of their actions, each of these removals can be taken, I think, as a part of the "production of innocence."

It struck me that I, too, had been scapegoated, washed off in one of these rituals of purification. And that insight felt evocative and strange. Purification through the removal of vulnerable people is a trope with deep roots in the worst parts of American culture. I had been washed off right as people were all asking: What does Donald Trump's victory mean for the media? Will the media stand up to him? Will they say "lie," will they say "racist"? This purity ritual is part of what allows news media to forever avoid the implications of actually standing for something or other—or avoid facing that they stand for little but profits and private interests.

Sandy Nelson and Desmond Cole were pushed off of their career paths by this form of scapegoating. Linda Greenhouse avoided such a fate—in part by playing by the rules, stepping back and apologizing, and in part, I'm guessing, by being a white, cisgender woman who had already met with a fair amount of success before accusations of bias flew her way. But even without her being fired, the scouring of her choices as a citizen and as a woman is a part of journalism's purity ritual.

Something happened in 2017 that made it clear just how troubling these demonstrations were. On January 25, the day I was suspended from my job, NPR senior vice president for news Michael Oreskes defended NPR's choice not to use the word "lie" to describe Donald Trump's frequent falsehoods. Not using the word "lie," not calling Trump a liar, is a classic case of false balance, and an easy one to call out. After all, in regular life, someone who says untrue things several times a day is generally not hard to categorize, and politicians arguably should be held to a higher standard for truth than regular people. In any case, Oreskes's statement on that particular day was a painful example to me of how far journalism was willing to go to protect its self-image—so far that it seemed this self-protection mattered more than speaking plainly about the truth.

More painful still, Oreskes resigned from NPR in 2017 after it was revealed that he had sexually harassed women who were seeking professional guidance from him, at both the *New York Times* and NPR. I later learned that in the 1980s, during his tenure at the *New York Times*, he was one of the reporters criticized by the gay community for homophobia in his coverage. It seemed a certain type of biases—homophobia and sexism—had been acceptable not just for months or years, but for decades in his case. While women, people of color, and LGBTQ were pushed out for questioning "objectivity," Oreskes had been promoted again and again while upholding the biases of the status quo, homophobia, and sexism.

Similarly, for ten years John Hockenberry was the host of the show *The Takeaway* that fired freelancer Caitlin Curran for her connection to Occupy in 2011. In 2017 he was revealed to have pushed out multiple women of color as cohosts due to his gendered and racial harassment. Hockenberry was never fired; these revelations came after his resignation.

Public radio saw an exodus of white male hosts at the time: WNYC's Leonard Lopate and Jonathan Schwartz were both accused and eventually fired. Tom Ashbrook, host of the national show *On Point* at WBUR, lost his job after eleven men and women came forward with accusations against him. It was a seeming watershed as men were revealed as sexual harassers at the *New York Times*, the *New Yorker*, VICE News, *Vox*, NBC, Fox, and the list goes on. Mostly white male hosts, reporters, and editors had made many, many women's lives miserable, in some cases over many years. Yet none of them had been accused of having a conflict of interest for being unable to respect women. Could they report fairly on women? The question had never been asked.

As 2017 swept along, it only became more clear to me how retrograde the whole situation is. You couldn't be an activist against sexual assault or harassment and hold a full-time job in most national media.

And yet, it seems, you could still assault and harass people. None of us live free of conflicts of interest—and it's worth engaging what the appropriate line is for individual news organizations and having clear policies that can be fairly enforced. But we also need journalism to change. We need new institutions, with new policies and practices, to put an end to double standards and harassment. Being political about it, being a walking conflict of interest, wasn't really a choice for me, or for Sandy Nelson or Desmond Cole or Linda Greenhouse. The #MeToo movement has been, like #BlackLivesMatter, a visceral and viral reminder of the fact that our very lives, our bodies, our careers are political—all of us, not just those of us targeted by abuse and harassment.

Journalism's production of innocence, its purity ritual, needs to become a thing of the past. It is intellectually and morally dishonest. It encourages cynicism about our profession and works to keep oppressed people out of journalism entirely. The courage of people coming forward in the #MeToo movement doesn't restore all the lost careers, all the discouraged young women and people of color who left reporting and never came back. But even more revealing is the fact that the media has seemingly been more fixated on keeping political signage off its reporters' front lawns than keeping the bosses' hands off its reporters' bodies. Maybe a few more advocates in the ranks could have helped.

"I did not live in the apolitical vacuum my employer carved out for me," Sandy Nelson wrote in 1996. "I had not succumbed to the cynicism of my profession and my generation. I believed—and still believe—that humans are capable of changing the conditions of our existence."

8

"CAN'T YOU FIND ANY MORE WOMEN TO ATTACK?"

What Happens When Facts Don't Matter

> Criticize other people for not being objective. Be as subjective as you
> want. It's a great little racket.
>
> MATT LABASH, writer for the *Weekly Standard*

"I do not lie on this program," Rush Limbaugh told his millions of listeners in 1993. "And I do not make things up for the advancement of
my cause. And if I find that I have been mistaken or am in error, then
I proclaim it generally at the top of—beginning of—a program, or as
loudly as I can."

Limbaugh, at the time, was barely clear of the era of his "AIDS
Update," a regular segment during which he complained about the
militancy of anti-AIDS activists over soundtrack of Dionne Warwick's
"I'll never love this way again." Another regular segment on Rush's
show in the late '80s, the "Gerbil Report," concerned the practice of
"gerbilling"—a largely apocryphal sexual practice involving a tube,
an orifice, and a gerbil (if you're still curious, feel free to Google it).

Rush loved to play both sides: he claimed the title of journalist only
when it served him and denied it when he was accused of bending
the truth. But he had some favorite journalists. One of them, a then-
closeted gay man named David Brock, made his name with a 1992
article called "The Real Anita Hill" in the *American Spectator*. At the
time, the entire country was obsessed with the lewd "he said, she said"

that had emerged in the confirmation hearings for Clarence Thomas, who was nominated by George H. W. Bush to replace the Supreme Court's only Black justice before him, Thurgood Marshall.

Anita Hill, who is also Black, alleged that Thomas had sexually harassed her while he was head of the Equal Employment Opportunity Commission—the federal agency in charge of preventing workplace harassment. Conservatives, hungry for a solidly right-wing justice, immediately set out to paint Hill as a liar, and Brock in "The Real Anita Hill" presented plenty of reasons why she might lie: he called Hill "a little bit nutty and a little bit slutty." Limbaugh gleefully read Brock's copy on the air, making Brock famous overnight.

What he didn't say was that Brock's "investigation" into Hill had been requested and paid for by a wealthy North Carolina conservative heiress, funding that was never mentioned in the *Spectator*, either. As Brock would later write, "I saw the offer, my introduction to right-wing checkbook journalism, as a big break."

Brock has a lot to teach about how the misinformation sausage is made. He would go on to write a best-selling book, *The Real Anita Hill*, based on his "nutty, slutty" article. Later, he confessed to bending, warping, and even fabricating facts in the name of the right-wing cause, defending Clarence Thomas at all costs. Brock's story provides insight into both the rise of right-wing media, and the production and popularity of stories that are only partially true.

I knew I needed to consider the problem of misinformation and disinformation—"fake news" is, after all, the eternal bogeyman that threatens real news and is a part of the argument for a return to traditional "objectivity." And in the last fifty years, arguably the greatest shift in how we think about "objectivity" in mainstream media didn't come from left-wing activists or diversity advocates. It came from the conservative movement, which built up a powerful machine to propagate spin without abandoning the claim of "objective" journalism. But the problem with conservative spin isn't that it comes from a political or an ideological place, or even that it is "biased." The problem is that much of it is unattached to fact and, more importantly, that readers and writers alike are being trained not to care. Ultimately, fake news isn't a symptom of the death of "objectivity"—it's a symptom of a much deeper American disease, what the poet Kevin Young calls the "colonization of doubt."

The fear, of course, is that without objectivity, we risk descending into a chaos of "he said, she said" stories, tales based on rumor and accusation rather than fact and verification; without objectivity, everything will be motivated by crass partisanship and propaganda. David Brock's story (which is also Anita Hill's story) affirms that this fear is partially founded. But it also shows why "objectivity" can't save us from ourselves—it's too easily deployed to uphold the status quo, its good intentions too easily undermined by attempts to colonize doubt.

· · ·

Anita Hill was a law professor at the University of Oklahoma who had worked for several years for Clarence Thomas at the U.S. Department of Education and then at the Equal Employment Opportunity Commission. The night her allegations against Thomas hit the newswires, a long October Saturday, Hill writes that she was tossing and turning in fear and trepidation. Her interview with Nina Totenberg would air the next morning on NPR. Before dawn, she checked herself into a hotel to hide from the suddenly descending press and the constant phone calls to her home; family and friends snuck in and out of the hotel to see her. She came home a day later to a television crew on her front lawn and then held a news conference at the University of Oklahoma Law School that was broadcast live, nationally. In her memoir, *Speaking Truth to Power*, she recalls eating out for dinner that Monday night: "This was the last time I would eat in a public restaurant with some sense of anonymity."

The story that emerged later was this: Hill was contacted by staffers from the Senate Judiciary Committee, responding to rumors that she had alleged sexual harassment while she worked for Clarence Thomas. She *had* made that allegation—in private conversations with a limited number of close friends. As she tells it, she went back and forth about whether to speak to the committee, ultimately deciding to do so because she felt responsible to the public. Thomas was, after all, being considered for a lifetime appointment. Hill spoke to Senate staffers and sent a written statement with her name attached, though she also expressed a desire not to testify publicly. When the Senate Judiciary Committee moved sluggishly to address her allegations, members of the press caught wind. Hill got a call from NPR's Nina Totenberg on a Saturday, and by Sunday morning, the story was out.

Days later, Hill was paraded before the Judiciary Committee, where she repeated the shocking allegations that Thomas had talked to her in graphic terms about pornography and penis size, and pressured her to go out with him, at multiple points over several years. Hill was treated to a scalding interrogation of her motives, her background, and her trustworthiness. The committee asked her, among other things, if she was a "scorned woman" or had a history of sexual harassment complaints (as if being harassed once means you sacrifice the right to complain the second time); senators implied that she suffered from "erotomania," a quack psychiatric condition. Thomas denied it all, famously invoking the phrase "high-tech lynching" to describe his experience. The national media flocked to the story, and the committee hearings were live on TV around the clock.

Anyone who was alive and cognizant in America at the time remembers it. I was seven years old, and I can remember my parents looking ashamed, shaking their heads, unsure what to make of the whole thing. Black men were saddled with the horrible stereotype of being hypersexual and intimidating, while Black women were saddled with the stereotype of being slutty and not-to-be-believed. My liberal parents hated the idea that either of these stories were true.

The hearings blew by in a week in 1991 at the end of which Anita Hill's credibility had been thoroughly undermined—polls showed a majority of Americans believing Thomas over Hill.

"In my first dealings with the press on October 2," Hill later wrote, "I was cautious though naïve. By October 13 I was thoroughly skeptical and doubted that the press would discuss sexual harassment with any insight or sensitivity. Nor did I believe that all the journalistic prying was motivated by service to the public's right to know."

. . .

As Hill's story gained traction, so did David Brock's reporting. "The Real Anita Hill"—the 1992 article and later the 1993 best-selling book—was a breakthrough. On the success of the initial piece, he ascended to the heights of 1990s neocon inner circles, a dramatic overnight success he describes in his 2002 book *Blinded by the Right: The Conscience of an Ex-Conservative.*

Brock was born during the decline of what some refer to as the age of American consensus—a brief window after World War II during which white patriarchs on the right and left managed to agree on a shared reality and shared enemies, no matter how tenuous the agreement. Communism was bad, capitalism was good; cities were dangerous, suburbs were safe; social services were good, fascism was bad. As this sense of consensus devolved into the raucous '60s and the depressed '70s, he describes an insecure childhood—his father a far right Catholic conservative with little time for the kids, his mother less politically right wing but generally tightly wound. He began to develop feelings of same-sex attraction at age eleven and worked hard to hide this from people through his teen years in New Jersey and then Texas.

He went to UC Berkeley for college, where he joined with a cadre of campus conservatives—students and a handful of professors who saw themselves as victims of the politically correct left. His great humiliation in college was that he was pushed out of the student newspaper, the *Daily Cal*, after many clashes over his conservative beliefs and bristly personality. A series of emotional episodes of rejection from campus liberals led him to take a conservative reactionary stance: "I now viewed politics as a knife fight, my critics as blood enemies."

It was with this mentality that Brock went to DC to become a conservative writer after college. In 1986, at age twenty-three, he went to work for the *Washington Times*, the conservative daily rag run by the cult known as the Unification Church, or the Moonies. At the *Washing-*

ton Times, there were many rewards for pushing a right-wing agenda, and few checks on truth or factuality. He recalls once interviewing Chilean dictator Augusto Pinochet without asking him about his record of abuses. And the *Washington Times* had an aggressive culture, which he adopted fully: "When I harassed and humiliated one woman, targeted as a liberal, to the point that she stormed into my office in tears, dumped two feet of research files into my lap, and quit, John and Tod [the editors] high-fived me." While he doesn't give his status as a homosexual as an excuse, he does cite it as a factor in his extreme desire for acceptance from these men, who were known homophobes.

In the late 1980s, Brock started writing for the *American Spectator*, a magazine that was underwritten by billionaire philanthropist Richard Mellon Scaife. He shifted from cranking out daily news stories to right-wing muckraking. He describes his *American Spectator* editor as harried and credulous, "rarely questioning the reporting in a piece, so long as it bludgeoned the predictable liberal targets"; the magazine employed no fact-checkers and rarely questioned writers' assumptions. Meanwhile, Brock, who'd been out as gay in college, went quietly back into the closet, avoiding the topic of sexuality with his friends and mentors in conservative media as he sought success within the movement.

He did find success with "The Real Anita Hill," publishing unsubstantiated accusations that she had littered pubic hair into a student's paper while working as a law professor and getting help in his smear campaign from top Republican aides as well as friends of Clarence Thomas. He protected their anonymity while attempting to destroy Hill's reputation.

"As is always the case with sexual harassment, there were weak spots in the story told by Hill and her witnesses, and I portrayed them as intentional lies," he later wrote in *Blinded by the Right*. He describes himself as reaching hard to find an explanation for why she would go under oath to testify against Thomas. And he was willing to go on the offensive: "No respectable publication, not even the *Spectator*, had ever seen the likes of the sexist imagery and sexual innuendo I confected to discredit Anita Hill. These were but two ingredients in a witches' brew of fact, allegation, hearsay, speculation, opinion, and invective labeled by my editors as 'investigative journalism.' And, well, it did *look* like journalism."

It helped that Anita Hill was never a real person to him—just a great source of attention. After Rush Limbaugh promoted Brock's piece on his show, *American Spectator* circulation tripled. He recalls that his editor at the *Spectator* asked him, in passing, "Can't you find any more women to attack?" Brock brushed it off. In his mind, "I was doing good, getting out the truth by any means necessary."

. . .

When he expanded "The Real Anita Hill" into a book with the same title, Brock sought out any and all dirt he could find, rarely depended on solid verification, and didn't care that he didn't include voices who might tell a different story. The book is a mess, but what's important about it is that it doesn't read like a mess: it reads like a regular old researched book and includes things people really did say. It was not fair or impartial, by Brock's own admission, but its tone and style imitated traditional "objectivity."

This attempt to perform the role of "objective" journalist begins in the author's note: "Though readers may be struck by the book's seemingly single-minded focus on Hill, as opposed to Thomas, this should not lead anyone to conclude that only Hill's testimony was subjected to close scrutiny. . . . If the evidence had come out the other way, I was fully prepared to write a book that questioned Thomas's credibility and character and redeemed Hill's." He has since admitted the lie.

Brock spends much of the introduction carefully casting himself as an impartial observer, while creating Anita Hill as a subjective (and therefore untrustworthy) character. "Until now, there has been no effort to examine Hill's account on the evidence and to 'reconstruct a narrative' dispassionately, and from a factual foundation. Readers will have to decide for themselves whether that alternative construction is persuasive."

Brock uses second- and third-hand sources, rumor and innuendo, to imply every possible motive for Hill to lie about Thomas: she had a "civil rights" agenda or a feminist agenda, she had a special interest in Thomas as a mentor or a lover, she struggled with rejection and saw herself as a scorned woman, she was martyr-like in her workplace behavior. His depiction of her, by his own later admission, is incoherent—a hodgepodge of stereotypes used to discredit Black women.

Throughout *The Real Anita Hill*, Brock also frequently indicts Hill's supporters on the basis of their lack of objectivity. For example, he calls the conclusion that Clarence Thomas was guilty "a subjective, emotional, and political reaction to the event of a woman's charge of sexual harassment against a man, not an objective, reasoned assessment of the facts and evidence of the case at hand." (The irony, of course, was that the Republicans on the Senate Judiciary Committee had in fact concluded that Thomas was innocent *before* they investigated the accusations, not after.)

The dangerous reality, he later wrote, is that he believed his own propaganda. "For many readers, my inability to take in other points of view was, perversely, the source of my strength as a political writer," he said—a profile of him in the *Washington Post* called him a "young warrior." He later admitted he was no warrior, but a journalist who'd been trained only in how to look "objective," not in how to actually seek out truth: "Like a kid playing with a loaded gun, I didn't appreciate the difference between a substantiated charge and an unsubstantiated one."

His approach had spoils galore: *The Real Anita Hill* was a best seller. After Anita Hill, he targeted the Clintons with his "investigative" reporting. His social circle included close friends of Clarence Thomas, an early career Laura Ingraham, Matt Drudge (the blogger who broke the Lewinsky scandal), and some of the most notorious homophobes of the 1990s. Rush Limbaugh was only a degree removed from Brock, and as Brock tells it, they all saw themselves as warriors for the same cause: the conservative movement, by any means necessary. It was a lovely time to be a conservative—their once-fringe perspectives moving into the mainstream at a breakneck speed.

Clarence Thomas may have been many things, including a serial sexual harasser. But one thing he was for sure was a Rush Limbaugh listener, a die-hard fan of the dog-whistling radio host. In 1994 Limbaugh got married for the third time. The officiant at his wedding? Supreme Court Justice Clarence Thomas, who was sworn in on October 18, 1991, less than two weeks after Anita Hill's testimony. Thomas hosted the Limbaugh wedding at his home.

. . .

"Screw journalism," Matt Drudge once said. "The whole thing's a fraud anyway."

Matt Drudge, David Brock, and Andrew Breitbart—rock-star journalists of the conservative movement, as detached from accountability and fact-checking as the coastal elites are from Middle America— did not emerge out of a vacuum. Their careers were the result of a concerted, decades-long effort on the part of the conservative movement to gain control over the media—and thus, the narrative—in the United States.

Historian Nicole Hemmer, in *Messengers of the Right: Conservative Media and the Transformation of American Politics*, gives a detailed history of the early conservative media movement, explaining that conservative media as we know it today actually began as a reaction to that postwar era of consensus. It turns out (surprise!) that period in the 1940s and 1950s wasn't so much a consensus as a concentration of power among centrists.

"This consensus was, paradoxically, understood as both liberal and nonideological," she says. The liberal center opposed Communism and fascism and believed in New Deal democracy and free market capitalism. But outside the power structure, not as many people were buying it. "Viewed from the progressive left or the conservative right, the neutrality of the vital center was a farce," Hemmer writes.

A critique of this supposedly objective center was a zone of agreement between radicals at opposite ends of political poles—both felt their views were marginalized by the status quo.

"Activists on the left and the right found themselves tarred as extremists and ideologues, politically illegitimate in a post-ideology age. Both sought to expose the ideological agendas of these purportedly neutral institutions, attacking the press's claims of objectivity, the universities' claims of neutrality, and the government's claims of technocracy," says Hemmer.

But it was conservatives who launched the more successful movement to undermine the legitimacy of the center. This movement began with the premise that objectivity wasn't real—that it was merely an expression of center-liberal ideology. As early as the 1950s, rightwingers began a concerted resistance to centrist beliefs, attempting both to discredit "objective" media and build out their own media infrastructure that would counterbalance liberal consensus. The *National Review* was founded in 1955 to advocate a conservative position while critiquing mainstream media for liberal bias. Another influential publication, *Human Events*, said it was objective and concerned with accuracy, but not impartial—like many nineteenth-century papers, it rejected neutrality without rejecting facts.

At first, these conservative rags were bit players in a world dominated by TV news and daily papers. But the conservative movement developed a strategy to propagate its ideas much more widely. A key player in that effort was Supreme Court Justice Lewis F. Powell. Months before his appointment in 1971, he wrote a memorandum at the behest of a friend of his who worked for the US Chamber of Commerce. Now known as the "Powell memo," the document urgently asserted that free market capitalism was under attack, and that business interests were insufficiently represented in the politics of the day. Powell was frightened that consumer advocates, environmentalists, and campus leftists were driving a conversation that could only lead to more stringent regulation of big business. The memo, which circulated among powerful businesspeople and politicos, called for a coordinated propagandist response, a full-court press for free enterprise.

Powell had powerful allies, including *Wall Street Journal* columnist Irving Kristol, and a growing group of CEOs and trade associations who agreed on the need for a well-funded defense of unfettered capitalism. Out of his call grew the conservative think tanks—the American Enterprise Institute, founded in 1938 but expanded with an influx of corporate funding in the '70s, and the Heritage Foundation, founded in 1973 with the financial support of the Coors Brewing Company and Richard Mellon Scaife (who later supported David Brock's work). Heritage and AEI, with millions of dollars in funding, began to grow a national network of think tanks, media organizations, lobbyists, and eventually journalists who would advocate pro-business, anti-regulation conservative causes under the guise of "objectivity" and balanced scholarly study. It was a shift from the earlier approach of right-wing media, which had been to critique the whole idea of "objectivity." Along the way, these activists abandoned that critique in favor of a less transparent strategy: they would critique others for bias, but claim the conservative perspective was, in fact, "objective."

It worked: by the late 1980s, when Brock entered the fray, there was a network of powerful conservative media outlets and think tanks, working together to advance pro-corporate beliefs under the name of fact-based research and media. Talking points produced by Heritage Foundation writers or corporate lobbyists would be repeated on right-wing radio shows, papers, and eventually websites and blogs across the country, creating the image of consensus (or at least a lively debate) on issues that had previously been at the fringes of the national conversation.

An important part of the strategy was to attack "liberal bias" in mainstream media and academia. An organization called Accuracy in Media, founded in 1969, focused not on accuracy but on this perception of bias. Anything that didn't reflect a conservative worldview was smeared for "liberal bias." By the 1990s, these conservative media activists had tapped into an approach that wasn't just politically powerful, but profitable.

Matt Labash, a writer for the conservative *Weekly Standard*, summed up the strategy concisely in an interview with the website JournalismJobs.com: "We've created this cottage industry in which it pays to be un-objective. . . . It's a great way to have your cake and eat it too. Criticize other people for not being objective. Be as subjective as you want. It's a great little racket." This "great little racket" of feigned objectivity, however intellectually dishonest, was what David Brock keyed into in his attacks on Anita Hill and the Clintons in the 1990s. He followed

Labash's formula: you attack your foes for being unobjective, present yourself as objective, then proceed to produce distorted news that is also unmoored from practices of fact-checking and thorough sourcing.

· · ·

Brock took this strategy and ran with it, pointedly excoriating others for their rejection of "objectivity." In the epilogue of *The Real Anita Hill*, Brock openly scorns the idea that patriarchal or sexist thought might make it hard for men to hear or understand what women are saying, quoting the feminist legal scholar Ann Scales with a sense of horror. In "The Emergence of Feminist Jurisprudence: An Essay," published in the *Yale Law Journal* in 1986, Scales had written: "Feminist analysis begins with the principle that objective reality is a myth. It recognizes that patriarchal myths are projections of the male psyche." Feminists wanted to redefine sexual harassment laws to make them more focused on the subjective interpretations of women, a prospect that deeply disturbed Brock. "Notions of logic, objectivity, equality under law, and the common good are all regarded as reflections of this patriarchal bias," he wrote with obvious distaste.

It's funny that he brought up Ann Scales, because I later discovered she had warned of this precise problem with supposedly "objective" approaches to law and science. "Neutrality is dangerous: if one group can take a decidedly non-neutral point of view and get people to buy it on the grounds that it is neutral, the game is over," she wrote in a 1992 article in the *UCLA Women's Law Journal*. Scales pinpointed the trouble: we depend on subjective interpretation to decide what is neutral, and those subjective decisions about neutrality tend to uphold the perspectives of those defining the terms of the debate. In other words, "objectivity" always protects the status quo, interpreting the powerful as "neutral" because it is they who create the frame—and people like Brock can easily exploit it.

Feminist method, she writes, "does not criticize objective reality because it is insufficiently objective, or even because that reality has failed to incorporate women's voices. Rather, it is objectivity itself—

entailing objectification, unacknowledged self-reference, and protection of the status quo—that is criticized." In other words, "objectivity" could be deployed by anyone in power to protect against criticism. It was dangerous because it claimed "neutrality" without a mechanism for investigating the motives of the people involved. It was dangerous no matter what.

Scales was sounding the alarm against people exactly like Brock—those who would claim "objectivity" as a guise for upholding oppressive power dynamics, in which men could harass women with impunity, and women, seeking to prove it, would have nothing but their word to go by.

As Scales points out, there can be multiple truths without sacrificing truth and fact altogether. In the case of sexual assault, this is pointedly, scarily vivid: one person can be raped, while another person sees himself not as a rapist, but as a man engaging in a consensual act or even fulfilling a God-given role. Establishing that it is rape *is* a subjective process, dependent on our understandings of gender roles and the bodily autonomy of people who are raped. But this is all the more reason to clearly define the values that drive our inquiry: When a man and a woman disagree over whether an encounter was a rape, whose perspective matters more? Can we evaluate both claims neutrally? It's unavoidable that establishing rape or even workplace harassment as a fact involves weighing one person's perspective over and against another, giving real-life weight to a victim's feeling of having been harmed. "Objectivity" can't save us from this conundrum—though it has protected many a rapist and harasser.

We need to muddle through it on our own, calling on our values and explaining the reasons we have to believe or disbelieve a claim. I can't tell you for sure what happened in private between Anita Hill and Clarence Thomas—no one can. But "objectivity" allowed David Brock to claim that he could—it provided shelter for his particular distortions, because they aligned with the culture of the times.

· · ·

Anita Hill is gracious and measured, almost painfully so, about her own objectification by the likes of David Brock. In her memoir, *Speaking Truth to Power*, she writes: "The event known as the Hill-Thomas hearing has been described variously as a watershed in American politics, a turning point in the awareness of sexual harassment, and a wake-up call for women. For me it was a bane which I have worked hard to transform into a blessing for myself and for others." She was thirty-five when she was pulled into this scandal, and to this day, very little factual information has been unearthed to suggest she had any reason to fabricate a story about Clarence Thomas. Nonetheless, he came out on top: he's a Supreme Court justice, while she is a law professor still navigating the constant glare of the public eye.

Brock's "fraudulent portrayal of me, presumptuously entitled *The Real Anita Hill*, hinged on sexual mythology about black women and society's willingness to believe it," she writes. "Because Brock supported his case with fabricated and misquoted sources, I was at first amazed that the press gave him such broad license to define me."

Hill avoids personal attacks in her discussion of Brock—focusing instead on the system that created him.

"David Brock is a product of the times in which we now live. As a white male he is given permission to define me, a black woman, on whatever terms he chooses, without establishing any credentials to do so. He is presumed to be free of bias, no matter how obviously biased his work may be," she writes, noting the positive reviews his book received from major outlets. "Responsible journalists failed to see that there is a special danger in this approach, where it targets individuals who have been historically portrayed negatively without support."

Brock's own conclusion about his book *The Real Anita Hill* later on was that "the case made in the book was not only wrong and false, it was almost precisely the opposite of the truth." But Hill adeptly points out that the problem lies less with Brock himself, and more with the cultural surroundings that made Brock's story about her believable.

"All of Brock's false claims, accusations, and theories fall into a void about black women, another void about women who raise harassment claims, and still another, even larger void of misogyny." Anita

Hill's own humanity disappeared into this void: she became a symbol, not a human being.

It wasn't out of care for Anita Hill or Hillary Clinton or any other woman that Brock left the conservative movement—he left to save himself. His fast rise to fame led to an equally inglorious fall: when he published his second book, pitched as a takedown of Hillary Clinton, die-hard right-wingers were disappointed by the forgiving tone he ultimately took toward the hated first lady. Following the publication of that book, Brock was outed as gay. That didn't lead to immediate expulsion from the conservative movement, but it did lead to his eventual alienation and defection. He writes that he left behind "six-figure salaries and seven-figure book contracts" and started working as an actual journalist—not unbiased but aiming for the truth. "I'll never forget the panic that came over me when I received the first call from a fact-checker at *New York* magazine, asking me to submit my notes for a story." In his twelve years in conservative journalism, he had never once been fact-checked.

. . .

In later reflections on the problems with conservative media, David Brock never makes quite clear what he thinks would be the best response to the way conservative media has bent the truth toward its interests. Is his answer that everything is ideological, and left-wingers just need to push harder in the marketplace of ideas if they want a fair shake? Or does he believe there is an "objective" place to return to? And, more fundamentally, is the problem with conservative media of the type he worked for primarily that it is *biased*, or is the problem that it is not sufficiently interested in facts? Does bias inevitably lead to this disconnect from facts?

I feel a kind of desperation around addressing these questions, in part because one of the fears I've heard most often about abandoning objectivity is that it must mean a descent into pure partisanship. Without objectivity, I'm told, we are all ideologues, unmoored from the truth. And what if we are all ideologues anyhow—just some of us are more aware of it than others?

The biggest bogeyman here, of course, is "fake news"—a loose term for the falsehoods, disinformation, half-truths, and lazy reporting that fly free across the internet these days. But one of the chief problems with our analysis of disinformation today is that's it's ahistorical—it assumes fake news is a by-product of the internet age, or the work of Russian hackers, or the result of right-wing political activists and their parallel hacks on the left. The cries to return to an age of "objectivity" assume such an age ever existed—and that it protected us from lies and propaganda. And they presume that objectivity is the opposite of "alternative facts." But what if the antidote to disinformation and misinformation isn't "objectivity," but curiosity?

"In the face of the inexplicable, audiences will settle for unbelievable," writes Kevin Young, a poet and the director of the Schomburg Center for Research in Black Culture. I was at the gym listening to WNYC's *On the Media* when I heard Young explaining the connections between Barnum & Bailey and reality TV, the early penny press newspapers and the internet. He explained that the biggest, baddest success in the earliest days of the penny paper came from a fabricated story, the now-famous Great Moon Hoax. In 1835 a story about a scientist discovering life on the moon helped make the *Sun* the best-selling newspaper in the country—its descriptions of man bats, biped beavers, and even unicorns astonished and delighted readers, even after it was revealed to be fake news. The Moon Hoax took a pseudoscientific tone, bringing the modern scientific fetish for classification to bear on a series of creatures discovered on the moon (and imagine this: some were superior to others).

I bought Young's poetic history book, *Bunk: The Rise of Hoaxes, Humbug, Plagiarists, Phonies, Post-Facts, and Fake News*, and read it hungrily. It's a dense and thorough examination of the history of hoaxes and fake news in the US. To the extent that the book makes a single argument, it is that hoaxes, fake stories that pretend to be true, end up succeeding when they speak to our most misguided fantasies about ourselves. "There is of course no larger mass hysteria in American history than the epidemic of racism," he writes. Race was asserted as biological fact for decades before it was debunked by later iterations of scientific research—race, it turns out, is little but a cultural construct, a language of power and control.

"The hoax regularly steps in when race rears its head—exactly because it too is a fake thing pretending to be real," Young says.

From hoaxes and bunk, he explains, we can learn a lot about the gap between what we hope to be true and what is happening in reality—hoaxes speak to those hopes, even where they are base and unkind. The slave owner, for example, hopes that the slave is subhuman. The rich CEO hopes that the poor people working for him are happy in their place. The American hopes that the parts of the world our country invades are both lawless and helpless. That's why hoaxes are littered with dark "others," characters who represent what we wish was true about race—birtherism is a prime example from our current era. For some, a more believable President Obama would have been one who was lying about where he really came from, a cheating Black man; it was on this precise racial hoax that Donald Trump rose to become the 2016 candidate for the US presidency. Trump's other racial hoaxes include "Mexican rapists" and a supposedly violent caravan of Central American migrants.

Young argues that the problem with hoaxers isn't that they get facts wrong sometimes (as all journalists do), or even that they are ideological (as all journalists are, whether it's the ideology of the center or another one). It's that they *don't care* what is true. They're not interested in multiple truths or subjectivities—they're interested in bullshit, in making truth and fact feel obscure and impossible.

"Calling *bullshit* isn't easy," Young writes, but it is urgent. Young urges us to notice that we're descending into a euphemistic age, with a president who lies daily and news media who call his lies a "changing narrative" to avoid sounding accusatory. Trump reminds me of the Queen of Hearts in *Alice in Wonderland*, so addicted to bullshit she doesn't know the difference between that and reality. I think of her cronies, painting the roses red to please her. This is *Fox News* and much of news in general today: red roses and Trump tweets and emperors with no clothes.

Young says this Trumpian idea that anything and everything might just be a total hoax makes journalistic practices like fact-checking and healthy skepticism irrelevant. "Unlike a novel, the hoax feigns certainty yet depends on doubt, so much so that it might be said to colonize it."

Doubt is necessary for journalists—we need skepticism and doubt to ascertain facts and come up with new theories, and we need to question endlessly, relentlessly. But when doubt becomes cause to give up, rather than open up a new line of inquiry, it's been colonized, indeed. Half-truths like the ones David Brock told about Anita Hill help colonize doubt: they reinforce the fallacy that nothing can truly be known. Aided by racism and sexism, all he had to do to stir up disbelief in her story was suggest a few racial and sexual stereotypes; the dominant culture filled in the gaps.

If nothing at all can be true, nothing new is worth knowing. True stories seek meaning, diving ever deeper, while hoaxes and disinformation perpetuate meaninglessness, foreclosing the possibility of learning more about the world. Understanding Anita Hill and Clarence Thomas requires an interest in details, a curiosity, an acceptance of ambiguity. Brock's story was easy; the "true" story is complex. It should be no surprise that a later figure, President Donald J. Trump, has focused so heavily on claims of "fake news" against facts he doesn't like, while creating and perpetuating his own share of hoaxes: it's a double-whammy tactic that works, again and again.

"There are still mysteries," Young writes. "This is exactly why we cannot abandon investigation, or science—but true investigation often admits when it isn't exactly sure."

I agree. Certainty is usually a mistake (notice I said *usually*). But there are also facts, truths out there in the world; reality, however fractious and prismatic and magical and ugly, does exist. To look at it, we need to become comfortable with both wonderment and mystery, to accept that mystery is uncomfortable and imperfect and sometimes even ugly, to humble ourselves in the search for truth. It's uncomfortable to make a claim that something definitely happened, and the most responsible journalists covering the Hill-Thomas debacle took their time to investigate the facts. But Anita Hill had no reason to lie, while

Clarence Thomas had every reason in the world. That this context wasn't made clear in every story about the both of them speaks to just how deep our culture's racism and misogyny runs.

. . .

The Hill-Thomas hearings had a long shadow: journalist Jill Abramson—who coauthored an excellent book with Jane Mayer in 1994, *Strange Justice: The Selling of Clarence Thomas*—returned in the midst of the #MeToo movement to lay out an argument that Clarence Thomas perjured himself and should be impeached. In a February 2018 piece in *New York Magazine*, she pointed to an abundance of largely overlooked evidence. There were the four other women who were never brought before the Senate Judiciary Committee to testify, one who said she was also harassed, others who could have in one way or another corroborated Hill's accusations or contributed to their legitimacy. Later a lawyer named Moira Smith said Thomas groped her in 1999, an accusation that was corroborated by a witness as well as her husband. Thomas's ex-girlfriend Lillian McEwen has spoken out in recent years to say that the behavior described by Hill was consistent with her memory of Thomas.

A few days after Abramson's report, the Heritage Foundation's news site published a post using a number of its now-familiar tactics: insulting and undermining Abramson as a journalist; calling into question the factuality of her research even with little evidence to the contrary; and race-baiting those who would question Thomas, saying some people simply can't accept a Black man as a Supreme Court justice. It is a careful exercise in bullshit—nothing that could be taken as an outright lie, but plenty that disregards the importance of curiosity and fact.

The Heritage writers, Tiffany Bates and Elizabeth Slattery, conclude that Abramson is a raw opportunist seeking to "humiliate an honest and decent man." And ironically, they invoke the most sexist image of all, but invert it: "The witch hunt against Clarence Thomas must stop."

The problem with Heritage's assertion isn't that it is biased or lacks "objectivity." It's the authors' bald disinterest in the truth—any truth. "There was a hearing," they write. "All of America saw it. And the American people believed him."

That "the American people" believed him is hardly evidence that he was telling the truth. And the hearing was, after all, not a trial, but a rushed political event. Clarence Thomas has never been tried for harassment, nor has all the evidence yet been heard. How can you know the answer to a question you haven't even asked?

Two and a half decades later, the conservative media would descend similarly on Dr. Christine Blasey Ford, who in 2018 accused Supreme Court nominee Brett Kavanaugh of a violent sexual assault while they were both in high school. Blasey Ford wasn't subjected to quite the same kinds of attacks as Hill, but the outcome was the same: after taking the huge risk of coming forward and giving emotionally intense testimony to a Senate committee, Blasey Ford was systematically undermined, witnesses who might have supported her were never called, and Kavanaugh was confirmed to the high court for a lifetime appointment, with little curiosity on the part of most Republicans about whether he did what she claimed. Again, key questions were simply never asked, and key evidence ignored. Power won out over truth, and many were left, again, with the feeling that the truth didn't matter anymore.

Some will still say all this rancor, all this falsehood and disinformation, is all the more reason to return to the principles of "objective" news reporting. And maybe they are right. But I suspect that this treatment addresses the symptoms and not the cause. We've had fake news and bunk since we've had news, regardless of whether we've indulged in the fantasy of objectivity. To me, this also isn't a partisan issue: lies and hoaxes and the colonization of doubt can happen from any camp, and politicos are particularly likely to partake—although right-wing media has made it an art, plenty of left-wing media dabble in the same shallow water. Balancing right with left solves nothing if everyone is feeding us half-truths and bullshit.

US law protects the language of hoax and "alternative facts" as free speech, and that's a value worth protecting even if it means the freedom to fabricate. Perhaps the *possibility* of being fooled is a price we pay for the responsibility of freedom of the press in this country—we can't eliminate that possibility or wave a magic wand that makes disinformation disappear. It's the *likelihood* of being fooled that's a problem, the cultural and economic forces driving which stories gain traction. If that's true, then real balance doesn't mean rebutting every half-baked hoax or self-righteously claiming that David Brock and the Heritage Foundation are not "real journalists"; it means exposing and shifting the power structures that make these hoaxes possible. The question then becomes why do we buy these lies? Who benefits? What do we get from the thrill of believing? What if our job as journalists isn't to pummel people with "objective" facts, but to help them keep asking questions?

9

TRUTH AND THE LOST CAUSE

"So funny to watch Fake News Networks, among the most dishonest groups of people I have ever dealt with, criticize Sinclair Broadcasting for being biased," Donald Trump tweeted in March 2018.

Sinclair Broadcast Group typifies much of what is wrong with news media today: it is a network of local television stations that have become an increasingly powerful propaganda arm for the right-wing movement since Nixon. Sinclair started in 1971, and the number of stations it owns almost tripled from 2010 to 2018, with 191 stations by early 2019. Sinclair has been a friend to President Trump from the start. The group sends out must-air videos to its stations that encourage fear about terrorism and curry support for Trump. In early 2018, Sinclair drew attention by broadcasting simultaneous statements across many of its stations decrying "biased and false news"—the right-wing term for any news critical of the president. During this time period, any news questioning Trump's connections to Russia, the ethics of his international business dealings, his xenophobic immigration policies, or his leadership of a high-turnover White House was decried on the right as "fake news."

A couple of historians noticed a curious parallel between Sinclair's cries of "bias" and a conservative media movement of the past: the efforts of southern Confederates to remake the story of the Civil War after they lost. That movement, known as the "Lost Cause," depended on white supremacy and historical revisionism to reshape the story of the Civil War, glorifying the "Old South" and touting the benefits of the Confederacy. In a *Washington Post* article "The Lost Cause Roots of Sinclair's Propaganda," historians Ethan J. Kytle and Blain Roberts wrote, "Sinclair is building on a time-honored American tradition that dates back to the 19th century, when defeated Confederates and their offspring used allegations of 'bias' to rewrite the history of the Civil War."

The Lost Cause claims that white southerners stood not for slavery but for "states' rights, low tariffs and constitutional liberty," and its advocates pushed to get this framing into official histories, calling for "impartiality" in the history books. The relative glory of the Confederacy was depicted as a perspective in need of a fair shake. Suddenly slavery was relatively civilized, the Civil War a righteous cause—false balance at its best.

Why did people believe this story? Well, for many whites, both northern and southern, it was a comforting revision of an uncomfortable truth. Just as we see today in Trump's tweets, the cry of "bias" works well to bolster racism while also appealing to the cultural fantasy of objectivity.

"A century ago, Lost Cause champions routinely maintained that their histories of the war were unbiased. It was a shrewd rhetorical strategy, a preemptive strike that discouraged potential challenges to their claims," Kytle and Blain wrote. Importantly, the purveyors of the Lost Cause narrative knew what they were doing. "The Lost Cause was not the product of an honest disagreement over how to interpret historical facts but a willful distortion of them."

This distinction between disagreement and distortion matters. The tone and content of the Lost Cause story felt eerily similar to what I'd witnessed while covering white supporters of Donald Trump—and watching the devastating media denial about the role of whiteness in the 2016 election. Make America Great Again only applied, of course, to those for whom a great America was available to start with. It was starting to feel clear to me, as clear and messy as truth ever will: To fight disinformation, we don't need more neutrality, or more calm, or fewer fighters in the ring. We don't need more "both sides" reporting as a matter of course. We need a reckoning with the cultural forces of white supremacy and patriarchy themselves—these animating fantasies of superiority, with deep roots in US history. That requires a new framework for journalism—one that doesn't shy away from analyzing and naming power and oppression.

. . .

When I lived in southwest Ohio from 2013 to 2016, I covered a Democratic multiracial city and a hippie-laden college town, with John Boehner's congressional district next door, and some of the most conservative suburbs and rural areas around. This was a place where Black Lives Matter demonstrations happened down the street from facilities where young men piloted drones over Yemen, where Tea Partyers might show up at street fairs next to peace protesters, where white suburbanites kept moving farther out to get away from Black people they perceived as "violent" and schools they perceived as failing. The city and the countryside were plagued with drugs. New technology and post-industrial decay cozied up to each other in the central city. There were gorgeous hills and valleys next to devastating industrial wastelands. It was true Middle America, weirder and cooler and worse and better than most outsiders imagine.

One of my last big assignments, in March 2016, was covering a Trump rally in the Dayton suburb of Vandalia during the primaries. Hours before the rally, thousands of people, almost entirely white, lined up at dawn. The energy was electric and excited. People were happy, and at midmorning they crowded into an airplane hangar to see Trump step off his plane. They hooted and howled as he whipped up the crowd with thinly disguised ethno-nationalism and calls for violence. That was the day that a young theater student bum-rushed the stage, producing a clip of Trump wincing and ducking in fear as Secret Service agents hustled the candidate off the podium. (The young man hoped to grab the mic and call Trump a racist. He was charged with a felony.)

I watched from the press box as the crowd got more and more belligerent, screaming angrily at protesters as they interrupted the speech and the Secret Service dragged them out one by one. The lightness and excitement faded to something darker, a tone of racial resentment and fear. Trump told an apocryphal story about US General John Pershing dipping bullets in pigs' blood before shooting down forty-nine accused Muslim terrorists and dumping their bodies in a mass grave, leaving the fiftieth alive to warn off others. "I'm not saying it's a good thing," he said, dog-whistling furiously into the crowd and shrugging.

"Off with their heads!" someone near me yelled. At some point, Trump asked for a pledge that each person would vote for him, and hands went up in the air and held there, scarily reminiscent of a Nazi salute. Between filing live reports for NPR's *Weekend Edition* and listening carefully to these stories, watching the crowd's bitter response, I felt my blood run cold. This was a side of Ohio I had rarely seen, despite knowing it was there.

I talked to dozens of Trump supporters that day, but one interaction stuck with me. On my way out of the rally, I ran into a man I had met before. Just a few weeks back, I had knocked on the door of his mobile home in a trailer park with no running water. I was doing a story about water shutoffs in mobile homes, going door to door to ask people about the landlord who refused to fix the faulty water system. The problem was national in scope, and my story had aired on *Marketplace*, complete with tape of the trailer park managers slamming the office door in my face when I knocked to demand an interview. Anyhow, this man showed up drunk at the trailer door around noon, in boxer shorts, and chatted with me warmly but declined to go on record, returning instead to his TV blasting *Fox News*. He didn't want to get involved.

On this day in March 2016, he recognized me emerging from the hangar (not hard: I had a giant microphone and am ambiguously gendered, a relatively rare sight). "What did you think about the rally?" I asked.

"It was nice, it was great," he said, grinning. "Trump says things no one else will say."

When I called my dad sobbing later, it was this man I talked about: I could see the appeal of Trump, for him. And I was fearful of what I'd seen—not so much Trump himself as the willingness of the crowd to rally around racial resentment, to chant "Build the wall!" without a thought for the human beings literally drowning in the river, dying in the desert trying to get over that border. The man from the trailer park probably hadn't participated in anything political for years, but this rising white supremacist movement was exciting to him, affirming of a worldview he'd absorbed from *Fox News*. What disturbed me about it was how normal he was—maybe not a great person, but not the worst, either. Trump's appeal had reached this guy, gotten him out of his trailer on a Saturday morning.

Seeing him woke me up to something deeply unsettling: that white supremacy sometimes feels good. That's what makes it insidious, a dangerous worldview rather than an absurdist plot easily defeated by rational argument. The narrative that white people are more deserving of safety and success than people of color, and that people of color are to blame for all of their own problems, is a tempting one. Racism gives a leg up to people who would rather feel rage than guilt, rather feel deserving than unsure, rather have privilege than give anything up for equality.

That's what I saw at the Trump rally. But on NPR that day, I didn't talk about Trump's racist dog-whistling or the man from the trailer park. I called in live and talked about the crowd size, the heightened security, the Trump supporters who said they were tired of seeing jobs leave the area, tired of seeing immigrants flow over the border like water in an undammed river. And yet I know these views were upside down, produced through the looking glass: employment had been rising in southwest Ohio for a couple years, and immigrants in Dayton were the sole reason for a population turnaround after forty years of decline. In this radio segment, there wasn't time for that, and those weren't the questions the NPR host was asking me. Live on air, I told Melissa Block about how thrilled these Ohioans were with the idea of Donald Trump. But I wasn't allowed to say why—not really. Because racism was a big part of the real reason, and calling Trump's movement racist wasn't an option. That could have been seen as partisan, and perhaps it was also just too painfully true.

. . .

A few months later, I moved to New York. I was stunned by what I saw there. As Trump took the lead in the Republican primary, a kind of massive anxiety began to overtake the liberal coastal media. Who are these people who are surging in favor of the despicable, misogynist reality TV star? What god-forsaken boonies do they live in, and where in the hell are they getting their news?

Of course, it's too easy, almost a cheap shot at this point, to talk about the coastal national media being out of touch and elite. Let's accept that this is largely true, and I won't put too fine a point on it, other than to say that before the election, I knew we were missing something big. The talk in the newsroom at *Marketplace* was all about the role of economic anxiety, the former factory workers and disengaged Middle Americans, the rural opioid addicts and run-down white towns. I'd seen all of that—I knew it was real. And it was also on CNN and NPR and even Fox.

But what I'd seen in Ohio told a different story: by and large, Republican voters (the people we now call "Trump supporters") weren't fired factory workers or down-and-out addicts—they were suburbanites, business owners, middle-class and sometimes rich white folks who actually had figured out a way through this economic transition our country was in. The thing they'd collectively lost in the transition wasn't jobs or money but identity: a sense of order as their privilege and power seemed to slip away, the country careening toward being majority people of color, gender equality and gay civil rights threatening the old order. Following the presidency of Barack Obama, Trump allowed them an outlet—a way to play the victim while also reclaiming their stance at the center of the narrative. There was nothing new about this: in 1984 Reagan ran on making America great again. Revanchism, this belief that a privileged people have been cheated and deserve revenge, has worked again and again with white Americans, a perfectly forgiving narrative that also forgets.

Still, to the East Coast liberals making many of the editorial decisions in national newsrooms, widespread white supremacy and anti-Blackness seemed an embarrassing reality, so troubling that it was almost impossible to point out. They must really be victims of something, the liberals insisted. Let's find a fired factory worker (implicitly: a white one) and interview him about Trump. So the stories went, and went. White factory guys in Michigan, where I'm from, and in Ohio, where I'd last lived, were paraded proudly across Trumpism stories, with the occasional opiate story to accentuate the sadness and badness of poor Middle America. Low-income people of color, who voted overwhelmingly Democratic, didn't appear in these stories about poverty; it was as if they didn't exist.

And this is key: whiteness appeared constantly, but without analysis or criticism—taken as a state of being instead of a structure of power. The idea that there is a "white working class," for some reason separate from people of other races who work for wages, was accepted as naturally true, rather than socially constructed. And their resentment was presented as a sort of natural outcome. White nationalism was normalized as working-class "populism."

Statistics trickled out that showed it wasn't sheer economics, but racial animosity and segregation, that drove a propensity for Trump support. I asked to be sent back to Ohio to report on this. I wanted to ask Trump supporters about whiteness, about why they feared Mexicans and Islam and "Chicago" (a place Trump particularly loved to dog-whistle about). At that Trump rally, I'd spoken to person after person who had a job, a house, a decent retirement—and yet they described America in decline, growing crime, shrinking resources, no future for the children, and so on. I had seen desperation before and they didn't represent it. Send me to Ohio, I pleaded, let me talk to these people— and to the other people, the working-class and poor folks whose reaction to their own troubles is *not* to support a white supremacist who thinks sexual assault is fine.

My superiors at *Marketplace* declined. We were focused on planning our post-election coverage, predicated entirely on the assumption that Hillary Clinton would win. In a private bet on election outcomes in the New York bureau, I don't recall a single reporter, producer, or editor predicting a Trump victory—many, including me, had Hillary winning by large margins.

Then Trump won, the stock markets soared, and the production crew in LA suddenly agreed: I should go to Ohio.

On November 12, I was back in Dayton, driving to the Cincinnati suburbs to see a white factory owner named Greg Knox, who had Trump signs out front and believed in Trump's economic ideas—lower taxes, higher tariffs, America First. He also believed in Trump's racial ideas. "My ancestors were immigrants," he said, "but they were good, hard-working immigrants." I asked him what he made of the fact that many people were afraid as a result of the anti-immigrant violence and xenophobia following the election.

"I don't want anyone to be afraid," he said, "but I want an America that's for Americans," as if his Irish ancestors had been Americans when they came. I went in fearful and left sad and frustrated—Knox wasn't a fool, but his intellect seemed wasted on the desire to have power over others, to compete and win. I almost liked this man, and he respected my probing questions. But there was no reason for him to develop any more empathy for others, especially people of color—he didn't need it, and the system didn't reward it.

Another woman, Kate Geiger, was a Republican (and now a Trump supporter) who I'd known since I interviewed her about the last GM truck plant in the area—she'd been a pensioned worker at the notorious facility when it finally closed in 2008. In 2016 she was working at a MillerCoors factory, making a good wage with benefits. I sat down on her cushy couch in her living room to talk to her for hours about the Trump victory. How did she feel about his views on women? She said she didn't care; all the men around here were misogynists, too. How did she feel about his views on immigrants? She said she agreed with him: we need to put Americans first. How did she feel about his idea of banning Muslims from the country? She couldn't really agree with that, but she was as afraid of terrorism as the next person. I asked her if she'd ever known anyone Muslim, and she said no. I asked her what she thought about the recent rise in hate crimes against Muslims.

"A lot of Muslim women are afraid," I said. "They're afraid of people like you." Geiger thought for a while. "If I were a Muslim woman, and I didn't know me, I'd be scared of me," she said.

This was one of the most remarkable quotations I'd ever heard from a source, but when I filed the story, show producers tried to cut it out, claiming it veered off into unrelated territory. When I filed the Greg Knox story (which also featured a Latina small business owner who was fearful for her family's future under a Trump presidency), producers proposed cutting his quote about being a nationalist. I can't tell you why I had to fight for these quotes to stay in, but the sense I had was that the show's mind-set—that nothing was *really* about race, that it was all *actually* about economics—was seeping into these editorial choices. I won some of these arguments, and they weren't the best stories of my life, but they weren't the worst either.

The story with Kate Geiger in it ended on the words of a Black woman, Robin Pink, another worker at the MillerCoors factory, whose class experiences mirrored Kate's, but whose take on politics came out dead opposite. She had supported Hillary in spite of reservations; anyone but Trump, she said. And as to whether the election outcome had to do with racism?

"This country has been about race from the beginning," she said, sitting in a Mexican restaurant on Dayton's segregated West Side. "You know, that hasn't changed."

. . .

Reckoning with race and power in reporting requires intellectual rigor—a framework to counter the racism and white supremacy that often underlie national conversations, whether we are aware of it or not. It requires us to challenge status quo understandings of racism, such as the idea that racism is primarily an individual belief system reflected by the use of racist language (Donald Trump is not a "racist" unless he can be caught on tape saying the N-word). The belief that people are oppressed because they're "different" rather than because someone benefits from oppression is another relatively permissible framework, appearing often in "objective" news reporting. What if in order to counter the lies and fantasies of white supremacy and anti-Blackness, we need a framework that embraces curiosity and fact-finding, while recognizing the systems and structures that hold oppression in place? In other words, what if journalists need to learn to identify and talk about ideology—not as a bad thing to be avoided, but as an inevitable part of how we frame our stories?

If ideology is journalism's hot potato, whiteness is journalism's other hot potato, something always there but seemingly untouchable—perhaps because talking about race would mean talking about racism, and about the bias that comes with being white. These fears, these restrictions, made it hard for mostly white newsrooms to actually talk about what happened in 2016, what I saw and what lots of people were seeing. To call it white supremacy (as I did in the blog post I was fired for) seemed ideological, but I believe it was also true—and that it is equally ideological *not* to call it white supremacy. It became abundantly evident during and after the 2016 election that I would need to push back on whiteness and white supremacy in my pursuit of truth-telling.

The question was, how? I didn't see many models out there for how to interrogate whiteness through curious journalism—until I found John Biewen, a North Carolina–based audio journalist at Duke's Center for Documentary Studies (CDS) whose series *Seeing White* was about just that.

. . .

Biewen, who produces a podcast for CDS called *Scene on Radio*, launched his series *Seeing White* not long after the election, driven by some of the same questions I had: How can we describe institutional white supremacy and its role in this political moment? How can we address the construction and propagation of whiteness, which is not a biological category but a cultural and political one? The "post-racial" story of Barack Obama's presidency couldn't explain the events of 2016 and 2017, so John was left searching for a framework that made more sense. He said he had a lightbulb moment: "I've been a reporter for thirty years and hadn't done something about whiteness." He'd focused instead on stories about people of color as a way of reporting on race.

After attending an anti-racism training session and watching the role of race in the election, he said he realized that white people are *a story*—and not a story that should always be left to people of color to interpret and tell. "My feeling was that white people need to be doing this work."

At the same time, he realized white people's perspective on race can be suspect—he enlisted fellow journalist and media studies researcher Chenjerai Kumanyika, a Black man, as a collaborator on the show, giving feedback and criticism in each episode. Like me, Biewen had confronted a contradiction within liberal public media. Talking about institutional white supremacy—about racism as more than just individual attitudes—was basically off-limits. "Just the use of that kind of language is seen as radical and ideological," he said. Biewen had become convinced that the false narratives of white supremacy, like the Lost Cause narrative, are making it hard for us to see, hear, and understand true stories about our country. "I had been, as a white American, steeped in more reassuring narratives about who we are and our history," he said. These narratives minimized the harms of slavery, invisiblized the torture, rape, and murder of Native Americans, and convinced people we were on an inevitable march toward racial progress and unity.

The first reassuring narrative Biewen destroys in his series is the story of his own hometown, Mankato, Minnesota. Growing up white in Mankato, Biewen never learned that it had been the site of the largest mass execution in US history, the 1862 hanging of thirty-eight Dakota Indians after losing the Dakota War against white settlers. The story is gory and sad, and the sites of death are presented today in purportedly "neutral" terms that make the trauma of the Dakotas invisible and the victory of the whites inevitable. But of course, what really happened in the Dakota War is a matter of perspective—as Biewen reveals in his hour-long piece (originally aired on *This American Life*), the Dakotas tell a story of being worn to the bone by white occupation and finally rising up in the war, while the whites tell a story of being under attack and taking fair measures to punish the attackers. The institutions, however, ended up squarely on the white side: the mass execution took place and was virtually erased from local histories, the story of the war told forever from the perspective of the victors.

For Biewen, confronting the silences of white folks on the topic of indigenous people was a way to peel back the layers, to report honestly on his own origins. "In this series we were presenting a version of the nation's history that frankly is closer to the truth than the one that we get in school."

Biewen says he's always been a reporter first—not an activist or an advocate. But working on *Seeing White*, he developed more of a sense of mission than he'd ever had before in his career. "Can we get more white people having a truer analysis? And being more thoughtful about having a truer understanding of how we actually got here and who we are?"

Even with that sense of mission, Biewen maintains that his goal isn't to promote his individual point of view—it's to acknowledge it. He doesn't believe in objectivity, but he does believe in being as fair as possible with our sources and representing them carefully. "I'm not going to dwell on myself or tell you a whole bunch of stuff about my opinions and my presumptions," he said. "But I'm also not going to be shy about giving you a general sense."

But he does have an agenda in *Seeing White*: to expose whiteness as a lie that can't be untold but can be questioned and undermined.

"There's no capital-T truth there, but some things are certainly more true than others based on the evidence," he said. And the evidence often remains obscure if we aren't looking at whiteness, acknowledging the role of white supremacy in this country.

Still, I can see the problems that arise when you start to be perceived as a partisan, an opinion writer. No one likes being misrepresented, and conservative sources considering speaking to me might fear that they would contribute to a cause they didn't sign on to. A "neutral" journalist from *Marketplace* was a disguise I wore, in part to gain access to people and stories who might reject contact with a "biased" freelance reporter. Biewen said he's thought about this but has yet to encounter a source who felt he was unfair to them. I, too, continued to have good relationships with conservative sources, who seemed to appreciate my ability to listen.

And importantly, admitting where he's coming from is a way of deepening his ability to understand the world around him. As Biewen goes further into his study of whiteness, he remains a bastion of deep inquiry—more concerned with producing good questions than with settling on final answers. He still believes that there is always more to know.

· · ·

A journalist named Gary Younge also reports unflinchingly about white supremacy—both the overt kind and the kind that is reflective of a status quo of structures privileging white people in the United States. Younge is British and Black, and he traveled the US to report on white America for the *Guardian* after the 2016 election.

Mostly, he talked to regular white people—people who wanted a border wall or hated Obamacare or feared terrorism. Interviewing an avowed white supremacist was a choice he didn't make lightly. A short of video of him interviewing famed neo-Nazi Richard Spencer went viral in early 2017.

Much of the coverage of white supremacists in mainstream media has gone easy on them: calling them the "alt-right" (their preferred term), depicting them as surprisingly smart or handsome or normal, and just generally giving them plenty of space to air their confusing, delusional views. From the start, Younge gives these views no quarter, pushing hard with his questions. After Spencer calls white ethnostates a "safe space," Younge responds: "Safe space? Why do you need a safe space?" On the defensive, Spencer quickly spins out, telling Younge that "Africans have benefitted from their experience of white supremacy." Younge calls that "a ridiculous notion," and Spencer digs his heels in. "I'm proud to be a white man," he says, claiming that Black people have contributed nothing significant to world history. After less than three minutes, Younge says, "You don't know what you're talking about," and spins on his heels, ending the interview as Spencer smirks in front of the camera.

Younge said he mostly got positive feedback for going this hard on Spencer—especially from Black audiences. Some white people did tell him they thought he should have given more time for Spencer to talk, listened to his arguments more carefully. Younge laughs that off: "It comes from a position of, he's got a point of view and you've got a point of view, and you know reasonable people might disagree on whether white supremacy was good for black people, or black people benefit from slavery." Again, the Lost Cause echoes through our discourse, making a dishonest argument out of something that should have been settled long ago. An honest debate about the legacy of slavery in this country cannot start with the premise that it may or may not have even been bad.

This was a rare decision on Younge's part to provide coverage of a white supremacist who was *seeking* coverage for his ideas, which he felt could only be accompanied by tough questioning and immediate, on-camera challenges to Spencer's Lost Cause lies. And Younge is careful to distinguish between his interviews with neo-Nazi activists, and those with white Americans who benefit from whiteness and hold racist views, but don't necessarily seek a platform for those views. Younge didn't want to write takedowns of these Americans—he wanted to understand how their beliefs came to be, to put their beliefs in context.

"I think journalists should be curious, even with people that you don't like," he said. "It's a less inquisitorial and more kind of exploratory method. I actually want to know why people vote for Donald Trump. I don't want to tell them not to vote for Donald Trump. . . . My job is to find out what the hell is going on."

Younge strove to understand the grievances of white Americans, whether they aligned with his shared reality or not. By listening carefully, he came up with some incisive analysis. In an article in November 2017 about his travels in white America, he wrote, "Increasingly, for many white Americans, their racial privilege resides not in positive benefits of work and security but in the sole fact that it could be worse—they could be black or Latino. In other words, their whiteness is all they have left."

He observed that, as parts of the national media had reported already, much of white America *is* suffering—from cultural and economic loss, gun violence, opioid addiction, and suicide. Whites have privilege and power that people of color don't, but they are often unaware of that, by design.

"When your privilege amounts to this amount of pain, no wonder you can't see it," wrote Younge. "But just because you can't see it, doesn't mean it's not there."

This is a conundrum of the journalist documenting whiteness: white people experience it and benefit from it, but often they don't even believe it's there. It takes the form, instead, of insidious fantasies about people of color—they are terrorists, they are taking our jobs, they are going to mug us in the inner city or rape us in a back alley. No matter that all of that is statistically unsound and obscenely unlikely. These racial myths live on, making whiteness hard to look at, if not hard to see. It's a fiction with real consequences, and as journalists, we come seeking truth.

. . .

The fictions of white supremacy and anti-Blackness too often lead to mass violence. In 2018 writer Rachel Kaadzi Ghansah won the Pulitzer Prize for Feature Writing for a story in *GQ* about white supremacist Dylann Roof, who killed nine Black people in an AME church in Charleston while Barack Obama was still president. Roof is from the same place as my mom's family—Columbia, South Carolina—and Ghansah spent months in Columbia and Charleston, studying white supremacy by talking to Roof's family and friends. She was amazed by their passivity, their confusion about what had happened.

I heard her on a podcast talking about her original motive for doing the story: she hated the way Roof sat silently through his own trial. "Over and over again, without even bothering to open his mouth, Roof reminded us that he did not have to answer to anyone," she'd written in the 2017 *GQ* article.

She wanted to make the people in his life explain themselves, to force blood from a stone, to understand the cultural and political forces that made him. The story should be read in its entirety, but this part in particular stood out to me: "Roof is what happens when we prefer vast historical erasures to real education about race. The rise of groups like Trump's Republican Party, with its overtures to the alt-right, has emboldened men like Dylann Roof to come out of their slumber and loudly, violently out themselves. But in South Carolina, those men never disappeared, were there always, waiting. It is possible that Dylann Roof is not an outlier at all, then, but rather emblematic of an approaching storm."

She suggests a wisdom about racism that much of the reporting on Roof shied away from: It is always there, waiting. She is open about her perspective, the framework that underlies her deep curiosity about the fantasy of white supremacy. She's not "objective." But "objectivity" asks that we accept our current structures of dominance as inevitable, that we accept Roof's silence as the final explanation for what he did. Reporting on whiteness, too often, has stopped at that silence, ended with a shrug.

Rachel Kaadzi Ghansah, John Biewen, and Gary Younge are just a few examples of journalists who challenge white supremacy through their journalism: they reject the premise of whiteness and explore alternative ways of looking at it with depth and honesty. By questioning whiteness itself, their work suggests that being oppressed, poor, or targeted for being Black is no more inevitable than being privileged for being white. They're not advocating a policy position or a partisan stance, and they're not being dishonest about their sources or distorting their perspectives. But they *are* doing ideological work: they put their sources' words into a different frame than the one that normalizes and accepts white male superiority and privilege.

If embracing anti-racism is a path to more true stories, and to more justice in the world, I can only believe that it's a path more journalists should walk. How we understand power structures—as either inevitable or constructed, natural or learned, consensual or forced—matters a great deal to the questions we ask about race, class, gender, and identity in this era. The answer isn't to settle for less truth, or to give up on skepticism in favor of cynicism, but to stay vigilant about the role of power and oppression in our search for stories that are true.

10

THE "ASSAULT ON REALITY"

Trans People and Subjectivity

> In reality, is the subject a boy or a girl?
> DR. GAFFE, writing in a French medical journal in 1885

I went in for a diagnosis, but I already knew what I had. The trick was to tell the symptoms just as the doctor wanted to hear. And I knew, from reading and from hearsay, what she'd require me to say: I can't stand my body. I have been wanting to live as male for as long as I remember, and I have been living as male for at least a year. All I want in the world is to make my femaleness disappear.

With that, I could get a letter saying I had gender identity disorder, in the psychiatric parlance of the early 2000s. That letter would allow me to get a surgery to alter my body to feel more aligned with my inner sense of self, my inner "sex."

These psychiatric appointments were absurd, a performance for an audience of one who was also in on the joke. But the shrink wrote me the letter, which I showed to my parents and to a plastic surgeon in Texas before I got my breasts removed in 2005.

I was twenty-one when I had the surgery—a double mastectomy with nipple reconstruction—and I had been out as transgender for a little over five years. How did I "know" this was the "real" me? Why would someone as effeminate and soft as I was want to "live full-time as a man," as I had told the psychiatrist at the free clinic in San Francisco?

Well, I had lied. I didn't want to live full-time as a man. I wanted surgery in order to align with an inner sense of self that had little representation in either medical or media discourses about trans people at the time. I had to lie to get the letter, and I had to get the letter to get the surgery. So, I pretended to be normal, or at least normative, a normal male stuck in a female frame, despite the fact that this story never resonated with me.

When I made this choice, I was changing my own body, but through this change, I was also helping to change what was possible in the world. It was a world, at the time, that said that people like me—nongendered, genderqueer, or nonbinary people—simply didn't exist. There were men, and women, and a few folks born in the "wrong" bodies who simply needed to be corrected through medical intervention. I knew I was none of these, and so I had to help create a new language, both linguistic and somatic, a new kind of body for myself. In doing so, I also changed reality. This insight that we have the power to change reality has been with me since I was young, and it is key to my understanding of what journalism is—and could be.

Throughout my exploration of "objectivity," there remains a nagging question for me about the underlying philosophical problem of facticity and truth claims themselves. "Objectivity" isn't only a set of protocols for being unbiased, fair, and balanced that I reject because it is impossible, impractical, or oppressive (though I think these are all true). It hinges on a more fundamental belief that there is a knowable world, a way of seeing that, once we set aside our own subjectivities, can be universally achieved or at least universally agreed upon. It hinges on an understanding of truth that turns all bodies and shapes into objects—the ocean, the human body, human events can ultimately be known and spoken of and described from some unassailable point of view. It is this objectification, not just the protocols of journalistic "objectivity," that I believe make it an unsalvageable framework. I'm far from the first, of course, to come to this conclusion. "Objectivity" has been debunked and debated for decades now in the fields of history, philosophy, anthropology, gender and race studies, to name only a few.

If we can only ever see through our own subjectivities, isn't the attempt to tell true stories futile? If nothing can be definitely "proven," can anything at all be true? In a way, that one's easy to answer: Dispensing with the myth of objectivity is not about rejecting the possibility of truth altogether; it's about accepting the possibility of multiple truths.

I have found that trans experience—my own and other people's—is great material through which to look at these questions, because it has always been filtered through clearly subjective lenses, and the terms of the discussion continue to change constantly. And trans experience has granted me an insight into journalistic work: we may be trapped in our subjectivities as writers and as human beings, but that only serves to highlight the importance of choice in our public and private lives—of choosing our values and practices and frames, as people and as storytellers. These choices are powerful, because stories don't just reflect reality, but they help to create it—just as I created a new reality when I came out as trans at age sixteen.

. . .

In 2010, while studying religion in college, I read a medieval text called *The Romance of Silence*. Written in the thirteenth century, it's the story of a child born female to a pair of British nobles. Her parents, aware of the patriarchal inheritance laws at the time, decide to raise her as a boy so that she can inherit their land when they die. Silence—that's the child's name—is sent to the woods just after birth, to be reared in secret by a nanny who will teach him to be a boy, and then a young man.

It's a fabulous narrative. At fourteen, Silence runs away with a couple of traveling minstrels and becomes a celebrity in the courts of France, beloved for his gorgeous voice and cherubic face. There's drama and intrigue, queens and princesses who fall in love with him, near-misses with robbers and murderers on the streets of Dark Ages Europe.

But the part of this old French *roman* that most fascinated me was a strange scene that takes place in the woods during Silence's travels. Silence is alone, and two characters emerge from the forest, debating fiercely. Their names are Nature and Nurture, and they are arguing over who Silence is going to be—Nature claims that Silence is truly a woman, unable to ever fully inhabit manhood due to her nature. Nurture claims that Silence is truly a man, trained and reared as a man and therefore only skilled in the ways of manhood.

Silence listens to the debate, trapped between two worlds. When he finally weighs in, it's only to say that he doesn't know for sure. He can never be truly womanly, he reasons, because he hasn't been taught how. But he's not sure his nature is as a man, either—if he could be a woman, would he want to? Maybe. The story goes on, Silence a "he" until nearly the end of the dramatic tale (no spoilers here, just in case I ever get to make that *Romance of Silence* Netflix series one day).

Silence and his body become a symbol—in medieval times, perhaps a symbol of femaleness or vulnerability. For me, reading the story in the twenty-first century, he becomes a symbol for the ways in which transgender people are debated and discussed, without being granted the authority to weigh in. This symbolism goes all the way down to his name: in the nature/nurture debate, he has the most information about the tension, and yet it is he who is silent.

. . .

Since I've been looking for discussions and debates over realness, bias, and objectivity, I have started to see them everywhere. Recently I clicked on a link to an article in the conservative *National Review*, "The Assault on Reality," by freelance writer Rachel Lu.

The article is a review of a new book by an activist named Ryan T. Anderson, *When Harry Became Sally: Responding to the Transgender Moment*. "The Assault on Reality" is a perfect specimen of the problem that "objectivity" presents for transgender people. Behold the opening lines: "What is it like to be a bat? In a famous 1974 article, philosopher Thomas Nagel addressed this question and declared, brazenly, that we can't know. That may not sound like an impressive conclusion, but it's actually an interesting essay. Nagel's point is that subjective experience is by nature a closed book." (Nagel was an influential philosopher, whose book *The View from Nowhere* has helped shape my thinking about the limits of subjectivity and objectivity alike, and his argument in the bat article was about the limits of objectivity.)

Lu's point, however, is that being a man or a woman is *not* like being a bat. The second paragraph of the article ridicules the idea that gender is subjective—a personal experience that can only be described by the person experiencing it. She and author Ryan T. Anderson consider this thinking not just ideological, but impossible. Impossible because so-called transgender ideology begins with the premise that someone who is assigned female at birth can simply declare that they are male.

"It's easy to lose track of reality when we *begin* by elevating subjective experience to a position of infallible authority. The popular transgender narrative offers a harrowing illustration of how this can happen," Lu contends. She writes disparagingly, almost desperately, about the existence of children much like the one I had been: "The child who gleefully exchanged her bunny slippers for soccer cleats might end up as a weirdly androgynous, baby-faced 20-year-old, scarred by surgery and sterile for life."

There is still relatively little data on transgender people and identities, even in the arena of health. But anti-trans advocates nonetheless point to whatever evidence they can find for the failure of what they call the transgender agenda. In her article Lu, like Anderson in his book, cites a small group of highly publicized stories of "detransitioners," people who transitioned gender in some way and then changed their minds and regret that transition, as evidence of the potentially damaging effects of the trans movement. Most frequently, though, they cite biology itself: they believe contemporary gender theory is a hoax, with the only reality for them being biological alignment between being male and being a man, being female and being a woman.

"In a better world," laments Lu, "transgender theory might provide promising fodder for philosophical debate. Unfortunately, it's escaped from the ivory tower."

But the possibility of a gender-transgressive identity predates some recent descent from an ivory tower—it spans thousands of years of global history. People were asking whether gender was a matter of nature or nurture, soul or body, as early as there was inquiry, and cultures around the world have also recognized third genders in many cases.

It's only been around 150 years since the Western medicalized model of sex/gender alignment took hold. While the concept of men and women had existed in many cultures for a long time, what "made" someone a man or a woman started out hazy. A binary model for primary and secondary sex characteristics, determined by X and Y chromosomes at birth, first appeared in the mid- to late 1800s alongside advancements in the study of biology, and when these categories first emerged as medical "realities," they were not entirely easy to narrow down. There were people with ambiguous chromosomes, genitals, and secondary sex characteristics, some of whom would now be called intersex. There were also people we'd now call "trans"—born one way but seeking gender expressions and bodily modifications early on out of a deep desire to appear another way.

Nonetheless, this new medicalized understanding of human biology began to explain sex as a natural, scientific, and predetermined category, with gender identity following naturally along. Medical science became a justification for performing nonconsensual surgeries on people born with intersex characteristics as well as an explanation for the danger or even the impossibility of transgender existence.

This same binary understanding of sex became the framework for early trans medicine. Records of the "treatment" of transsexuals for their condition first begin to show up in the 1930s and 1940s—as surgical technologies developed, people who felt an innate sense of being a different gender than their assigned one sought out surgical and hormonal assistance. In the beginning, in order to access medical services such as hormones and surgeries, transsexuals were required to attest that their transitions would turn them into "normal" heterosexual men or women—extreme typologies of masculinity and femininity. Unless one's innate sense of being female aligned with hyperfemininity, that sense wasn't "verifiable" by the doctors in charge (and vice versa for transmasculine people, who had to show they were both straight and hypermasculine). These standards, first codified in the 1970s by Dr. Harry Benjamin and still in use by some doctors today, became a self-fulfilling prophecy—only those with the most extreme binary gender expressions could access care, which created a story about trans people that said we all wanted to be hypermasculine, or hyperfeminine, and straight.

Perhaps counterintuitively, the movement to make trans identity visible also eventually led to its categorization as a mental illness. Gender identity disorder (GID) appeared for the first time in the third edition of the American Psychiatric Association's *Diagnostic and Statistical Manual of Mental Disorders* (*DSM-III*) in 1980—the same year homosexuality was removed from the psychiatric guide. Mental health, like journalism and social science, is a subjective and socially shaped practice and study, further complicated for trans people by the fact that barriers in health care mean we often depend on diagnoses to access care that we need, however subjective the acquisition of these diagnoses might be. In addition, these barriers and definitions are shaped by cultural and health care systems—in the US, federal and state agencies and insurance companies are among those involved in defining and gatekeeping gender nonconformity.

Gender identity disorder, for which I received a diagnosis in 2005, was replaced in the *DSM-V* by gender dysphoria in 2013. I "objectively" had a mental illness that now no longer exists. Was it I who committed the assault on reality?

· · ·

"Objectivity"—and the matter of what a person's objective, true gender or sex actually is—courses through all of these categorizations and debates. The general belief has been that trans people must be studied, "proven," before we can be validated or helped. As trans activist and psychotherapist Patrick Califia wrote in 1998, "To be differently-gendered is to live within a discourse where other people are always investigating you, describing you, and speaking for you; and putting as much distance as possible between the expert speaker and the deviant and therefore deficient subject." Like Silence in the medieval *roman*, trans and gender-variant people have been subjects; others look at us objectively. That was the paradigm into which I came out as trans in the late 1990s.

It's only in these last two decades that the word "transgender" has

come into popular use, and transgender identities are evolving rapidly—in the mid-1990s, female-to-male and male-to-female transsexuals were still broadly assumed to be the only kinds of transgender
people. My discovery of my trans identity coincided with a massive
expansion of possibility—trans, genderqueer, gender nonconform-
ing, nonbinary, agender, Two Spirit, and many other categories were
birthed or rebirthed in the United States. By the time you're reading
this, it's nearly guaranteed that new words will have been coined, new
identities spawned. Many young trans activists today reject the medical terminology of "transsexual" altogether. When I was a teenager, my
friends and I advocated for the use of "ze" and "hir" as gender-neutral
pronouns. These days, "they" and "them" as singular, gender-neutral
pronouns are in use everywhere from classrooms to NPR and the *New
York Times Magazine*.

Much of this social change has been driven by media, although not
always the news media: transgender culture in the 1990s depended
on a robust network of 'zine writers, self-publishers, musicians, and
word-of-mouth storytellers to spread ideas. I was an active part of creating and sustaining this culture, writing 'zines about gender identity as
early as 1998. I met some of my longest-term friends and collaborators
through this underground media, where we carried out debates that
were many years from appearing in mainstream papers or TV news.

. . .

I remember clearly the first time I saw a mainstream media representation of a trans person who seemed at least somewhat like me. It was in
the movie *Boys Don't Cry*, a 1999 release that told the story of the 1993
murder of a young transgender man named Brandon Teena.

The movie was inspired by a long report in the *Village Voice* about
Teena and his two friends who were also killed—but the story, written by cisgender lesbian journalist Donna Minkowitz, led to criticism
and protest from trans advocates because it referred to Brandon as
"she" and assumed that he was a lesbian living out a male fantasy due
to childhood trauma. Minkowitz believed she was doing a fair story
about the murder; transgender activists saw her take as offensively off-

base, so much so that they showed up at the offices of the *Village Voice* to confront her. Such has been the relationship between trans activists and news media for much of the intervening period.

In 2018 someone forwarded me a long piece in the *Village Voice* in which Minkowitz apologized for the ignorance that led to her original take on Brandon Teena. She had fretted about it for years. Over time, she'd realized that her view of Brandon was not his own view—and that was a problem. Trans activists contended that because he lived as male and went by male pronouns, Brandon Teena was a man. He died for his choice to live as male. In retrospect, Minkowitz figures the least she could have done is respect this choice. Her searing self-critique ends with this: "All stories are partial, but the deaths go on in their fullness."

These problems of "objectivity" and choice, and of the partialness of every story, show up again and again in the battles over trans representation. Put simply, there is no "objective" criteria for reporting on trans people. For example, if someone's legal name or gender differs from the name or pronouns they use, an "objective" take could mean giving their legal name, or it could mean giving the name and gender of their preference. It could mean both. Some will argue that trans people are in fact "objectively" who we say we are—a useful argument, say, if you are talking to a journalist who prides themselves on their "objectivity." But I think our response to trans identities is a value judgment for journalists, not an "objective" one based on agreed criteria available in the observable world. In short, objectivity isn't the right frame for talking about trans folks—not because it arrives at "wrong" conclusions, but because gender is subjective and ever-changing. It can't be proven, but it still seems to exist. For trans people, our view of our own bodies and lives, our view from somewhere, is precisely the thing we need to be respected. We could try to establish ourselves as "objective," as I did when I got my GID diagnosis, but it invariably leads to more gatekeeping. Subjectivity isn't the problem here—it's the answer to the problem.

· · ·

When Meredith Talusan, a PhD student in comparative literature, found herself thrown into the world of journalism in 2014, she knew she would never pretend to have a view from nowhere. Like me, she had half a lifetime of being out as transgender to tell her that one person's "truth" is often markedly different from another's.

When I interviewed her via Skype, she shared an anecdote from a recent work trip to Austin, Texas. A cabdriver had dropped her off and said, "Have a good trip, sir!" Ten steps later, in the hotel, the bellman said to her, "Have a good stay, ma'am." The day before she told me this story, I'd sold my car in the morning to a guy from craigslist who was calling me "he" and bought a new car in the evening from a dealership at which everyone referred to me as "she." In addition to our own experiences of gender being subjective, there's truly no accounting for other people's subjective experiences of our genders. We both laughed for a minute and moved on; gender whiplash is normal to us.

Talusan, who is a friend of mine from the small community of transgender journalists I know in New York, came into journalism in part because of the rising demand for trans writers with strong voices. She started out, as many online writers do, writing personal essays and "takes," and gradually developed a skill set as a reporter.

In the summer of 2014, after she'd been freelancing for a while and was working on her PhD, she traveled across the South to report on trans southerners. During the trip, she ended up randomly meeting someone in Atlanta whose friend was being tried for aggravated assault, but the friend said he had been gay-bashed and had responded in self-defense. Talusan took an interest in the seemingly strange details of the story—there were inconsistent accounts from witnesses, and the defendant himself, Luke O'Donovan, seemed to have struck the first blow. She found herself inclined to believe his claim of self-defense: he was queer and, like Talusan, identified as bisexual and poly. She wanted to believe him.

But she really wasn't sure whether O'Donovan was telling the truth, and she became fascinated with the conundrum. "I ended up being really interested in my position as a reporter in that story, as a trans person, and I wanted that to be in the story." The piece of writing that emerged was both an investigation into the stabbings, and a critique of objectivity and its limits. Talusan admitted that she could never know for sure what had happened, and that her own biases brought both insight and limitations to her investigation. The final line of Talusan's first feature report, which was published on the Medium website *Archipelago*, was "This is my stab at the truth."

She went on to publish a series of popular and influential articles, both essays and reported features, for national outlets, and in 2015 she became a staff writer at BuzzFeed News—the first out trans writer covering the LGBTQ beat on staff, and one of few openly trans writers at any national outlet. BuzzFeed had built its popularity on the basis of fluffy and often openly political "listicles" and clickbait cultural commentary, but at the time, it was expanding its journalistic offerings and aspired to a more traditionally detached, third-person stance.

Talusan says this created problems for her style of writing from the get-go—she was good at both first-person writing and at third-person reporting, and she was keenly interested in the relationship between the two. But she said her reported work was supposed to "follow a specific editorial template, which did not include the subject position of the writer."

Talusan and I were both working in Manhattan newsrooms in June 2016, when we woke up on a Sunday morning to the terrifying news about the Pulse massacre in Orlando: forty-nine people killed in a gay bar, many of them Latinx, Puerto Ricans, and immigrants. Our overlapping queer communities in New York were in deep grief, connecting to and identifying with the victims. And both of us, later that month, were sent to Orlando to cover the massacre—in Meredith's case, to do searing feature reporting on the victims for BuzzFeed, in my case, to report on job and housing discrimination against LGBTQ people in Florida for *Marketplace*.

Talusan worked her personal connections to gain close access to the surviving victims and their friends and families. She was present at the first gathering of Pulse employees after the shooting, sat in the dressing room during benefit drag shows with people who were performing and still grieving at once. She was aware, covering Pulse, of both her connections and her limitations: she was queer and trans and an immigrant (Talusan moved to the US from the Philippines as a child), but she was also an outsider who didn't speak Spanish, a reporter for a national outlet dipping into a strange community at a time of extreme trauma.

Still, what BuzzFeed wanted from her was, at a minimum, the performance of objectivity in her pieces. Talusan pushed back. "I didn't want to resituate myself as if I wasn't a part of the community, which I disagreed with from a philosophical perspective," she told me. "All of those assumptions are based on a notion of neutrality that doesn't exist, and that is fundamentally cis and white and straight and able-bodied."

In her BuzzFeed story "This Is How Queer People in Orlando Are Mourning after the Pulse Shooting," she was allowed to be somewhat transparent. She wrote that some of her sources "adopted her," making her part of their family during her week or so in Orlando. She shared intimate observations of these sources. But in the end, she wrote, "As much as I and so many other queer people have imagined and identified with what they must be dealing with, there's no way to fully understand what it's like to lose that specific friend or lover, that specific cherished sanctuary of a club—the one you've relied on as a home for your chosen family."

Her role as an observer was limited: identity is subjective, and so is grief. The beauty of her story is that she acknowledges both.

. . .

When I started in journalism, I had quickly adopted the supposedly impartial, impersonal tone of public radio despite my doubts about it. I was impressed with Talusan's clarity on the matter: she ended up leaving BuzzFeed News in part because even there, she didn't feel free to explore her own point of view in pieces.

"It's always been a really important facet of my work to be really clear about my subject position, and to assert my right to embed it in my stories," she told me.

Why had she been so attached to her subjectivity, I asked her. Why not strive for the tone BuzzFeed and other news outlets wanted?

"I find it retrograde and anachronistic in journalism," she said, "because these conversations have been so live in the past twenty years in history and literary theory. Assuming a neutral position, both in history and philosophy—there's so much evidence that what that really means is positioning the privileged majority as neutral. Even the very words, the very language that we're using to express ourselves is not neutral."

To her, it's absolutely not incidental that she's a trans Filipina writer, and someone who is often mistaken for being cisgender and white. (Talusan is albino and has light skin, eyes, and hair unlike many people from the Philippines.)

"People from my background so rarely get to be in positions where we can tell these stories ourselves," she said. "You're not gonna get me to behave like a cis white person, because that to me would be the very definition of being tokenized."

And yet I see a hole in her argument, and in my own. The problem comes back to "the assault on reality," the idea that some people have that the state of even *being* transgender is objectively impossible. If everything is, in fact, subjective, aren't our detractors as entitled to their point of view as we are to ours? I may believe I am trans; you may believe I am not. Right?

I asked Meredith this, and she rolled her eyes to the ceiling and back, making sure I saw her do it.

"That's a straw man," she said, "that's ridiculous. There's a set of facts that a vast proportion of people can agree upon by consensus. . . . There's a key distinction between your perspective on a fact and a person denying the existence of a fact itself, or reversing a fact."

In other words, for her, a big portion of what we cover as journalists, while it may not be "objectively" true, is factual by dint of collective agreement and empirical, observed data. The sky is blue; we have bodies and move around; the sun sets. We all see it, or experience it, and so it's there. That doesn't mean she's not constantly aware of subjectivity, even the relativity of truth claims. We talked about an article we'd both recently seen posted in which an anti-trans activist referred to transgender women as men, repeatedly. But if gender is subjective and constructed, what, I asked her, is your argument against this?

"My objection to calling trans women men is not because there is a fundamental or objective truth about calling trans women men," she said. She objects because it is disrespectful and goes against the self-determination of the group. She says that we live in a society that at least nominally strives to allow minority groups to self-define. We can acknowledge that gender identity is subjective, but the matter of respecting trans people's gender identities is a matter of social contract and respect, not "objectivity."

In other words, it's a choice.

Still, transgender people face practical problems when we depend on subjectivity to account for our truths. Accessing services and basic public and private safety measures requires some determination that we are "really" the gender we say we are, regardless of the fact that in a fierce search for a purely genetic explanation behind gender identity, biologists have found nothing definitive. Medical care in the United States, for example, is often gendered; prisons, bathrooms, and many other spaces in the United States are gender-segregated; and certain types of hormones and surgery, while freely available to those who are not taking them in order to change genders, are highly restricted for those who are. So trans activists have sought data, research, and some "objective" evidence of our need for various treatments and protections—and evidence of our existence, period. There is still no comprehensive survey of gender identity in the US, but a 2011 study by the Williams Institute at UCLA found that trans people made up 0.3 percent of the US population. That, too, appears to be changing quickly: a 2016 study by the Williams Institute doubled it to 0.6 percent.

· · ·

I don't propose that we try to prove the objective realness of trans experience; instead, we need to reframe the value of subjectivities. We can't see, can't know, can't verify one another's experience—creating a society that embraces trans people is inherently about accepting a multiplicity of truths. And this change requires a value system. The question becomes not whether transgender people can exist (we can and do), or even how many of us there are, but *how* we will exist. Anti-trans activists have coined the term "gender ideology" as a derisive phrase for all that's wrong with America today. But there's a funny way in which I agree with them: I, too, think that gender is ideological, and that how we engage with it is a choice that reflects our specific cultural, political, and historical frameworks. It's this shifting notion of choice, rather than the frozen accusation of "ideology," that interests me most.

"To Be, or Not to Be" is the title of a brilliant essay by Russian journalist Masha Gessen, published in the *New York Review of Books* in early 2018. Gessen, who does not have a preference as to pronouns, was speaking at the New York Public Library in December 2017 when they first presented the essay, which is organized around seven terms: *fetus, vulnerable, diversity, entitlement, science-based, transgender,* and *evidence-based* are the subject heads in the print article. The significance of these words was obvious to audiences in the US at the time: they were the seven terms reportedly discouraged from use in budget documents at the US Centers for Disease Control and Prevention. Under the Trump administration, CDC officials reasoned they'd have an easier time getting their proposals through if they just avoided words like "transgender," "diversity," and "evidence-based."

To me, it's no coincidence that "transgender" and "science-based" were struck out with the same pen. Their association with one another reveals the extent to which we in the United States are in a battle right now over truth and narrative. The use of the word "transgender" makes transgender existence possible; the use of "evidence-based" evokes the existence, too, of realities some conservatives would prefer not to face, such as the reality that abortion is usually a very safe procedure. This kind of censorship admits that language constitutes and creates reality—otherwise the word "vulnerable" wouldn't be so threatening.

Gessen comes at the discussion from a unique position—as a queer person born in Russia, whose parents brought them to the United

States as a child, only to see Gessen return to Russia as an American journalist in their twenties. Gessen stayed in Russia until they couldn't anymore—they were driven out in 2012 on the basis of being queer, the government threatening to send social services for their children.

On returning to the US, they describe coming back to a changed landscape, one in which many of the people they'd known as "women" had come out as transgender.

At first, Gessen was resentful of these choices. "I too had always felt like a boy!" But, they write, they adjusted to the idea of a different set of choices, of paths not taken because of their context: "Here I was, faced with the possibility that in the parallel life that my left-behind self was leading in the United States while I was in Russia, I would have transitioned. True gender (whatever that means) didn't have much to do with it, but choice did. Somehow, I'd missed the fact that it was there."

Gessen, who'd had a double mastectomy and their ovaries removed due to the threat of cancer in their genetics, quit taking estrogen and began taking testosterone—a low dose. "I have no idea how it's going to affect me," they write. "My voice has become lower. My body is changing. But then again, bodies change all the time."

Indeed, gender changes, bodies change, language changes. It is a gift of being human to have power and agency over these changes. And Gessen, expert at living under a totalitarian government, observes that agency—a sense of choice—is precisely the thing that threatens autocrats and dictators.

"Totalitarian regimes aim to make choice impossible," they write, arguing that autocracy is always about choicelessness: the autocrat relieves people of the need to make a choice, brings comfort to the masses by limiting their options. Choice, as they depict it, requires imagination, and imagination is the fabric of resistance.

Choice is a controversial way of talking about transgender experience, particularly within trans communities. After all, if it's "just a choice," then why should we have the right to health coverage or bathrooms that reflect our identities? But I think it's an empowering one, too. It acknowledges that this society hasn't always been safe for trans people—we have had to choose, to activate and push, in order to make it so.

"A choice may have to be defended—certainly, one has to be prepared to defend one's right to make a choice—while arguing that you were born this way appeals to people's sympathy or at least a sense of decency," writes Gessen. They don't weigh in on whether there could be something innate about being trans, but they suggest that the trouble with being "born this way" (queer or transgender) is that it doesn't make our choices less threatening to the status quo—the Russian autocrats and the homophobic parts of the Christian church don't care if we were born that way or not. They care what we do with our bodies, the choices we make.

. . .

I came out as trans very young, and it now feels inevitable that I would have—almost as if I had to. But I still believe it was a choice. If I'd been born in medieval times, like Silence, maybe I'd have made do as a cross-dressing minstrel or a secretly lesbian nun. Maybe I'd have found a nice effeminate man to settle down with, playing with our genders behind closed doors. Maybe I'd have had fewer choices than that: condemned to a life of sexual assault and servitude, as so many female-assigned people have been in European cultures. If I'd been born in the 1950s, maybe I'd have killed myself.

The point is, I view my own transness as both essential to my being and contextual: a choice that comes out of a combination of nature, nurture, and culture. This idea may be grounds for some to discount the likes of me as delusional—a mentally ill young woman unable to face my own womanhood. But rather than claiming some essential nature, I prefer to claim desire and choice—to claim the idea that gender, like language, is a form of expression I'm interested in liberating through my actions. If my existence, and my articulation of it, is an "assault on reality," so be it.

Journalists in the twenty-first century could use a similarly nuanced take on subjectivity and power. The journalist whose stories show what is possible threatens and undermines the concentration of power in the hands of a few. So does the transgender person, the queer person, the border-crosser. Black Lives Matter activists probe the role of choice and agency in police killings and racial profiling, calling for accountability. Young people advocating for gun control or against climate change ask what choices we can make now that will let them grow up into another world, one that is further from destruction, closer to safety and belonging for all. When we choose to tell these stories, or ignore them, we are shaping what is possible. The same is true when we choose to refer to transgender women as women, or use nonbinary pronouns in a story, or discuss trans people on their own terms.

I hope journalists can face these choices—and make them from a place of hope and principle, rather than hiding beyond "objectivity." Standing to the side of history is impossible when we are the ones writing it.

11

THE VIEW FROM SOMEWHERE

It was August again, hot and damp. I was back in the Midwest, this time for a ten-day reporting trip in Detroit. One of my stories was about a man, Kevin Matthews, who was killed by police, unarmed, near the border of Dearborn and Detroit just before Christmas of 2015. He had a serious psychological disability, someone his family described like a child in an adult's body.

I sat for an afternoon with Matthews's family in their suburban lawyer's office. His mother and sister and thirty-year-old younger brother eyed me suspiciously as I sat down, calmly set up my microphone, and began to ask questions, stretching my arm across the conference room table toward each of them as their great, unthinkable pain unfurled in front of me. His mother was a small woman, hunched and dark-eyed, almost unable to speak. She was a housecleaner by profession, but had barely worked since Kevin died, immobilized with grief. When Kevin's younger brother, thin and hunched like their mother, finally talked, he broke down into choking sobs. I could feel my eyes go wide trying to take in the pain of their stories, their collective grief, trying not to lose my cool. Maybe the worst part was that he'd been killed by people he had trusted. Kevin loved everybody, they said, even cops. They all wished they had done more to protect him.

This family probably met with me because they wanted desperately to have Kevin's story told to a national audience, a power I had at the time. There had been protests, but they had never grown big enough to get his name in national news, to force his memory onto the world. I think I already knew then that my story on *Marketplace* probably wouldn't accomplish that. Of course, one hopes that listening and telling helps heal pain, but who knows. I didn't know, and I don't know if it felt that way for them, either. So while I absorbed this family's unbearable trauma, I remained clear with myself that I was no savior. I was there to get a story and go home.

I was also working on a series about the devastated mortgage market in the city, modern-day redlining. Since the housing crash, lenders weren't making mortgage loans in Detroit; the vast majority of transactions were happening in cash, and investors would scoop up houses for $1,000 or $5,000 a pop, speculating on which neighborhoods might "come back." In large swaths of run-down neighborhoods, unless you had cash, the only way to buy a house was through the unregulated market in land contracts. These unregulated land contract sales were often predatory—giving people homes cheap, but with high interest and hidden costs. Often enough, the buyer would fall back on the payments, and the seller would repossess the house, a few thousand bucks richer, then "sell" it again to someone else.

I was looking for a "character" for this story, someone who'd been sold a house in Detroit under a bad land contract. After some door-knocking and a day in eviction court, I met a lawyer from a nonprofit who connected me with a Black man in his fifties named Eddie Cave.

I rolled up to Cave's place, and at first it seemed that no one was there. It was a two-story house, blue-gray, with a pretty peaked roof on a quiet street north of downtown. There was a classic car with flat tires in the driveway, and out front, an electric wheelchair sat empty, connected to a cord that ran around to a generator in the back. I called Cave's cell over and over, and finally he picked up, apologizing profusely; he was upstairs, and he'd taken some pain pills earlier and fallen asleep. Eddie struggled down the steps on crutches and met me out front, where he collapsed into the chair. I pulled out my recording equipment and sat on the cement steps in the sun to interview him.

It turned out this house, which he'd "bought" for just $2,500 on a land contract, had no running water, no electricity, and no heat. He ran space heaters from the generator out back and cooked on a propane stove inside the dark kitchen. When his legs were feeling better, Eddie had been painting the place, beautiful blue shades that complemented the Victorian-style oak woodwork. It was a classically beautiful Detroit house, but shadowy, and marked with Eddie's obvious loneliness. Now the trouble was that the "sellers" were trying to take the house back after he fell behind on payments—he hadn't realized he would owe thousands of dollars more in back taxes that the seller had dropped into the contract, which he signed with no lawyer advising him. A local nonprofit was trying to bail him out so that he could keep the house from tax foreclosure.

Cave had wire-rimmed glasses and a giant smile, salt-and-pepper whiskers on his gaunt face. He reminded me of people I'd known, queer men (although I never asked his orientation), and he alluded to a past in which he was part of a big, active community. He'd been a DJ in New York City, where he's from, but most of his friends had died, he said, from AIDS or crack. He'd been in Detroit for a couple decades, surviving his own disability and trying to do work in his community. I listened for hours, letting Cave offer up anything he wanted to share as I prepared to create an image of him as more than just a victim of his circumstances, a full person. At some point, sitting in the sun together, he hugged me from his chair and started to sob freely. He'd bought this house because he wanted a safe haven—for himself, and for the kids on the block. He just wanted to get back to where he could DJ block parties, he said, give back to his neighborhood. He didn't want to be the one getting help. He wanted to be a journalist. "You're a beautiful person," he said, smiling into my eyes. "So are you," I said, unselfconscious about the microphone between us.

. . .

I sat in the Detroit Airport later that same day, drinking hard liquor at 2 p.m. next to this fountain that sends sculptural streams of water shooting across a pool in hypnotizing patterns. I'm sensitive to anniversaries: August was when John Crawford III was killed in Beavercreek in 2014, the year #BlackLivesMatter really took off. Now it was 2016, the end of the Obama era with an election on the way, and from where I stood, Detroit looked like a devastating expanse of unanswered calls for help. I had grown up with the idea of this city, forty-five minutes away, seared in my mind: it was "dangerous" and "sad." Now, the image of Eddie Cave moving slowly through his home on crutches, lighting his propane stove, eclipsed those old images. My mind filled with the sound of Kevin Matthews's younger brother, sobbing in that conference room, the sterile fluorescent lights beating down on all of us.

Growing up, so many white people had talked about "helping" or saving Detroit, and now there was this narrative that the city was "coming back" because white people were moving there. I hated this story. I wanted to resist any sense of white saviorism, any idea that my journalism was somehow going to save people when it wasn't. Grief-stricken as I was, I really *didn't* see myself as helping my sources—I was aware that probably they were helping me more than I was them.

I got back to the shiny high-rise where *Marketplace*'s New York studios were housed, loaded with what radio people call "good tape," powerful stories plucked from the ruins of decades of racial segregation and institutional white supremacy, tears and lonesomeness, captured with deep empathy. I tried to do stories that talked about all of this in context, put a finger on who and what is to blame, but ultimately Eddie Cave got four minutes, hardly time to explain the mortgage market and paint a quick picture of his quiet block. Kevin Matthews and his family got six minutes. Later I would use my Detroit clips to apply for jobs and fellowships.

Periodically during my years in public radio, I descended into a similar despair about what I saw as the extractive, exploitive nature of my work. I wanted to reconcile the contradictions, to believe I was doing right by people, but it called to mind one of my favorite books, Janet Malcolm's *The Journalist and the Murderer*. It's a story about a journalist covering a murder, but she also compares journalists to murderers—in that we are people whose vocation calls on us to deceive our sources, make them believe we are their friends when in fact we are just purveyors of whichever part of their story we deem the most useful, the most true. She implies that journalism is a sociopathic calling, at its root.

As journalism is taught and practiced today, I can't say I disagree. Good intentions aren't enough when you're dealing with entrenched power structures. I'd always tried to push past my own comfort zone in the search for more justice, which in this case meant abandoning the fantasy that I had truly "helped." But the version of myself that had parachuted in to Detroit, and left with a bitter picture, another sliver of poverty porn, was a version of myself I didn't really like: the journalist as murderer, or at least as miner, extracting people's pain to craft a story whose beneficiaries are the audience, the radio show, the reporter—other people, elsewhere. My empathy, no matter how deep and real, could not undo this power dynamic. I was another white person profiting off of Black people's pain. I knew there had to be another way.

. . .

Detroit in 2016 was a low point. Since then, and since the weirdly disguised blessing of losing that job, I've begun to map out a new path—to clarify what accountable, subjective journalism might look like, what it might mean to transform the relationships through which we produce and distribute journalism. While I was working in national media, it was *hard* to look at the extractive nature of the work, and nobody talked about it. That's because the conversation was still catching up with reality: we were still talking about newsroom "diversity" and the need to even *do* stories about Black life and death. Talking about the exploitive nature of the entire structure was not really on the table. Now, I have the privilege of standing outside of that model, identifying its problems, and suggesting new ways.

When I was with Eddie Cave and with Kevin Matthews's family, I felt wrong not because it was wrong to tell their stories. I felt wrong because I was working from a model of extraction rather than collaboration. Detroit, police violence, Blackness, poverty, and death all become products, packaged for the consumption of some other person far away.

The extractive approach to journalism treats facts like coal in a mine, using sources and places the way mining companies use land—as a resource to dig into, and then leave behind. It's the most common model for journalism today, particularly journalism about marginalized communities, and it goes hand in hand with "objectivity": the outside observer objectifies the people and places the stories are about, who become "sources" rather than human beings. It is deeply grounded in capitalist ideology: people, experiences, and events are turned into commodities, things that can be sold as "clickbait" or pushed as "shareable content." Such objectification bolsters journalists' careers, but it doesn't build trust or necessarily reflect a truer version of the world. It also limits the action and agency of the people and things we write about and claim to know, freezing them in place.

In 2018 I was back in Detroit for the Allied Media Conference, where I co-organized a roundtable called "Objectivity, Intimacy and Integrity." The idea was to hold a discussion in which we rejected "objectivity" as a premise, and then talked about other ways of working with integrity. During the panel, Jade Begay of Indigenous Rising Media described a model of journalism that's not about storytelling *for*, or *about*, but *with* a community—more than just "service" or "solutions" journalism, she pushes for the decolonization of storytelling itself. In her context, that means returning the tools of making stories to the communities from which they came. And it means not rushing the process—she's from the Dine tribe and, she explained, "for my people, we take ten minutes to introduce ourselves. It's a life way." Introductions are only the start: before reporting with a community, Begay said she spends a lot of time getting to know the people she's working with, getting to know their values and modes of communication, and building trust. Her work is grounded in indigenous values and centers around indigenous voices, taking the time that trust requires rather than moving at the speed of the twenty-four-hour news cycle.

. . .

For another journalist at the Allied Media Conference, Sarah Alvarez, accountability and collaboration didn't require shared experiences or even deep empathy. Alvarez started Outlier Media in 2016, based on the premise that low-income people in Detroit were underserved by their local outlets. She had worked for NPR affiliate Michigan Radio, and before that she'd been a lawyer for public interest organizations. Her interest in accountability and social change brought her into journalism, but she was quickly frustrated with the lack of accountability to low-income audiences. She saw that public media often talked *about* poor people but didn't often produce news that was actually *for* them, based on their needs or interests. Public radio's programming reflects its high-income audiences. The audience, in turn, is built based on the programming, and then the programming is further tailored to the audience, and so on in perpetuity. She thought public media lacked a vision for interrupting this cycle. But where I had seen a gaping hole I had no idea how to fill, she saw an opportunity: use data to create accountability and produce information that underserved audiences actually need.

"I don't see a lot of journalism organizations being like, 'who are we not serving.' And how do we bring them into the audience and how do we create content that is of value to more people," Alvarez said in an interview.

She figured if low-income people weren't listening to public radio, it was because they didn't find it useful or interesting. So when she started Outlier Media, she used data, mostly United Way's 211 call records, to figure out what kinds of information residents were most often seeking. Housing and utilities were at the top of the list; as I had learned in my own reporting, the city is overrun with predatory landlords, shady housing transactions, tax foreclosures, and bad contracts that leave people like Eddie Cave exposed to exploitation. But instead of waiting for the Eddie Caves of the world to come out of the woodwork *after* they'd been exploited or misled, Alvarez created a news service to meet their information needs *before* they signed bad land contracts or leased homes that were in foreclosure. She built a database with public information where you can search any address for background.

Then, she went to her customers directly. She bought lists of phone numbers in the poorest neighborhoods and sent out automated texts inviting people to inquire about any house—their own or one they were considering buying or renting. A person could find out easily if the seller or landlord actually owned the house (deed scams are common in the city) and learn whether the house was in tax foreclosure or had other unpaid debts. This information helps tenants and prospective buyers hold landlords and owners accountable directly. After they text to receive data, they get a follow-up text encouraging them to contact Alvarez with further questions; she often answers dozens of calls a week, and the automated service is used by hundreds of people per month.

"My news consumers are very focused on accountability, as am I," she told me. "There are many people who have saved their homes with this information. There are many people who have avoided eviction with this information."

She also wants to create accountability between herself and her customers—so she follows up with everyone who texts or calls to ask them how they have used Outlier's information. "I want to know if this information was valuable or not, what questions people have that I might not be able to answer."

Alvarez considers herself an independent journalist, but not an "objective" one.

"I definitely have an agenda," Alvarez said. "My agenda is for low-income Detroiters to have the same access to information as high-income Detroiters."

Learning about Alvarez's work in Detroit was a lightbulb moment for me: when I came to Eddie Cave to ask him to tell his story, he had already bought that house with the back taxes attached, and it wasn't even clear if the "sellers" held the deed. The story I was there to tell wasn't really for him or for people in his situation. But Alvarez's form of journalism could have shared the information that Cave needed *before* he signed a contract. And unlike models I was familiar with, this journalism didn't depend on deep and empathetic relationships with each "source"—the people usually treated as sources, low-income Detroiters like Cave, are also the *audience*. Where I had come to Detroit looking for a sad story like Cave's to extract for an outside audience,

Alvarez's role in Detroit is based entirely on accountability to people like him.

She has gotten pushback from other journalists on her ideas. "Journalists don't want to be accountable to their sources, to their communities, because they feel like it threatens their independence," she said. But she thinks this threat to independence isn't borne out in reality. "I don't know that that fear has a lot of basis in fact. I have never felt threatened by being more accountable."

Another criticism has been that her approach is more a charitable service than a news service; she disagrees, and to me the evidence is obvious. High-income people get reports on the stock market daily from TV news tickers and shows like *Marketplace*. Outlier Media is simply economic information for low-income people. Both the information and the delivery are different because this audience has different needs. It is news, but it's news that upends and unsettles the power dynamic of much of the mainstream media right now: in most news organizations, oppressed and marginalized people are treated as characters whose stories are there to be extracted and told, rather than as engaged audiences or community members or, god forbid, journalists themselves.

· · ·

As I continued in my journey out of public media journalism, I was exposed to more and more examples of people trying to create more accountable and less extractive forms of journalism. At another conference, I met Bettina Chang, who came into journalism through a more traditional means than me or Sarah Alvarez. After growing up in Chicago's suburbs, she studied at Northwestern's Medill School of Journalism and went from internships straight into an editorial job out of college. After a few years, she started working for what she imagined was the gold standard for a writer: a national print magazine, *Pacific Standard*, which focused on social science and printed beautiful full-color editions.

Chang, a fast-talking millennial midwesterner, seems just the type to be a liberal magazine reporter—incisive and passionate, contained and meticulous. Like Alvarez, though, Chang had different ideas about accountability than the institutions where she worked. In the national magazine world, there were few systems in place for assessment or feedback, for the sort of evaluation Alvarez was doing of community information needs. Chang found that journalists at national magazines seemed most interested in what *other* journalists were talking about, not the conversation in the communities they wrote about. There was also a continuous system of reward for the most outrageous, clever, or clickbaity stories. Within a year, Chang was disillusioned. "Actually getting in there and seeing how insular it was . . . that started to really grate upon me," she said.

If the process of producing the journalism seemed strangely hollow, so did the process of reaching audiences. Even when she wrote something that felt meaningful, she explained, "it was this overwhelming feeling that every time I published a story, it was just going out into the ether and I had no idea who I was writing for. . . . People would say, 'Oh, you're writing this to change the conversation,' . . . but the conversation for whom, whose conversation?"

Maybe the type of journalism Chang was witnessing was inevitable, even when an individual editor or publication resisted it: the rewards for clickbait were too high. But the audience ultimately loses out in this oversaturated environment where the focus is clicks and shares. We can get all the facts we want, but we're starved for meaning, context, and connection. "A lot of the stories that we read nowadays especially like these outrage stories are just meant to rile you up and then make you feel powerless," Chang said.

Click, read, and get riled: the model is great for advertisers and social media platforms, bad for journalists and the public. These concerns eventually took Chang back to Chicago, first to work for the hyperlocal outfit DNAinfo (which was eventually shut down by its billionaire owner after workers tried to unionize), and then to start a new kind of organization with a small group of young media-makers. She teamed up with reporter Darryl Holliday, educator Andrea Hart, and publisher Harry Backlund to found City Bureau, a nonprofit civic journalism lab based in the South Side, the mostly Black part of segregated

Chicago. Their vision was something that would engage the parts of the city that are often misrepresented in coverage, a newsroom where the staff reflected the community and received ongoing and robust feedback on the stories they produced. An immediate goal was to build accountability for good local journalism; a long-term goal was to build trust and a journalism organization that audiences would directly support with their dollars as well as other forms of participation.

"I started to realize that when people do know about our process, then they can trust and feel invested in it, and then they see value in it," said Chang. They started training journalists and non-journalists from Chicago in the nuts and bolts of reporting. But City Bureau's journalism fellows didn't just report—they also did outreach and held community meanings, not only at the end of the reporting but at the beginning and middle. Reporters talked to and heard from people affected by the issues they were working on, integrating their ideas about how to tell the story. And instead of journalists pretending that there was no power dynamic with their sources and audiences, they'd acknowledge it openly and try to build a more equitable process. Instead of "we want to help you," she said the message was "journalists have power and we want to be able to share that power with you."

Training people who don't consider themselves journalists is equally important at City Bureau, she said, because journalists have an incentive to hoard their power. She reminded me, again, of my own reporting on Kevin Matthews: "When journalists extract the sad stories of downtrodden people to publish for an audience of mostly privileged people, we are endorsing a particular theory of change for journalism: that powerful people read a sad story, feel bad about it, and are therefore spurred to change things from their seat of power," she wrote to me in an email. "This keeps journalists in a powerful position, because ONLY WE can translate that sad story to the 'only' people who can create change . . . rich, powerful, privileged people. We reject that theory of change. We believe that journalism instead should enable change coming from people who are most affected by issues that we write about—which means putting the information and tools directly into their hands."

Within a few years, City Bureau had created the most diverse and representative newsroom in the city, with many of its fellows going on to report for larger organizations, and many of its stories co-publishing with citywide papers like the *Chicago Reader* and national outfits like the *Guardian US*. The reporters were no more or less "objective" than anyone else, said Chang, but they were more connected and more collaborative, more understanding of the reasons for the widespread distrust of news media. They learned to build bridges in both directions: helping communities rebuild trust with media and helping more mainstream media receive feedback from people it had long been ignoring. "There is no such thing as coming from no point of view," Chang said. "You're always going to fight for the survival of yourself."

. . .

I don't believe in silver bullets, and I also know journalism in the information age serves more than one purpose. For some people, it's a source of data and facts, organized in such a way that they are useful or necessary. For others, it's a source of stories to give meaning or perspective to our confusing, overstimulated lives. And for still others, journalism is a way to build community, to find connection or cohesion around an idea or an experience. So while journalists are never neutral purveyors of "just the facts," some will focus more on organizing facts while others will focus more on interpreting them or extrapolating solutions from them, and others will focus on building communities surrounding them.

Call it all what you will: data journalism, interpretive reporting, engagement journalism, solutions journalism, movement journalism, advocacy journalism—buzzwords come and go, and often get stale along the way. For me, examples like Outlier Media and City Bureau are just good journalism that answers the demands of the current age. And they are examples of how journalists can resist the objectifying, extractive model of journalism, while holding to our role as purveyors of truth in the world.

Both organizations were founded on the hope that when the broken trust between audiences and news outlets is healed, the audiences will see real value in their local news outlets and support them directly. Many more news organizations have since been founded on this premise, using a combination of membership models, cooperative ownership, and nonprofit funding. The experiment is ongoing and could yet be overpowered by economic and political forces that continue to oppose the equitable distribution of meaningful, useful information to the public.

In order to ensure that an equitable future is possible, I also believe media production *needs* to be paired with media activism. That means everything from working for freedom of information and protection of net neutrality, to creating robust and representative local newsrooms with clear mechanisms for accountability and feedback, to defending the free speech rights of both individual journalists and media organizations.

Building equitable, accountable organizations also inevitably means facing the power dynamics of race, class, gender, and exploitation. After all, people aren't "underrepresented" in newsrooms because they want to be, but because racism, heteropatriarchy, ableism, classism, and xenophobia are built in to the way we do journalism and the way we talk about ethics and "objectivity." And I'm afraid that until we let go of the activist/journalist divide, our hands will be tied each time we try to address inequity and power. Activism is not, and cannot be, a dirty word in journalism anymore: we need activists in our newsrooms, and activists in the street defending our newsrooms.

But I do think it would be a mistake to settle in to just one form of activism, to align with a political party or a rigid platform. At its core, journalism should always remain curious and open-minded. Ideally, mission-driven journalism organizations and networks melt the barriers between journalists and "the public," journalism and activism, and they seek out a representation of "the public" that reflects the communities they are speaking to and about. They also aim to change the power dynamics in journalism, rethinking everything from news judgment, to the way stories are written and distributed, to the process of reporting.

And these journalistic experiments open up questions that need asking again and again: What is a story for? Who gets to tell stories? What would it mean to transform our relationship to truth, to resist authoritative and propagandistic voices and develop a truly critical, curious public? What if the role of the journalist today was something closer to a community organizer? What can we learn from storytelling models in Native American and indigenous communities, or the West African tradition of the griot—a poet, musician, and storyteller all in one? What can we create by telling the truth?

My friend Jennifer Brandel once said that the purpose of journalism is to show people what we are capable of—the beautiful and the bad. We have a choice about the world we depict in our stories, and that choice matters because it helps us see what is possible. Maybe the news alone can't teach imagination, curiosity, and social change, and maybe journalism alone can't end exploitation or enact justice, but it can acknowledge these values, bend toward them. We need to imagine that we are capable of changing the world just as we are capable of destroying it.

CONCLUSION

THE END OF JOURNALISM

My generation, my upbringing, was defined by lies and conspiracy. In the 1990s we had Y2K and Troopergate; in the 2000s, we had truthers and weapons of mass destruction and "Mission Accomplished." On September 15, 2008, when Lehman Brothers and AIG went under, an NPR host said, "Remember this day . . . it will go down in history." It was my younger brother's twentieth birthday, and I still remember where I was standing, in my kitchen in Chicago. In my neighborhood, condo developments would stand half-built for years while rents sky-rocketed. Years later, I would report on how the same investors who'd made a fortune off the crash bought up rental properties en masse across the country, making a fortune off the people who'd lost their homes.

Ten years have passed and I still remember the progress we were promised when Barack Obama was elected, the promise of an end to the wars in Iraq and Afghanistan, the promise of a post-racial era and a return to socioeconomic progress. None of that has materialized: instead we got government shutdowns, a half-assed health care bill, birtherism, drone strikes. Later we got an election that may have been stolen by Russia and a legislature without the will to find out, a sinister Rudy Giuliani on TV spouting, "Truth isn't truth." As I write this, the economy is strong again, but the benefits are being sucked up by the fabulously wealthy, and for the rest of us, nothing is guaranteed—not health care, not retirement, not personal safety, not a safety net. What little social change we made in the last twenty years around gay rights, anti-racism, and the rights of people with disabilities is being chipped away. Trans people are a lightning rod; gender and racial scapegoating is at a new high. No wonder people seek refuge in near-reality, in the Kardashians and *Naked and Afraid* and President Trump's tweets.

I'll admit: I seek refuge in the NPR newscast at the top of every hour—even though, for my whole life, it's given me a vision of the world that doesn't align with my own. Still, there's something comforting in a world that seems fundamentally the same as it did last week, last month, last millennium, something comforting in the distillation of the news of the day into a three-minute clip. My friend Ramona Martinez, who used to be a producer at the NPR newscast, once said that "objectivity is the ideology of the status quo." On the one hand, as this book has made clear, I can't stand the status quo: it doesn't have room for me and my communities, it's an emperor with no clothes, it's a mess. But on some days, for me, that status quo can feel like a refuge—it relieves me of responsibility and fear. Let's just pretend those are clothes on that monarch, that everything is fine. Wildfires and hurricanes, wars and mass shootings, celebrity deaths and congressional stalemates become something easy to digest. The calm voices keep the listener at a distance, and I get to be the listener, a member of the anonymous crowd.

That distance, the sense that we are not implicated, yields a temporary comfort—probably a false one, but this, too, is part of the promise of "objectivity." If you can stand outside of the world, you can afford not to change it.

Mine is not an argument against the rigorous pursuit of facts, or even an argument that the job of every journalist is to write opinion pieces all day and then protest by night. I love the NPR newscast like a childhood stuffed animal (in an alternative universe, I once fancied myself a less-cool Korva Coleman). I feel sure that there is still a place—a big, important place—for people who seek the truth, who shape and give it meaning. But we have to know what power we have in the shaping.

. . .

At this point, an "objective" approach to news is easy to poke holes in. As we've seen, news judgment is never neutral, and movements like #BlackLivesMatter and #MeToo have shifted the way we think about what's news for the better. And not affiliating with political parties may be valuable and possible, but not when it's conflated with impartiality on issues of justice—many Black journalists like T. Thomas Fortune, Ida B. Wells, and Marvel Cooke have stood outside of political affiliation while also speaking out against racism and their own erasure. But because it is so often conflated with the viewpoint of people in power, "objectivity" has been used again and again for gatekeeping, to discourage labor organizing and exclude diverse voices. "Objectivity" also excludes certain people by suggesting that a detached observer is a better one, even as many of the most important stories of our times have been told by people who were close to the issue, not detached outsiders. Finally, "objectivity" has a tendency to objectify, turning people into flattened-out "sources" whose stories are there for the taking, encouraging an extractive approach to journalism in which the journalist is never implicated or accountable.

These are the problems of the practice of so-called objectivity. There is also the more insidious problem of performed "objectivity" and false balance. The need to appear "objective" permeates newsroom culture, especially in mainstream national outlets, often to the detriment of truth and honesty. The attempt to "balance" left with right has often led, in practice, to stifling the voices of people of color, LGBTQ people, and low-income people as well as giving platforms to white supremacists, climate deniers, and transphobes. The right wing in the US has run a campaign to smear the powerless as unruly leftists rather than people speaking up for themselves, and mainstream media outlets have too often given in to this false framing. Performed "objectivity" also often means sidelining women, trans people, and people of color who call for real social change in newsrooms—the fear of being deemed "activist" for standing up for ourselves is very real. This attempt to appear impartial has clearly led to excluding diverse voices from newsrooms over the years. And of course, performed "objectivity" can help journalists avoid bringing an analysis of power and oppression to bear on our own work; looking honestly at power might require us to radically transform how journalism is done.

For me, that transformation can't come a minute too soon. But if not "objectivity," what makes journalism trustworthy and good? Even as I expand my ideas about the process of truth-telling and the meaning of balance, I propose hanging on to some basic tenets of traditional journalistic ethics: verification and fact-checking, editorial independence from political parties and corporations, clarity and transparency about financial and political conflicts of interest, and deep, thorough sourcing. I also join a chorus of journalists who have been gradually replacing objectivity with the practice of radical transparency about both our values and our methodologies. Finally, I think defining our values as journalists when journalism is under attack means admitting that we are activists and becoming clear about what we are activists for.

Transparency has also been a focus of ethics in the information age, with good reason: these days, audiences can find out everything about journalists and our stories, even fact-checking or verifying our work on their own. Journalism is exposed from every corner, and this isn't a bad thing. Journalists make mistakes, and also bias is real. When audiences get information about the reporter's biases, methodologies, and intentions straight from the reporter or outlet, they can evaluate the trustworthiness themselves. Checking in about, acknowledging, and working within our biases is not the same as doing away with them, or pretending they aren't there. Transparency can help build trust, letting our audiences in on how we decided what stories to report and how we arrived at our version of the truth.

Of course, the idea that every journalism outlet should be values-based raises up the fear that such a situation will undermine trust in the news media—"objectivity" is still a part of many audiences' expectation and hope. But the cat is already out of the bag. The information age presents us with more information than any one human, or any one news outlet, or any one algorithm can possibly process. It *requires* us to bring value systems to bear in evaluating what matters, what's news, and how stories should be told. Audiences know this but are left with a confounding situation in which everyone claims "objectivity," but it's still not clear whom to trust. The least that the news producers can do in this confounding, polarized environment is offer a sense of why and how we report what we do.

Many news organizations already are going further, actively participating in community-based collaboration, media education, and the promotion of curiosity as a part of their news production. And others are also beginning to add another key ingredient for making good journalism that actually reflects the communities we cover: a systemic and ongoing analysis of power and oppression, not just in our reporting but in our assessment of the field of journalism itself.

. . .

I don't like coming to conclusions, or particularly seeming sure of things. This is one of the traps of putting things in writing: it seems we have come to a stopping point, decided that there is nothing left to consider. The postmodern era has been defined by anxiety over truth claims, reality, and subjectivity, and I share that anxiety. In 2018 Trump henchman Rudy Giuliani made a meme out of the phrase "truth isn't truth," and then dug his heels in. In his case, it was a way to avoid the truth (and the law), but the trouble is, he was playing effectively to this shared anxiety. If nothing is entirely true, what does truth matter? While plenty of disciplines have embraced the conundrum, journalism has struggled to catch up; we are still expected to write as if we are sure, to come to conclusions.

More damaging still, journalism is still grieving its lost heroes, looking back at a golden age that never was. Fragmentation in media has made more space for diversity, and the stubborn nostalgia for a more homogeneous era of true "objectivity" has also created an ugly opening, easily exploited by people who actually just don't like racial, sexual, or gender equity. We need to "go back," they say, to make journalism great again. We need to purge all these "liberal-bias" identity-politics

fake-news journalists—who are often Black or gay or trans or immigrants. In 2018, as I was working on this book, journalist Don Lemon
reported that President Donald Trump had privately told him he
thought Lemon was unable to be objective about race because he is
Black. Meanwhile, Trump and his supporters regularly made public
statements against any media critical of him, accusing them of bias
and unfairness and calling them "fake news," railing particularly hard
against women and people of color. This kind of talk perfectly exploits
both the fear of diversity and the dated attachment to "objectivity" that
continue to hold back much of journalism today.

What to do about "alternative facts," about the bullshit and dishon-
esty that dominates our political discourse today? The truth is, I don't
know. And one of my deepest beliefs, one of the practices I value the
most, is admitting what we don't know—allowing our minds to swim
in the questions, to be submerged. If autocracy and racism and fake
news foreclose imagination and colonize doubt, I believe curiosity lies
at the center of a framework for resistance that cultivates imagination,
that cultivates the skill of living in questions. And when journalists
offer this to the world—the attitude of not knowing, and of endlessly
seeking to know more—I think we can gain the power to change it.
When we foreclose imagination and curiosity, foreclose fierce analysis in favor of feigned objectivity, we sacrifice that power—feeding,
instead, into cynicism and indifference. Truth isn't truth, so what's the
point? This is just the way things are, people say, and then they change
the channel, click back to puppy pictures on Facebook.

Journalism without bias is impossible, and our audiences know it.
In the postmodern era, and in the internet age, readers and listeners
can also always look elsewhere, for a voice they like better, someone
they find more honest or identifiable. Rather than making truth impossible, I think accepting the possibility of multiple truths is a positive element of the fight against binary thought and intellectual foreclosure. It doesn't solve "fake news" or insidious bullshit, but it does
give us more narratives and more voices, tools with which to fight back
against falsehood.

Kevin Young writes, "What if truth is not an absolute or a relative, but a skill—a muscle, like memory—that collectively we have neglected so much that we have grown measurably weaker at using it?" Maybe what we're trying to work out here is how to build back up a muscle that has become atrophied in this country: our ability to ask questions. But inquiry is hard to do, humility before the terrible wide world too easy to forget in favor of simplicity. If we understand truth as a skill, it requires us to break down the barriers between journalists and "the public"—to move toward the end of journalism as profession and toward new models driven by collaboration and education. What if exercising our ability to seek out truth, using our muscle of curiosity and questioning, was a job for all of us?

One thing I do know is that we should not succumb to hopelessness in the face of "alternative facts." Truth matters even when it is multifaceted, prismatic, and strange. If cries of "fake news" lead us to the conclusion that nothing at all can be true, then the game is pretty much over. The winners are the people in power, the people with something to hide.

. . .

Recently I had a dream full of rising water. I was on a ship with my dad and a whole lot of other people, and the ship hit an iceberg. The water was cold and high, and the ship was sinking, like the *Titanic*. There was a way out, which involved scrambling across the deck of the ship to the bow, jumping onto lifeboats. But as it started to tip and go down, the bow extending upward, lots of people were still caught below deck. There were dozens of children down there, and we knew it. My father and I realized we could save ourselves by following everyone, scrambling and jumping, but instead we headed back down to help. Right as we approached the door to go below the deck, an automated metal gate started to come down. Someone was locking the kids inside the ship to drown. In my dream, my father and I ran toward the gate, wedging our bodies between the gate and the floor and screaming. We tried to hold it open, but we weren't strong enough. Then I woke up.

We've all wondered what we would do in the worst conditions— war, disaster, slavery, prison. Would we be empathic and kind, protective and suspicious? Would we stand up to tyrannical authority or back down, maybe to protect ourselves or our children? Would we protest if it were *our* children locked in the bottom of the ship? Who would we be, faced with the most limited of choices? Would we stand to the side, looking on as people died? What if it was our job to be a journalist, and that job instructed us to stand to the side?

When the climate changes—politically or otherwise—we come to see ourselves anew. I remember Hurricane Katrina like it was yesterday. I was in Texas in a cheap motel, healing from a surgery when the storm hit. I was pumped up on Percocet, reading Truman Capote and watching the TV news, an unfamiliar treat to me. I remember seeing the newscasters standing waist-deep in the water, the detritus of people's homes and livelihoods floating by. I watched as one of those newscasters broke down in tears, trying to rattle off the numbers of homes underwater, the numbers of people evacuated, the numbers of dead bodies out there floating, in a disaster that was preventable and human-made. I remember clearly the images that emerged later of President George W. Bush flying over New Orleans in Air Force One, never touching down to see the human suffering. At the motel where I was staying, stranded people showed up from the Gulf Coast for long stays.

I wondered what I would have done if I were caught in that rising water, if it were my job to tell that story? Could I have stood there in the revolting floodwater full of toxins and talked clearly, dispassionately, like Korva Coleman giving the day's headlines? I imagine myself, the NPR newscaster I'd once hoped to be, standing in the Louisiana humidity, soaked through and telling it straight: It was a Category 5 hurricane. Thousands displaced. Hundreds dead. Here is the temperature. It smells like a dead body. The Dow is up, the S&P 500 is up. Let's do the numbers: The costs of property damage are in the billions. The levees broke in over fifty places. One thousand eight hundred thirty-three dead, more than a million displaced. A dog's body is floating by now, next to a torn-off trailer door.

At the time, 2005 was the warmest year on record, but the record keeps being updated. Years later, reporters stopped having to "balance" stories about climate change with climate deniers. I imagine the climate like that rising water, testing our empathy as we grit our teeth and give the news: It's hotter still this year, and hotter again. We're hearing reports of flooding and wildfires. We're hearing reports of drought and displacement. Let's do the numbers: twenty-five million to one billion people could be displaced by climate change by 2050, one study finds.

How do we balance a story about the sixth extinction, the end of the world? How do we make ourselves human again, after turning the whole world into an object, holding it at a distance, telling its stories without letting our voices crack? If I'm standing in the rising water, am I too close to the story? What does it mean to show vulnerability when you're the one after the truth, the one gathering the facts?

Stories shape reality and suggest possibility. They can spark curiosity or foreclose it, drowning us in facts and figures. It is possible to make the world new through stories, but it's also possible to create a world we don't want. During Hurricane Katrina, a lot of the reporting focused on "looters" and violence, turned away from stories about dozens and then thousands of deaths, dozens and then thousands of people helping each other survive. I imagine myself on the NPR newscast, voice cracking. Nearly two thousand people died here. I'm standing in this water. Hundreds of thousands still displaced. It smells like sewage and death. There is a dog's body, a trailer door floating past. There's someone on her way to help; there's someone on that roof, yelling. What can we do to make this picture different? How can we stop the water rising, hold open the gates so no one is trapped inside? In my little fantasy, my newscaster job doesn't last long, but it's okay. I really don't have time to wait around for the climate to change.

ACKNOWLEDGMENTS

I have had more support through the process of making this book than I can possibly acknowledge here. Thanks first of all to the very first people I turned to after I lost my job: my parents, Bruce and Raven, and my wonderful expanded family, including Nick, Clint, Jenna, Susie, Thorne, Nina Feldman, and the Comptons. Community is everything when your life is a mess, and I won't forget the ways I was also supported during that time by Sam Worley, Elzbieta and Medha at the Peace Palace, Eli Oberman, Jessie Dunn Rovinelli, Laura Wernick, Causten Wollerman, Amita Lonial, ChaNell Marshall, Mariame Kaba, Sarah Lu, Jane Hereth, Neenah Ellis, Janada Halbisen-Gibbs, Jocelyn Robinson, Mia Henry, Neena Pathak, Morgan M. Page, and Emily McCord, among others. Jennifer Brandel's advice as both a media maven and a compassionate human has been invaluable. I'm indebted to the friendship and allyship of Scott Tong, Amy Scott, Deidre Depke, David Brancaccio, and Kimberly Adams at *Marketplace*, and to many journalists and organizers who have since helped me out or become my friends through this ordeal; they include Adam Ragusea, Steve Henn, Brenda Salinas, Andrew Ramsammy, Enav Emmanuel Moskowitz, Harron Walker, Barbara Feinman Todd, John Biewen, Celeste Headlee, Jay Rosen, Jenni Monet, Sarah Alvarez, Alicia Montgomery, Cass Adair, Ramona Martinez, Anna Simonton, and the entire amazing crew at *Scalawag Magazine*. Steven Thrasher and Meredith Talusan have gone above and beyond in their friendship and camaraderie; they both make me proud to be a queer journalist. One very special person proposed a professional connection but ended up sending me snail mail—our shared love language—and ultimately supporting me in every imaginable way, Cole Parke.

Many people read these chapters, beginning with Carrie Frye of Black Cardigan Edits, who reconnected me with my childhood role model, Harriet the Spy. I'm thankful for the feedback from Katherine Webb-Hehn, Raven McCrory, Bruce Wallace, Tom Warhover, David Mindich, Nina Lary, Kaitlin Ugolik, Lynette Kalsnes, Alexander Eastwood, Lauren Sharp, Ramona Martinez, Meredith Talusan, and all the members of Ronnie's Children in New York. Ruth Samuel and Hideo Higashibaba took on some fact-checking in a pinch, and Juliet Fromholt at WYSO helped me access needed information from the archives. My younger brother Nick Wallace gave great feedback and caught mistakes for me and was generally generous with his time and insights.

I'm so grateful for the inspiration and ideas of my brilliant friends Micah Bazant, Ariel Springfield, Jesa Rae, Sinan Goknur, Autumn Meghan Brown, Catherine Edgerton, and Devi Vaidya, all of whom listened to me blabber and gave me ideas and great questions along the way. Gabrielle Civil and Billy Dee were brilliant critics who brought poetry, art, and vision into the mix, and the McCrory family gave us a place to retreat to at Mac's Acres. My research about gay media history was supported by a Heidrich Research Fellowship at the University of Michigan, and the original idea for this book came from Priya Nelson, my wonderful editor.

Finally, Carrie Frye encouraged me to think about one "ideal reader," the person whose questions I'm directly addressing in this book, whom I trust to be as curious as I am about the answers. That person for me, a sort of muse in addition to being a great friend and journalist, is Hideo Higashibaba.

FURTHER READING

This book, and the ideas behind this book, began with contemporary Black liberation movements and their stories: Wesley Lowery's *They Can't Kill Us All: Ferguson, Baltimore, and a New Era in America's Racial Justice Movement* (New York: Little, Brown, 2016); Patrisse Khan-Cullors and Asha Bandele's *When They Call You A Terrorist: A Black Lives Matter Memoir* (New York: St. Martin's Press, 2016); and Keeanga-Yamahtta Taylor's *From #BlackLivesMatter to Black Liberation* (Chicago: Haymarket Books, 2016) are all excellent starting points. The first chapter also depends on Steven Thrasher's journalism, and interviews with him, Mervyn Marcano, and Aislinn Pulley.

On the early history of "objectivity" in journalism, I found two texts invaluable: David T. Z. Mindich's *Just the Facts: How "Objectivity" Came to Define America Journalism* (New York: New York University Press, 1998) and Michael Schudson's *Discovering the News: A Social History of American Newspapers* (New York: Basic Books, 1978). While Schudson's approach is sociological, Mindich's is primarily historical and focuses heavily on the lessons to be learned from purportedly "neutral" coverage of the Civil War, slavery, and lynching. Another book on which I depended for general journalism history was Christopher B. Daly's *Covering America: A Narrative History of a Nation's Journalism* (Amherst: University of Massachusetts Press, 2012). Finally, I recommend *News with a View: Essays on the Eclipse of Objectivity in Modern*

Journalism, edited by Burton St. John III and Kirsten A. Johnson (Jefferson, NC: McFarland, 2012).

All of those books are academic; the most straightforward reading I have found that summarizes the origins of journalistic "objectivity" is in a memoir by retired *New York Times* journalist Linda Greenhouse, *Just a Journalist: On the Press, Life, and the Spaces Between* (Cambridge, MA: Harvard University Press, 2017). Onnesha Roychoudhuri's fabulous new book, *The Marginalized Majority: Claiming Our Power in a Post-Truth America*, contains a cogent analysis of the problems of "objectivity" for the political left (Brooklyn: Melville House, 2018). My own original posts about "objectivity" and the story of my firing are available at https://medium.com/@lewispants/objectivity-is-dead-and-im-okay-with-it-7fd2b4b5c58f and https://medium.com/@lewispants/i-was-fired-from-my-journalism-job-ten-days-into-trump-c3bc014ce51d.

The early twentieth century was when "objectivity" started to formalize as an ideal and began to be taught in journalism schools. I looked to Hazel Dicken-Garcia's *Journalistic Standards in Nineteenth-Century America* (Madison: University of Wisconsin Press, 1989) for further context on journalism education, and Nelson Antrim Crawford's wonderful text *The Ethics of Journalism* (New York: Knopf, 1924) for information on early journalistic ethics. Crawford's book includes a delightful index of ethics codes from newspapers around the country. Walter Lippmann's *Public Opinion* (New York: Free Press, 1922) is a powerful snapshot of his times and includes his argument for an "objective" approach to reporting.

I came across a lot of characters who wrote about "neutrality" in reporting during its earliest days. I was particularly delighted by the words of Timothy Thomas Fortune in *T. Thomas Fortune, the Afro-American Agitator: A Collection of Writings, 1880–1928*, edited by Shawn Leigh Alexander (Gainesville: University Press of Florida, 2008), and Fortune's own words in his 1884 volume, *Black and White: Land, Labor, and Politics in the South* (reprint; New York: Washington Square Press, 2007). There is only one biography of T. Thomas Fortune, Emma Lou Thornbrough's *T. Thomas Fortune, Militant Journalist* (Chicago:

University of Chicago Press, 1972), but Fortune's autobiographical works were published as a series of essays in 1927 in the *Philadelphia Tribune* and the *Norfolk Journal and Guide,* and later republished in T. Thomas Fortune, *After War Times: An African American Childhood in Reconstruction-Era Florida,* edited by Daniel R. Weinfeld, with an introduction by Dawn J. Herd-Clark (Tuscaloosa: University of Alabama Press, 2014).

Horace Greeley's take on neutral journalism is well summarized in "'Gagged, Mincing Neutrality': Horace Greeley on Advocacy Journalism in the Early Years of the Penny Press," by Daxton R. "Chip" Stewart in *News with a View: Essays on the Eclipse of Objectivity in Modern Journalism,* edited by Burton St. John III and Kirsten A. Johnson (Jefferson, NC: McFarland, 2012). I also read about Greeley in the words of his contemporary L. U. Reavis in *A Representative Life of Horace Greeley* (New York: G. W. Carleton & Co., 1872).

Possibly the best-documented life considered in the early chapters of this book is that of Ida B. Wells; her story is told clearly and passionately in her own book *Crusade for Justice: The Autobiography of Ida B. Wells* (Chicago: University of Chicago Press, 1970). I also depended on her pamphlets *Southern Horrors* and *A Red Record* republished as *On Lynchings* (New York: Arno Press and the New York Times, 1969); and on Mindich's excellent chapter on Ida B. Wells and "balance" in *Just the Facts,* which details the *New York Times'* equivocating coverage of lynching and its criticism of Wells.

Conversely, the least well-documented life discussed in this text is Marvel Cooke's, whose story in her own words was recorded for public record, as far as I know, only one time, in an oral history conducted by Kathleen Currie for the Women in Journalism Oral History Project of the Washington Press Club Foundation; I was also able to speak with Currie to get a clearer sense of who Cooke was. Based on Currie's interview, Cooke is written about in several volumes, including Rodger Streitmatter's *Raising Her Voice: African-American Women Journalists Who Changed History* (Lexington: University Press of Kentucky, 1994). Her five-part series "The Bronx Slave Market" for the New York *Daily Compass* (January 8–12, 1950), https://www.viewpointmag

.com/2015/10/31/the-bronx-slave-market-1950, provides additional insight into her voice and thought.

For the stories of Heywood Broun and the formation of the Newspaper Guild, I looked to Richard O'Connor's *Heywood Broun: A Biography* (New York: G. P. Putnam's Sons, 1975); *Heywood Broun, as He Seemed to Us*, produced as a memorial by the Newspaper Guild of New York (New York: Random House, 1940); and Heywood Hale Broun, *Collected Edition of Heywood Broun* (1949; reprint, Freeport, NY: Books for Libraries Press, 1969). I also referred to an article about the Newspaper Guild by Philip M. Glende, "Trouble on the Right, Trouble on the Left: The Early History of the American Newspaper Guild," *Journalism History* 38, no. 3 (Fall 2012); and to the text of the United States Supreme Court's decision in *Associated Press v. National Labor Relations Board* 301 U.S. 103 (57 S.Ct. 650, 81 L.Ed. 953).

Kerry Gruson spent several delightful hours with me over a couple of days in Miami sharing her story, which I first learned about from Schudson's *Discovering the News* and then from a *Wall Street Journal* article on "objectivity" by Stanford Sesser (October 29, 1969). I also depended on Gruson's autobiographical story for the *New York Times Magazine*, June 30, 1985, https://www.nytimes.com/1985/06/30 /magazine/the-long-road-back.html; and a column by her mother, Flora Lewis, "Trust, Arms and the Media," *Chicago Tribune*, December 11, 1984.

For broader context about coverage of the Vietnam War, I recommend Daniel C. Hallin, *The "Uncensored War": The Media and Vietnam* (New York: Oxford University Press, 1986); William M. Hammond, *Reporting Vietnam: Media and Military at War* (Lawrence: University Press of Kansas, 1998); and Clarence R. Wyatt, *Paper Soldiers: The American Press and the Vietnam War* (Chicago: University of Chicago Press, 1995). For Peter Arnett's story, I depended mostly on his *Live from the Battlefield: From Vietnam to Baghdad: 35 Years in the World's War Zones* (New York: Simon & Schuster, 1994).

Public media has many good books and memoirs written about its history, though strikingly few that deeply consider its political economy or the complex issues of "objectivity" for publicly funded outlets.

I could have written a whole book just about this but was relieved to find that someone else already had: journalist James Ledbetter's *Made Possible By . . . : The Death of Public Broadcasting in the United States* (London: Verso, 1997). For additional NPR history, I leaned on Jack Mitchell's *Listener Supported: The Culture and History of Public Radio* (Westport, CT: Praeger, 2005). On the early genesis of public broadcasting, I recommend Robert J. Blakely, *To Serve the Public Interest: Educational Broadcasting in the United States* (Syracuse, NY: Syracuse University Press, 1979); and Robert Waterman McChesney, *Telecommunications, Mass Media, and Democracy: The Battle for the Control of U.S. Broadcasting, 1928–1935* (New York: Oxford University Press, 1993). In my studies of public media, I also relied on interviews with Cecilia Garcia, Jack Mitchell, and Bill Siemering, and took bibliographic suggestions from Sarah Montague, Ben Shapiro, and Josh Shepperd. The online archives of *Current Magazine* are a trove and include Marlon Riggs's article "Tongues Retied," *Current*, August 12, 1991, https://current.org/wp-content/uploads/archive-site/prog/prog114g.html. Siemering's original mission statement for NPR is available at https://current.org/2012/05/national-public-radio-purposes/.

There are not enough books about public media that deal explicitly with race and gender, but I can suggest two for further reading: Christine Acham's *Revolution Televised: Prime Time and the Struggle for Black Power* (Minneapolis: University of Minnesota Press, 2004) and Allison Perlman's *Public Interests: Media Advocacy and Struggles over U.S. Television* (New Brunswick, NJ: Rutgers University Press, 2016). I hope their work will open up space for more women and people of color to write this important history.

For the history of gay media, I recommend Larry P. Gross, *Up from Invisibility: Lesbians, Gay Men, and the Media in America* (New York: Columbia University Press, 2001). I also depended on Barry Yeoman's preciously hard-to-find undergraduate thesis "Moral Judgments Before News Judgments: An Historical Survey of the Treatment of Lesbian and Gay Issues by the Straight Print News Media, 1897–1982" (Lafayette, LA, 1983), available in the Joseph A. Labadie Collection at the University of Michigan. Also at Labadie, I came across *Talk Back!*

The Gay Person's Guide to Media Action by Lesbian and Gay Media Advocates, an activist group in Boston (Boston: Alyson Publications, 1982); it's no longer a practical guide, but it is highly informative about the times.

Andrew Kopkind's brilliant collection, *The Thirty Years' Wars: Dispatches and Diversion of a Radical Journalist, 1965–1994* (New York: Verso, 1995), provides a hilarious snapshot into his early life as a reporter, which was augmented in my research by a long interview with John Scagliotti. The *Gay Community News* is archived almost in its entirety in the Labadie Collection, as is the *New York Native*; for further detail on those remarkable times in queer media, I also interviewed Larry Goldsmith and got background information from Cindy Patton, Michael Bronski, Sue Hyde, and Amy Hoffman. Hoffman's memoir, *An Army of Ex-Lovers: My Life at the Gay Community News* (Amherst: University of Massachusetts Press, 2007), is also peppered with fabulous anecdotes.

I used two key sources on the coverage of AIDS, namely, James Kinsella's long out-of-print volume *Covering the Plague: AIDS and the American Media* (New Brunswick, NJ: Rutgers University Press, 1989) and Randy Shilts's classic *And the Band Played On: Politics, People, and the AIDS Epidemic* (New York: St. Martin's Press, 1987). Cindy Patton of *Gay Community News* wrote two fairly academic volumes on AIDS: *Sex & Germs: The Politics of AIDS* (Boston: South End Press, 1985) and *Inventing AIDS* (New York: Routledge, 1990). Celia Farber takes a more international view in *Serious Adverse Events: An Uncensored History of AIDS* (Hoboken, NJ: Melville House, 2006).

My research into fired, punished, and scapegoated journalists brought me to Sandy Nelson, whose stories emerged in an interview and a number of articles still available online, including the 1996 piece in the *New York Times* that first brought me to her, "Gay Reporter Wants to Be Activist," by Timothy Egan, https://www.nytimes.com /1996/08/10/us/gay-reporter-wants-to-be-activist.html. Linda Greenhouse's story comes from her 2017 book, *Just a Journalist,* and Desmond Cole's story was sourced from his blog, *Cole's Notes,* https://thatsa truestory.wordpress.com/2017/05/04/i-choose-activism-for-black

-liberation/ as well as the *Toronto Star*'s website. Vox.com is keeping a running tab of sexual assault accusations against major public figures at https://www.vox.com/a/sexual-harassment-assault-allegations-list/les-moonves.

On the history of conservative media, the most useful source I found for broad context on its genesis was Nicole Hemmer's *Messengers of the Right: Conservative Media and the Transformation of American Politics* (Philadelphia: University of Pennsylvania Press, 2016); some of her main points are well summarized in "From 'Faith in Facts' to 'Fair and Balanced,'" in *Media Nation: The Political History of News in Modern America*, edited by Bruce J. Schulman and Julian E. Zelizer (Philadelphia: University of Pennsylvania Press, 2017). I found some additional context for the dominance of conservative thought in John B. Judis, *The Paradox of American Democracy: Elites, Special Interests, and the Betrayal of the Public Trust* (New York: Pantheon, 2000). To better understand conservative media leaders themselves, I read Andrew Breitbart's *Righteous Indignation: Excuse Me While I Save the World!* (New York: Grand Central Publishing, 2011); Matt Drudge and Julia Phillips, *Drudge Manifesto* (New York: New American Library, 2000); Edith Efron, *The News Twisters* (Los Angeles: Nash Publishing, 1971); and Bernard Goldberg, *Bias: A CBS Insider Exposes How the Media Distort the News* (Washington, DC: Regnery Publishing, 2001).

David Brock has published his own history of conservative media; although my reporter's instinct is not to rely on him alone for accounts of fact, *The Republican Noise Machine: Right-Wing Media and How It Corrupts Democracy* (New York: Crown, 2004) is riveting; his *Blinded by the Right: The Conscience of an Ex-Conservative* (New York: Crown, 2002) is a more personal account of his path into and out of conservative media. His best seller, *The Real Anita Hill: The Untold Story* (New York: Free Press, 1993), has been debunked, with Brock himself admitting to omissions and even fabrications; it's worth a read for analytical purposes if you can stomach it.

The best counter to Brock's account of Anita Hill is Hill's account of herself: *Speaking Truth to Power* (New York: Doubleday, 1997). For a more reportorial take, Jane Mayer and Jill Abramson's *Strange Justice:*

The Selling of Clarence Thomas (Boston: Houghton Mifflin, 1994) is the best. For an update from Jill Abramson, I read "Do You Believe Her Now?: It's Time to Reexamine the Evidence That Clarence Thomas Lied to Get onto the Supreme Court—and to Talk Seriously about Impeachment," *New York Magazine*, February 18, 2018, http://nymag .com/intelligencer/2018/02/the-case-for-impeaching-clarence -thomas.html. Finally, David Brock pointed me toward the work of feminist legal scholar Ann Scales: "The Emergence of Feminist Juris- prudence: An Essay," *Yale Law Journal* 96, no. 7 (1986), and "Feminist Legal Method: Not So Scary," *UCLA Women's Law Journal* 2 (Janu- ary 1, 1992), are but two of her brilliant articles that touch on the femi- nist argument against "objectivity."

The best book I know of on "fake news" is poet Kevin Young's *Bunk: The Rise of Hoaxes, Humbug, Plagiarists, Phonies, Post-Facts, and Fake News* (Minneapolis: Graywolf Press, 2017); this book by the current director of the Schomburg Center for Research in Black Culture dives deeply into the racialized history of fabrication and falsehood in our journalistic culture.

There are many great books about people of color in journalism, as well as media activism against white supremacy, which I don't have space to list all of here. A classic title is Juan Gonzalez and Joseph Tor- res's *News for All the People: The Epic Story of Race and the American Media* (London: Verso, 2011). I also highly recommend the personal memoir of former *Washington Post* journalist Jill Nelson: *Volunteer Slavery: My Authentic Negro Experience* (New York: Noble Press, 1993); it's hilarious, cutting, and contains a cogent critique of "objectivity" as it relates to Black experience in American newsrooms. Joshunda Sand- ers's *How Racism and Sexism Killed Traditional Media: Why the Future of Journalism Depends on Women and People of Color* (Santa Barbara, CA: Praeger, 2015) is a great primer on identity politics and representa- tion in journalism, including clear ideas about a path forward.

My research on covering white supremacy depended on a couple of excellent podcast episodes: *Reveal* host Al Letson saves the life of, and then confronts, a white supremacist in the September 23, 2017, episode "Street Fight"; *On the Media*'s episode "The Perils of Covering the Alt-

Right" (March 2, 2018) was guest-hosted by *Guardian* journalist Lois Beckett and features many other reporters. Rachel Kaadzi Ghansah talked to the *Longform* podcast in July 2018 about her *GQ* article on Dylann Roof and her own rejection of "objective" reporting on white supremacy (https://longform.org/posts/longform-podcast-rachel-kaadzi-ghansah-on-a-most-american-terrorist-the-making-of-dylann-roof). I conducted interviews with John Biewen and Gary Younge and got valuable historical context from Ethan J. Kytle and Blain Roberts, "The Lost Cause Roots of Sinclair's Propaganda," *Washington Post*, April 11, 2018.

The nature of my research led me to focus on discussions of the construction of gender and sex during the 1990s, with a brief foray into the thirteenth century: *Le roman de Silence* was published as *Silence: A Thirteenth-Century French Romance*, edited and translated by Sarah Roche-Mahdi (East Lansing: Michigan State University Press, 2007). I also revisited Judith Butler's beloved and maligned *Gender Trouble: Feminism and the Subversion of Identity* (New York: Routledge, 1990) and Alice Dreger's *Hermaphrodites and the Medical Invention of Sex* (Cambridge, MA: Harvard University Press, 1998). Kathy Davis's *Embodied Practices: Feminist Perspectives on the Body* (London: Sage, 1997) is another good '90s-era source on embodiment from a feminist, social constructivist perspective. That said, gender, queer, and trans studies have greatly expanded since then, as has Judith Butler's body of work.

On the history of trans movements and trans health care, I depended on Susan Stryker, *Transgender History: The Roots of Today's Revolution*, rev. ed. (New York: Seal Press, 2017), and Carolyn Wolf-Gould's "History of Transgender Medicine in the United States," *The SAGE Encyclopedia of LGBTQ Studies*, edited by Abbie E. Goldberg (Thousand Oaks, CA: SAGE Publications, 2016). I also highly recommend Pat Califia's *Sex Changes: The Politics of Transgenderism* (San Francisco: Cleis Press, 1997) as an early example of a powerful trans voice in this field.

The discussion of contemporary trans coverage was supported by interviews with Meredith Talusan; Masha Gessen, "To Be or Not to Be," *New York Review of Books*, February 8, 2018, https://www.nybooks

.com/articles/2018/02/08/to-be-or-not-to-be/; Donna Minkowitz, "How I Broke, and Botched, the Brandon Teena Story," *Village Voice*, June 20, 2018, https://www.villagevoice.com/2018/06/20/how-i-broke -and-botched-the-brandon-teena-story/; and Rachel Lu, "The Assault on Reality," *National Review*, February 16, 2018, https://www.national review.com/2018/02/assault-reality/. For a primer on the philosophical problems with "objectivity," I recommend Thomas Nagel, *The View from Nowhere* (New York: Oxford University Press, 1986).

My discussions of journalistic ethics in the twenty-first century were based on my experience as a working journalist and interviews with people like Bettina Chang of City Bureau, Sarah Alvarez of Outlier Media, and Alicia Bell of Free Press's News Voices program. The best and most surprising book I have read about journalistic ethics is Janet Malcolm's *The Journalist and the Murderer* (New York: Knopf, 1990)—it is not a guide to ethics, but a philosophical exploration of the ethical problem of telling someone else's story. For a more general guide, I recommend *The New Ethics of Journalism: Principles for the 21st Century*, edited by Kelly McBride and Tom Rosenstiel (Los Angeles: CQ Press, 2014), as well as the Society of Professional Journalists' online resources at www.spj.org and the ongoing research and reporting at www.poynter.org and www.niemanlab.org.

Finally, there were a number of journalists whose stories I learned but was unable to fit into this book. One of them is independent journalist Jenni Monet, whose work is online at jennimonet.com; I also interviewed Celeste Headlee, whose book *We Need to Talk: How to Have Conversations That Matter* (New York: HarperCollins, 2018) is full of practical skills for deep listening as journalists and human beings. Ramona Martinez and the *BackStory* podcast introduced me to Ruben Salazar ("Behind the Bylines: Advocacy Journalism in America," episode #0185, rebroadcast April 20, 2018). Salazar's journalistic work is available in *Border Correspondent: Selected Writings, 1955–1970*, edited by Mario T. Garcia (Berkeley: University of California Press, 1995). Salazar was killed by police while reporting on the Chicano movement in LA in 1970, and his biography has yet to be written.

INDEX